Marcel Bergen & Irma Clei

Amsterdam

The Guide

MokumBooks

Contents

The roof of NEMO in the background the Maritime Museum

Singel - Torensluis

Introduction

A msterdam is since the end of the middle ages has become one of the most beloved cultural cities of the world. The compact capital with its unique canals and impressive architecture invites many people out to visit the city.

With Amsterdam the Guide do you have a fine book in hands to get to know the city well.
You can use the Guide as city, hiking and architecture guide. In a series of ten walks you will be introduced to the city. You walk through shopping streets, but also quiet rustic streets and alleyways. Virtually all the major monuments, buildings and historic homes are described.

In the canal guide provides an overview of the most beautiful and major canal houses along the four main canals and zijgrachten. Using the extended register you quickly find the house or building where you stand for.
Your feedback is welcome for future editions of this guide, we are interested in your experiences, comments and suggestions.

Add your comment through **www.amsterdamtheguide.com**

Rijksmuseum

About Amsterdam

Amsterdam emerges in the 11th century when several settlements arise on the banks of the river Amstel, close to the present Dam. The settlers were in continuous strife with the water. To control the water they built a dam at the mouth of the river IJ. And in this manner a harbour and a village develop close to the present walls (Oudezijds Voorburgwal). Dikes are built along the Amstel to protect the settlements against the water.

In 1275 the inhabitants of the various villages along the Amstel receive from Duke Floris the Fifth the privilege of charging toll at Aemstelledam. Amsterdam's merchants do not have to pay toll (a charge to pass locks and bridges). This privilege gives Amsterdam quite an advantage above the other cities of Holland. It is also at this time that the name Amsterdam (or Aemstelledam) first came into use.

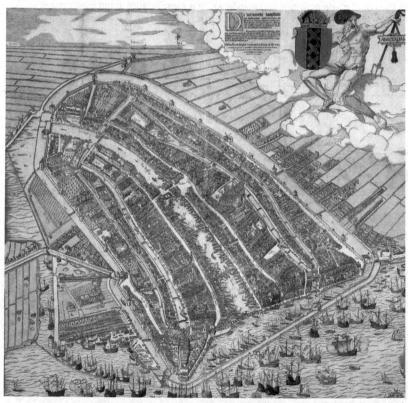

Amsterdam 1544 (Cornelis Anthonisz)

City rights

In 1306 Amsterdam receives city rights and a council is formed consisting of four mayors and the city council (board of 36 prominent merchants).
The centre of the old city lies between the Damrak and the Oude and Nieuwezijds Voorburgwal.
The charging of toll, around 1323, for the import of beer from Hamburg is the beginning of an intensive freight exchange with this German city. In the years that followed Amsterdam developed into the granary for the Northern Netherlands and an important trade junction between the Baltic Sea area and Flanders (Belgium).
The trade with the Rhineland begins, the seed for the economic expansion is planted.

During the middle Ages the rich merchants live on the Warmoesstreet. Around this street canals were excavated and walls were built up against the water. On these embankments houses were built: the Oude- and Nieuwezijds Voor- and Achterburgwal were created.
The economic growth is good for the city. At the end of the 15th century a new ring is laid around the city. This ring is formed by the Singel, the Kloveniersburgwal, and the Geldersekade.

The 17th (golden) century - Amsterdam world city

The Spanish rule of the Belgium Antwerp in 1585 is the great beginning of Amsterdam as world trade city. Merchants from Antwerp and Portuguese Jews flee to Amsterdam and take their total trade network with them. The Baltic Sea trade grows and Amsterdam becomes chief shareholder in the Dutch East India Company (VOC). The Stock Exchange and Exchange Bank are also established in Amsterdam. Through wealth and enormous economic influence Amsterdam is around

The VOC

On the initiative of the Staten (forerunner of the parliament) the Dutch East India Company was established in 1602 and had enormous powers. The company consisted of the twelve regional Netherlands companies that were united. The Dutch East India Company was managed by six chambers (Amsterdam, Middelburg, Enkhuizen, Delft, Hoorn, and Rotterdam) and Amsterdam was the most powerful. The Dutch East India Company was the first company in the world to issue stock to finance their expeditions to the East. The managers came together under the name the Gentlemen XVII. The Company had a monopoly on the trade around the Cape of Good Hope, and through the Straights of Magellan. Besides, the company could occupy land, make war, and sign international treaties. They were known for their brutal methods of extortion, murder, and colonization. The Dutch East India Company (VOC) drove the Portuguese out of almost all their areas of trade and got a monopoly on nutmeg and mace (Banda Islands), cinnamon (Ceylon), and cloves (Moluccas). The VOC centre of power was situated on Batavia (the present Djakarta). Because of its entanglement in various wars the VOC came into serious financial difficulties and was dissolved on March 17, 1798.
In Amsterdam there are still some buildings left that belonged to the VOC:
- Oost-Indisch Huis (1606)
- 's Lands Zeemagazijn (1656) (now Maritime Museum)
- the former admiralty building, the Prinsenhof (1666).

1620 the most important trade and financial centre of Europe. The population grows from 30,000 to 210,000 citizens. Between 1612 and 1632 there is a great expansion of the city. The ring of canals (Keizersgracht, Herengracht, and Prinsengracht) is constructed. The rich merchants establish themselves along these canals. The biggest and most imposing mansions are along the Herengracht (in the Golden Bend). The great numbers of labourers (mostly immigrants, foreign and domestic) establish themselves in small houses west of the ring of canals. The working-class neighbourhood the Jordaan is a good example of this. At the apex of the economic expansion in 1665 the new city hall was taken into use. The classical building was the largest city hall in the world at that moment.

Stagnation and growth

The economy continued to grow until the end of the 18th century. The first signs of stagnation appear during the 4th English War (1780-1784). The great reversal occurred during the French occupation. Napoleon closes the Amsterdam harbour in 1795. That in fact shuts down the import and exports through Amsterdam. A long period of economic crisis follows which results in a decline in population, the beginning of slums, and increasing poverty. About 1870 a new period of economic growth begins. The population grows from 180,000 (1810) to 520,000 (1900). The compact city cannot handle this growth. The city council decides to build new residential areas: De Pijp, Dapperbuurt, Kinkerbuurt, and Staatsliedenbuurt. These neighbourhoods are predominantly occupied by the working-class and lower middle-class. During the 20th century there is widespread city renewal. The old buildings beyond repair were replaced by new housing developments. The make-up of the population changes, also. In the 1970's and 80's many of the original families move to towns outside of the city to be able to live roomier. In 2014 more that 33% of the population of Amsterdam is of non-western origin. (National average is 9%).

Amsterdam not the seat of government

Amsterdam is a compact metropolis with a population of more than 750,000 and has a beautiful 17th century city centre. The great economic prosperity of the 17th century is still very evident everywhere. Canal-side houses alternate and join together many architectural styles: renaissance, classicalism, Louis styles, and a great number of surprising neo-styles. They make Amsterdam one of the most beautiful cities of the world. Amsterdam is the capitol of the Netherlands, but not the seat of government. In this Amsterdam forms an exception, along with five other countries in the world.

The government of the Netherlands (king, cabinet, and parliament) is seated in The Hague. During the French occupation Amsterdam was the seat of government for a short period of time (1808-1810). The brother of Emperor Napoleon I, King Louis Napoleon (1778-1846) was king of the Netherlands and established himself as the head of government in the Palace on the Dam. In this way Amsterdam was also the seat of government of the (occupied) country. After the liberation on 1813 the government returned to The Hague. In the first constitution of the Netherlands of 1814 Amsterdam was named as capitol, but in the later versions of 1815, 1848, and 1917 the status of Amsterdam is unclear. Only since the extensive changes in the constitution of 1983 is the formal status of Amsterdam as capitol restored. Even though there was no lawful status (between 1815 and 1983) Amsterdam was always considered to be the capitol of the Netherlands.

Heroic, Resolute, Merciful

The heart of the city's coat of arms is a red shield with a black band in the middle with three St. Andrew's crosses. The black band symbolizes the water in which the city is situated. The three crosses denote the Apostle Andrew who died a martyr's death on a cross. The crosses are also on the city coat of arms of two neighbouring boroughs, namely Ouder-Amstel and Nieuwer-Amstel. This might show that they originate from the family coat of arms from the family line of Persijn. This family owned much land in Amsterdam and surroundings in the 15th century. Another idea is that the crosses do not have a religious background, but are placed on the city coat of arms as a simple visual sign that can be easily recognized. In 1489 the emperor's crown was placed at the top of the coat of arms. The crown descends from the Austrian ruler Maximilian of Austria. The city got permission to use the crown in its coat of arms as a sign of appreciation because of the financial support Maximilian had received from the city. In the 16th century two lions were added as shield-bearers. The coat of arms is only completed in 1948 when Queen Wilhelmina gives the city the right to add the subscription Heroic, Resolute, Merciful. The city coat of arms, sometimes only in the form of the three vertically placed St. Andrew's crosses, is frequently used. It can be seen on many public buildings, but also on city folders, on the bus, the tram, on bridges, trash cans, street lights, and on anti-parking-posts called 'Amsterdammertjes'.

Climate

Amsterdam has a temperate oceanic climate.
This is characterized by mild (damp) summers. Inland the temperature can go up to 28 degrees C. On the coast it is generally somewhat cooler.

January-March	winter, temp. between 0-5 degrees C., lots of rain, some snow.
April-May	spring, temp. between 15-20 degrees C., changeable.
June-August	summer, temp. between 20-28 degrees C., June is often rainy, July/August are the best summer months.
September-October	autumn, temp. between 15-20 degrees C., September mild, October changeable.
November-December	winter, temp. between 0-5 degrees C.; November changeable, wet and/or stormy; December, most cold and dark month.

Amsterdam in numbers

Population: 834.713
Area: 219.07 square kilometres
Nationalities:180
Bicycles: 881.000
Trees: 220.000
Parks: 50
Trams: 216
Ferries: 9
Outdoor Markets: 38
Shops: 7.948
Canals: 165
Bridges: 1.281
Sight-seeing booths: 110
Houseboats: 2.500
Historical houses: 8.863

Historical gable stones: 654
Statues: 302
Windmills: 8
Museums: 75
Paintings by Rembrandt: 22
Paintings by Van Gogh: 207
Street organs: 4
Carillons: 9
Historical church organs: 42
Cafés and bars: 1.515
Discotheques: 16
Restaurants: 1.839
Hotel beds: 54.857
Camping sites: 6
Day visits per year:17.000.000

Typical Amsterdam
Amsterdammertjes

At many places in the city these red-brown anti-parking-posts are placed with the three St. Andrew's crosses. After the II World War they are placed to prevent cars from parking on the sidewalks. The policy of the city now is to allow the posts to disappear from the street.

Coffee shops

There are about two hundred coffee shops in the city. You might think the name applies to drinking coffee here. This is not the case, here soft drugs are sold. Amsterdam is not what is commonly assumed a 'Walhalla' for soft drugs. Please do not think that every Amsterdammeruses these mind-expanding drugs. Compared to other (European) countries the Netherlands has, a policy of tolerating the sale of soft drugs. This policy aims at regulating the (international) trade and use of soft drugs. The police allow the sale of soft drugs in special hotel and catering businesses that have a tolerance licence. The sale is only permitted to persons above the age of 18 and not more than 5 grams per day. Even though the government aims at containing the trade and use of soft drugs in the coffee shops, you might be approached by a dealer on the street. They offer soft and also hard drugs. It is best to just ignore them and keep on walking. In most cases they will not press on any further. The police are very strict and will prosecute against the (street) trade and use of hard drugs.

220,000 trees
There are 220,000 trees in Amsterdam along the canals, lining the streets, and in the parks. That makes Amsterdam one of the greenest capitol cities in the world (compared to Paris: 90,000 trees).

Canals
Amsterdam has 165 canals, of which the four main canals Singel, Herengracht, Keizersgracht, and Prinsengracht are the most important. Along these canals are the historical and imposing 17th century merchants' houses with their splendid step, neck, bell, and frame gables. Along the radial canals that connect the four main canals are the somewhat smaller 17th century houses.

Diamonds
Amsterdam has a rich history of processing diamonds. The diamond business is traditionally carried out by the Jewish community. For this trade there was no gild (trade union), so that many Jewish newcomers could become proficient in the art of diamond cutting. This rich tradition can still be seen in the city. A few diamond businesses organise free information meetings for those who are interested. At Gassan Diamonds you can take a free diamond tour.
Gassan Diamonds B.V.
Nieuwe Uilenburgerstraat 173
www.gassandiamonds.nl

Flowers, flower bulbs, and wooden shoes

Flowers, flower bulbs, and wooden shoes belong to Amsterdam. Especially in the city centre you can find plenty of flowers, flower bulbs, and wooden shoes. The famous floating flower market is on the Singel.

Bicycles

The citizens of Amsterdam prefers transportation by bicycle. There are more than 881,000 bicycles in the city.

Trams

The tram is the most important form of public transportation in Amsterdam. From the Central Station the trams run to the different parts of the city.

Canal tour boats

The canal tour boats dominate the tourist excursions through the canals. Especially in the high season it is a coming and going of the glass-topped boats of the different tourist carriers. Besides the tour boats, the boat taxi and the water-bikes are omnipresent on the canals.

Street organs

Since 1875 the street organ has characterized the musical street image of Amsterdam. In the last 40 years their number has gone back from fifty to just a few street organs. A street organ can still be regularly heard in the Kalverstraat.

Urinals

The green cast iron urinals, also called curls, are spread out over the entire city. The urinals are placed by the city to urge men to urinate where it doesn't do damage or offend. There is one urinal on the Oudezijds Voorburgwal that is built in the architectural style of the Amsterdam School.

Peppermills

You see them everywhere in the city: large advertisement pillars in the shape of a peppermill. Besides having the function of an advertisement pillar, they are often transformer houses.

11

Amsterdam - month by month

January

• **Chinese New Year**
The Chinese community in Amsterdam celebrates this traditional holiday with the dragon dance, lots of noise, and fireworks.
Date: between January 21st and February 20th.
Location: Nieuwmarkt-Zeedijk.

February

• **Memorial of the February Strike in 1941**
This general work strike was aimed at the German occupying force and took place on 25th and 26th of February in Amsterdam, Zaanstreek, 't Gooi, Kennemerland, and Utrecht.
Date: February 25th.
Location: Statue the Dokwerker on the Jonas Daniel Meijerplein.

• **Household convention**
Five hundred exhibitors present their newest products at Netherlands largest consumer's event. Visitors see the newest trends in the areas of living, interiors, fashion, cosmetics, health, and more.
Date: variable
Location: RAI
www.rai.nl (NL, Eng)

March

• **Silent procession - Miracle on the Kalverstraat**
On March 15, 1345, a sick man received a consecrated wafer in a home on the Kalverstraat. The man had to throw-up after which the vomit with the wafer was thrown into the fire. The next morning the wafer was found untouched by the fire and was carried in a consecrated box to the Old Church. Upon arrival at the church the wafer had disappeared out of the box. The next day the wafer was found again in the house and again the priest took the wafer back to the church. Again the wafer couldn't be found in the box and again it was found back in the house on the Kalverstraat. On the third day when exactly the same thing happened they concluded that God wanted to reveal a Miracle. Since then every year in the night around the 15th of March a sacraments' procession is held.
Date: around March 15th
Location: starting at the Begijnhof.
www.stille-omgang.nl (NL, Eng).

April

• **National museum weekend**
During this weekend almost all of the museums are open free.
Date: second weekend in April.

• **King's Day**
On this day the Netherlands celebrates the birthday of King Willem Alexander (April 27, 1967). At the time of his ascent to the throne (April 30, 2013), King Willem Alexander declared April 27th to be the national King's Day. Hundreds of thousands of Dutch people come to Amsterdam during the largest free market in the world to celebrate.
Date: April 27th
Location: the whole city, with the emphasis on city centre, Jordaan, and Amsterdam South.

May

• **National Memorial Day**
Remembering the casualties of the II World War. At exactly 8 PM two minutes of silence are held for all of the fallen in the period 1940-1945.
Date: May 4th
Location: National Monument on the Dam and other locations.

• **Liberation Day**
May 5th is the national holiday when the liberation of the Netherlands from German and Japanese oppression in celebrated.
Date: May 5th.
Location: the whole city.

June

• **Holland Festival**
Theatre, opera, music, dance, and film are presented in diverse locations in the city.
Date: daily in the month of June.
Location: diverse places.
www.hollandfestival.nl (NL, Eng).

July

• Robeco Summer Concerts
Classical concerts at a reduced rate in the Royal Concertgebouw.
www.robecozomerconcerten.nl (NL, Eng).

• Amsterdam Roots Festival
The Amsterdam Roots Festival is a annual festival of world music and world cultures with presentations of more than forty groups and artists from different countries.
Date: third week in June.
www.amsterdamroots.nl (NL, Eng).

• Julidans
Dance and ballet festival in diverse theatres in the city.
www.julidans.nl (NL, Eng).

• Kwakoe Summer Festival
Multi-cultural festival with song, dance, film, literature, and exotic cooking.
Date and location:
www.kwakufestival.nl (NL).

• Over het IJ-festival
Opera, theatre and expressive arts on the NDSM terrain.
www.overhetij.nl (NL).

August

• Sail 2020
Sail is a maritime festival that is held every five years. Sail is one of the greatest maritime manifestations in the world. The next sail will take place in August, 2020.
www.sail.nl (NL, Eng).

• De Parade
Much dance, music, and art and entertainment in and around theatre tents.
www.deparade.nl (NL, Eng).

• Canal Festival
Classical concerts at more than 35 locations in the area around the Prinsen-, Keizers- and Herengracht.
www.grachtenfestival.nl (NL, Eng).

• Prinsengracht Concert
Classical concert in the open air.
Date: 3rd Saturday in August.
Location: Prinsengracht.
www.grachtenfestival.nl (NL, Eng).

• Out Market
Opening of the cultural season. Many performances and promotion stands.

www.amsterdamsuitburo.nl (NL, Eng).

September

• Jordaan Festival
Festival of music in the Dutch language.
Date: third weekend in September
Location: www.jordaanfestival.nl.

• Open Monument Day
A great number of monumental buildings can be visited free of charge.
Date: first weekend in September.
www.openmonumentendag.nl (NL).

October

• Marathon of Amsterdam
Marathon through the city with many international participants.
www.ingamsterdammarathon.nl (NL, Eng, Ger, Fr, Sp, Jap).

November

• The entry of St. Nicholas
More than 300,000 people of Amsterdam welcome St. Nicholas and his Black Peters. The saintly man sails via the Amstel to the Maritime musseum where he is welcomed by the mayor. Then the procession follows through the centre of Amsterdam.
Date: 2nd or 3rd Sunday in November

December

• St. Nicholas Eve
The people of Amsterdam celebrate St. Nicholas Eve by giving each other gifts and special sweets.
Date: December 5th.

• Christmas
The Netherlands celebrates two days of Christmas (December 25, 26). The shops (most) are closed. Many of the restaurants are open.

• New Year's Eve and New Year's Day
In Amsterdam oliebollen (doughnut-like balls) and apple turn-over's are sold, that are eaten especially on New Year's Eve. At midnight firework is set off to welcome in the New Year. There are large parties especially on the Museumplein and Nieuwmarkt.
Date: December 31st.
www.amsterdamsuitburo.nl (NL, Eng).

Nightlife in Amsterdam

Nightlife in Amsterdam is a special experience. The historic city centre offers you a combination of a great number of atmospheric possibilities: cafés, restaurants, cinemas, theatres, and discothèques. The busiest evenings are Friday and Saturday. The entertainment centre is concentrated around four areas.

The **Leidseplein** is probably the most important entertainment centre. Many (dance) cafés, discotheques, and fast food chains can be found there. The square also functions as the way through to the cinemas and theatres that are situated around the square. On the square the Stadsschouwburg (city theatre) is also situated. Street entertainers give the square a cheerful atmosphere. You can also

Leidseplein

find many cafés in the area around the **Zeedijk**. In this old part of the city you can taste the atmosphere of the old Amsterdam.

Rembrandtplein has been an important entertainment area since the beginning of the last century. There are many cafés, betting alleys, snack bars, and sandwich shops to be found here. Next to the Rembrandtplein is the **Reguliersbreestraat**. In this street a visit to the Tuchinski Cinema is worth your while. Especially the auditorium is a experience to remember because it is in the art-deco style. Between the Reguliersbreestraat and the Rembrandtplein lies the **Thorbeckeplein**. The square is named after J. R. Thorbecke, an influential statesman who took initiative in 1848 to write the Constitution of the Netherlands. There are mostly student cafés on this square.

Eating in Amsterdam

Dutch food

Dutch food is characterised by a hearty meal that is very filling. The Netherlands have an extensive kitchen with many special dishes. The Dutch put a lot of emphasis on vegetables. The vegeta bles are usually cooked and served with boiled potatoes, meat, and gravy.

Stamppot

The different stamppots (boiled potatoes mashed with curly kale or potatoes mashed with sauerkraut and smoked sausage) are the most popular of the traditional forms of Dutch food.

Snert (pea soup)
Is a tasty, thick, nutritious, main course soup that is filled with vegetables, dried peas, bacon, and smoked sausage. Both the stamppot as well as the Dutch pea soup are mainly eaten in the wintertime (Oct - Mar.).

Bread
In the Netherlands the bakers have a very good selection of bread and pastries. The supermarkets also sell good quality bread.

Cheese
The Netherlands is a cheese country. Cheese has been made here since prehistoric times.
The first cheese making dates from 800BC; the cheese was made in earthenware with holes so that the whey could leak out and the curds could dry. In Amsterdam there are many cheese specialty shops and supermarkets with a large variety of cheese for sale.

Herring stand

The Amsterdammer likes to eat a salty herring at the herring stand. The herring is a healthy goody that is also called Hollands Nieuwe. After the catch the herring is gutted first of all and then salted. When they are cleaned the gills are also removed to promote the drainage of the blood and therefore the blood doesn't stay in the fish meat. Only the pancreas is left in the fish and these enzymes work to give the herring its typical taste and odour. The fishmonger removes the pancreas before consumption. Salty herrings are for sale the whole year round. The new herring are brought in June /July. The stands are mostly on the bridges of the canals.

Drop (liquorice)

The Dutch eat more than 30 kilos of liquorice per person a year. The black candy is made from liquorice root and gum and comes in many flavours (salty, sweet, bitter, hard, and soft) and can be bought at many places.

15

Snacking (Eating 'out of the wall')
Croquette, minced-meat hot dog, and nasi ball. 'Eating out of the wall' is a typical Netherlands phenomenon. At different places in the city you can get hot snacks out of a food machine. After inserting the correct coins you can open a little glass door and remove the snack of your choice located behind it. The snack bar also sells chips (French-fried potatoes) with mayonnaise.

Breakfast
A Dutch breakfast consists of bread or rusk with butter, cheese, chocolate sprinkles, peanut butter, or jam.

Lunch
The Dutch lunch consists of bread with butter, with cheese, sandwich meat, or salad.

Kitchens with Dutch food
A selection of the restaurants:

- **Tomaz**
Begijnensteeg 6
T 020-3206489
- **Dorrius**
Nieuwezijds Voorburgwal 5
T 020-4202224
- **Moeders**
Rozengracht 251
T 020-6267957
- **De Silveren Spiegel**
Kattengat 4
T 020-6246589
- **Haesje Claes**
Spuistraat 275
T 020-6249998

- **Haven van Texel**
St Olofssteeg 11
T 020-4270768
- **De Engelbewaarder**
Kloveniersburgwal 59HS
T 020-6253772
- **Restaurant Lt. Cornelis**
Voetboogstraat 13
T 020-2614863
- **Geef**
Willemsstraat 16
T 020-3348497
- **Hemelse Modder**
Oude Waal 11
T 020-6243203

Eat 10 x under fifteen Euros
The meals are good; the ambiance may have something to be desired.

- **A Fusion**
Zeedijk 130 hs
Asian food.
- **Aroy Dee**
Rozengracht 235
Thai.
- **Latei**
Zeedijk 143
Curiosity Shop annex restaurant.
- **Noodle & Go**
Prinsengracht 292
Noodles, rice, and beef served in cardboard containers.
- **De Vliegende Schotel**
Nieuwe Leliestraat 162
Vegetarian restaurant.

- **Bojo**
Lange Leidsedwarsstraat 49-51
Indonesian restaurant.
- **De Blaffende Vis**
Westerstraat 118
A complete main meal in a relaxed beanery.
- **Song Kwae Thai**
Kloveniersburgwal 14
Among other dishes, delicious chicken soup and curries.
- **The Pancake Bakery**
Prinsengracht 191
75 different kinds of pancakes and omelets.
- **Wagamama**
M. Euweplein 10
Japanese dishes served on large-wooden benches.

Amsterdam Museum City

A msterdam has at least 40 museums. Especially the Rijksmuseum (including the Night Watch by Rembrandt van Rijn), the Van Gogh Museum (most important works by Vincent van Gogh) and the Rembrandthuis (the home and place of work of Rembrandt van Rijn) are world famous. The Rijksmuseum houses the Netherlands' largest collection of 17th century art. In the Rijksmuseum the paintings of the Dutch masters like Rembrandt van Rijn, Johannes Vermeer and Jan Steen can be admired. The Stedelijk Museum is specialised in modern art, while the Amsterdam Museum, gives an overview of the (art-) history of Amsterdam. In short, Amsterdam is an exceptional museum city.

Museumkaart (MK)

If you want to visit more museums during your stay in Amsterdam, the Museumkaart is an advantageous solution. With this card you have free entry to 400 museums in the Netherlands. There are 38 museums in Amsterdam where you have free entry with this card. Price: € 59.90 per year, younger than 19 years € 32.45 per year.
The card can be bought at a participating museum. At the purchase you also pay a once-only charge for administration.

History of Amsterdam

Amsterdam Museum
Nieuwezijds Voorburgwal 357/
Kalverstraat 92 - **MK**
www.amsterdammuseum.nl (NL, Eng).
The museum is established in the former commoner's orphanage and offers an overview of the (art-) history of Amsterdam in 23 rooms. A few works by Rembrandt van Rijn (1606-1669) are exhibited including the copper etching plate with a portrait of Clement de Jonghe (1651) and the Anatomical lesson of dr. Jan Deijman (1656).

Amsterdam Museum

Herengracht 366-368 Bible's Museum in the Cromhouthuizen (1660)

National Maritime Museum

Kattenburgerplein 1 - **MK**
www.scheepvaartmuseum.nl (NL, Eng).
Het Scheepvaartmuseum, the National
Maritime Museum, shows how our
culture has been shaped by the sea.
Stimulating, interactive exhibitions allow
visitors to explore 500 years of maritime
history. Attractive object exhibitions
show the best of our world famous
collection. There are special exhibitions
for children, including 'See you in the
Golden Age' and 'The tale of the whale'.
One is for children under the age of 6:
'Sal & Lori and Circus at Sea'.
And last but not least: the exciting ride
Voyage at Sea is suitable for all ages
and the famous replica of the VOC ship
Amsterdam is back at the quay. There
are also various museum facilities that
are open to the public free of charge,
including the Central Square, the Open
Courtyard, the museum shop Het Pa-
khuys, Restaurant Stalpaert, the library
and the waterside patio.

Shipyard Kromhout

Hoogte Kadijk 147
Kromhout is one of the oldest shipyards
in Amsterdam. The museum tells the
expressive story of shipbuilding since
the Golden age.

Royal Palace on the Dam

Dam
www.paleisamsterdam.nl (NL, Eng).
The former city hall of Amsterdam is
one of the palaces that is at the disposal
of the king by Dutch law. The function
of the palace is primarily representative.
For example it is used at times of visits
of state, for the New Year's reception,
and for other official receptions.
The building is more than worth your
while. The Citizens Hall is very impressive. There are maps of the eastern
and western hemispheres in marble
in the floor. The Vierschaar (tribunal)
and the Courtroom give a good idea of
jurisprudence in the 17th century. There
are a large number of statues you can
admire, including Quellinius the Elder.

Museum Willet-Holthuysen

Herengracht 605 - **MK**
www.willetholthuysen.nl (NL, Eng).
The museum shows the life of rich
Amsterdammers in the 18th and 19th
century. The original and last inhabitants
were Abraham Willet (1825-1888) and
his wife Louisa Holthuysen (1824-1825).
In 1895 Mrs. Willet willed her house and
the enormous art collection to the city
of Amsterdam under the condition that
it would become a museum. In this way
the Herengracht is the only completely
decorated canal house that is open to
the public daily. Inside there is a large
collection of art, furniture, glassware,
and other arts and crafts collected by
Abraham Willet.

Geelvinck Hinlopen House

Keizersgracht 633 - **MK**
www.geelvinckhinlopenhuis.nl (NL).
The museum displays four rooms of
the Amsterdam regent family Geelvinck
Hinlopen in the period between the
Golden Age and the Industrial Revolution. The large garden is exceptional.

Museum Van Loon

Keizersgracht 672 - **MK**
www.museumvanloon.nl (Nl, Eng).
The museum is situated in a monumental canal side house (1672) and has an
especially beautiful interior with rich
wainscoting, plasterwork, and mirrors.
Through the centuries the interior has
almost remained intact. The Van Loon
family bought the house in 1884 and
lived there until 1944. In 1973 the Van
Loon family opened the house to the
public. The house has several historical
rooms where 80 family portraits, a large
amount of furniture, silver and china
can be seen. Behind the house there
is a garden in the French style and a
classical coach house.

Culture & religion

Museum Amstelkring Ons' Lieve Heer op Solder

Oudezijds Voorburgwal 40 - **MK**
www.museumamstelkring.nl (NL, Eng).
The museum is in the oldest part of

Amsterdam and is established in a 17th century canal side building. The upper three stories were renovated into a hidden Roman Catholic Church the 17th century, complete with ambulatories, an altar, and 150 seats. On the first floor there are 17th and 19th century style rooms to be viewed. Exceptional are: the Sael, a large reception room with marble floors and painted ceiling, and the confessional dating to 1740. Besides, the museum has a large collection of paintings, statues, and silver, that gives a good impression of Catholic Netherlands in the 17th century. On the website you can take a virtual tour through the museum.

Allard Pierson Museum
Oude Turfmarkt 127 - **MK**
www.allardpiersonmuseum.nl (NL, Eng).
Archaeological museum from the University of Amsterdam. The Museum has a large collection of art and utensils from old Mediterranean cultures. These objects, complemented with scale models and reconstructions (including the pyramid complex at Giza and the Zeus shrine at Olympia), give an impression of life in the great cultures of the ancient world. Besides the permanent collections, there are temporary exhibitions on themes from the ancient world, like shipbuilding and music. The Allard Pierson Museum is housed in the former neo-classic building of the Netherlands Bank (1869).

Bible Museum
Herengracht 364-370 - **MK**
www.bijbelsmuseum.nl (Nl, Eng).
The museum is situated in the monumental Cromhout houses and offers a fascinating exploration through the world of one of the oldest and most read books. The large collection of archaeological finds is special, Egyptian objects, pictures, and Bibles. You can also admire the world famous 19th century tabernacle by rev. Schouten.

City Archives Amsterdam
Vijzelstraat 32

www.amsterdam.nl/stadsarchief
Besides the archives and a historical topographic collection, there are two of three exhibitions a year on subjects in the history of Amsterdam.

Hermitage Amsterdam
Amstel 51 - **MK**
www.hermitage.nl (NL, Eng).
Changing exhibitions come from the State Hermitage Museum in St. Petersburg. In juli 2009 the Amstelhof became available for exhibitions. The display area in the Hermitage is over 4,000 m².

The Nieuwe Kerk
Dam - **MK**
www.nieuwekerk.nl (NL, Eng).
Changing exhibitions can be seen the whole year in the monumental Nieuwe Kerk on the Dam. Check the website of the Nieuwe Kerk for the most recent exhibitions.

The Old Church
Oudekerksplein 23 - **MK**
www.oudekerk.nl (NL, Eng).
This is the oldest church of Amsterdam. Besides its exterior, its interior is very interesting as well. The church is famous for its Vater Müller organ (1724). Among the 2,500 gravestones there is one for Saskia van Uylenburgh, the first wife of the painter Rembrandt van Rijn. You can visit the tombs online. Exhibitions, theatre productions, and organ concerts

are organised regularly. The Old Church has the title of European Monument.

Jewish Historical Museum
Nieuwe Amstelstraat 1 - **MK**
www.jhm.nl (NL, Eng).
The museum is established since 1987 in four High German synagogues. The starting point of the permanent exhibition is the model 'What Does it Mean to be Jewish' made by Amsterdam's philosopher Ido Abram.
According to Abram there are five aspects that play a role in some way or other in the life of every Jew:
1. religion and tradition;
2. the bond with Israel and Zionism;
3. war, persecution, and survival;
4. personal history;
5. the interaction between the Jewish and the Dutch culture.
The museum also has changing exhibitions on art, culture and photography.

Painting
Van Gogh Museum
Museumplein 6 - **MK**
www.vangoghmuseum.nl (NL, Eng).
This museum offers the largest collection of works by Vincent van Gogh (1853-1879) in the world. The museum consists of three sections: the work of Vincent van Gogh, the work of other artists, and the history of the collection. The work of Van Gogh is divided into five periods that correspond with certain phases in his life and work: Netherlands, Paris, Arles, Saint-Rémy and Auvers-sur-Oise. The museum also owns a large collection of Van Gogh's contemporaries like Henri de Toulouse-Lautrec and Paul Gauguin.

The Appel
Prins Hendrikkade 142 - **MK**
www.deappel.nl (NI, Eng).
Museum for contemporary art is mostly work by international artists. In consultation with the artists, the exhibitions are specially developed for the museum.

Museum the Rembrandt House
Jodenbreestraat 4 - **MK**
www.rembrandthuis.nl (NL, Eng).
It is one of the most visited museums in Amsterdam. Rembrandt van Rijn lived and worked here during the period 1639-1658.The museum is divided into two parts. In the living section you can get an idea of how Rembrandt lived and worked. In the museum wing there are 260 etchings of the great master. Besides a permanent collection, there are also temporary expositions. On the website of the Rembrandt House you can prepare for your visit by taking a virtual tour of the museum.

Rijksmuseum
Museumstraat 1- **MK**
www.rijksmuseum.nl (NL, Eng).
The Rijksmuseum is the largest museum in the Netherlands. It has more than 1,250 top pieces, including a great number of the Dutch masters, like 'The Night Watch' by Rembrandt van Rijn, and self-portraits of Rembrandt, The Kitchen Maid by Johannes Vermeer, realistic portraits of Ferdinand Bol and The Happy Drinker by Frans Hals. The museum also has a large collection of sculptures and a print collection and a collection of art from the Asian regions. If you pay a visit to the museum, it is wise to decide beforehand what you want to see. The website offers wide possibilities from which to choose from the extensive art collection.

Stedelijk Museum
Museumplein 10 - **MK**
www.stedelijk.nl (NL, Eng).
This is a museum of contemporary and modern art from the period 1850-present. The 'Stedelijk' is one of Europe's most important museums of modern art and has a comprehensive collection of works by Karel Appel (Cobra) and a collection of American and French abstract expressionists. There is also a collection of arts and crafts and industrial design (for example Rietveld). On the museum's website you can look at the most important works.

Second World War
Hollandse Schouwburg (Dutch Theatre)
Plantage Middenlaan 24 - **Free entry**

www.hollandscheschouwburg.nl (NL, Eng).
During the war years 1942-1943 the Hollandse Schouwburg was used as a place of deportation for Jews. From the Schouwburg thousands of Jews were transported to the transit camp Westerbork, and from there further to concentration camps in Germany and Poland. Since 1962 the Schouwburg is a place of commemoration for the Jewish victims.

Anne Frank House
Prinsengracht 267 - **MK**
www.annefrank.org (NL, Eng).
During two years Anne Frank wrote her world famous diaries from this place of hiding. The Achterhuis on the Prinsengracht 263 is still in original state. The museum contains a collection of original objects from Anne Frank and the other persons in hiding. Furthermore there are original diary citations, the original dairy, and other documents from Anne Frank.

Dutch Resistance Museum
Plantage Kerklaan 61 - **MK**
www.verzetsmuseum.org (NL, Eng).
The museum is situated in the Plancius building (1876) opposite the entrance to the Artis Zoo. By means of documents, films, sound fragments, artefacts and photos, the permanent exhibition represents life in the Netherlands during the Second World War. There are also regular changing exhibitions.

Education and nature
KattenKabinet
Herengracht 497
www.kattenkabinet.nl (NL, Eng).
The collection of the Cat Cabinet shows the role of the cat in art and culture throughout the centuries.

Tropenmuseum
Linnaeusstraat 2 - **MK**
www.tropenmuseum.nl (NL, Eng).
The core of the museum is the combined collection of the 19th century Colonial Museum in Haarlem and the old ethnological collection from the Artis zoo.

Madame Tussauds
Dam 20
www.madametussauds.nl (NL, Eng).
Museum of wax figures of many famous people. It has an extra perk: the beautiful view across the Dam.

NEMO
Oosterdok 2 - **MK**
www.e-nemo.nl (NL, Eng).
This museum lets you discover how science and technology have evolved from human creativity.It is an exploration trip between fantasy and reality. Interactivity is the key-word for Nemo. You must try computer games and make science experiments yourself. The museum can be reached via the quay around the IJ-tunnel. Via the stairs you reach the roof, where you have a fantastic view over the city.

Artis Royal Zoo
Plantage Kerklaan 38-40

natura
ARTIS
magistra

www.artis.nl (NL, Eng).
Artis (1838) is the oldest zoo in the Netherlands and one of the oldest in the world. The zoo contains around 9,600 animals (900 species) and a variety of monuments. One of Artis its major objectives is to keep the animals in their natural habitat. The Zoological Museum is part of the University of Amsterdam. The collection contains of more than 13 million registered objects.

Hortus Botanicus
Plantage Middenlaan 2a
www.dehortus.nl
The Hortus Botanicus (1638) is one of the oldest botanical gardens in the

world. In the garden and hothouses there are 6,000 plants of more than 4,000 species. Behind the 300 hundred year old entrance it is as if the city is holding its breath.

Theo Thyssen Museum
Eerste Leliedwarsstraat 16
www.theothijssenmuseum.nl (NL).
The museum is devoted to the Amsterdam writer, teacher, trade-union-man, and social democrat Theo Thijssen (1873-1943). He is especially remembered for his novel "Kees de Jongen".

Miscellaneous
EYE
IJpromenade 1 - **MK**
www.eyefilm.nl (NL, Eng).
EYE encourages debate and reflection about the role of film and media in society today. It preserves a collection of films that spans the whole film history.

Houseboat Museum
Prinsengracht opposite 296,
www.houseboatmuseum.nl (NL, Eng).
The HouseboatMuseum is an authentic freight ship that is renovated into a houseboat. On the ship the 'Hendrika Maria' you can experience what it is like to live on a houseboat on a canal in Amsterdam.

Heineken Museum
Stadhouderskade 78
www.heinekenexperience.nl (NL, Eng).
The museum is established in the old Heineken brewery (1867) and gives an extensive look into Heineken as the world's most leading beer brewer. In the museum you become acquainted with the malt silos, the brewing house, and the famous advertising campaigns.

Hash Marihuana Museum
Oudezijds Achterburgwal 148
www.hashmuseum.com (Eng).
You can see the hemp garden and the collection of hemp implements and paintings give a good picture of the role of marihuana and hash in history.

Amsterdam Tulip Museum
Prinsengracht 112
www.amsterdamtulipmuseum.com
(Eng).
The museum gives an overview of the history of the tulip, also a shop for flower bulbs.

The Amsterdam Dungeon
Rokin 78
www.theamsterdamdungeon.nl (NL, Eng).
Combination of museum, theatre and attraction. The history of Amsterdam is brought to life in a grizzly and thrilling manner. The Dungeon is not suitable for young children and people of the nervous type. Children are only allowed entrance if they are accompanied by an adult. Length: about 80min.

Ajax Museum
Arena Boulevard 29
www.ajax.nl (NL, Eng).
One hundred years of Ajax history that takes you from long before WW I, via Johan Cruyff up to now.

Museum Het Schip
Spaarndammerplantsoen 140 - **MK**
www.hetschip.nl (NL, Eng).
This is a Museum about the Amsterdam School, a stream in art and architecture, situated in the building 'Het Schip". The museum gives entrance to a restored working-class house, the world famous tower of architect De Klerk and the exhibition on the sources of inspiration of the Amsterdam School. The exhibition is accessible in French, German, English, Spanish, and Italian.

Huis Marseille
Keizersgracht 401 - **MK**
www.huismarseille.nl (Eng).
House Marseille is the first photo museum in Amsterdam. In contrast with the exposition programme which also contains historical photography; the collection at House Marseille mainly focuses on present-day photography.

Entrance of Museum Het Schip

Architecture in Amsterdam

A msterdam has rich (top) gable architecture. The different gable types were used to camouflage the sharp pitched roofs. In the past centuries many gable types were replaced and houses were demolished.

Presently the old gables are saved as much as possible and the houses behind the façades are restored. If this is not possible, a new house is built behind an authentic façade.

Gable types in Amsterdam

The wooden gable (1200-1669)

Until the middle of the 16th century there were mostly wooden houses in Amsterdam.

During the great city fires of 1421 and 1452 most of the wooden houses were lost. Local ordinances in

Begijnhof 34

1452, 1521, and 1669 finally forbid the building of wooden houses. There are still two wooden houses left in Amsterdam:

- Begijnhof 34 (1425)
- Zeedijk 1 (1550)

Stepped-gable (1600-1665)

In the 17th century the stepped-gable was the most common gable in Amsterdam.

In the following centuries most of the stepped-gables were rebuilt into neck-gables, Dutch gables, or frame gables. The

Geldersekade 97

distinguishing characteristic of the stepped-gable is that the top gable gets narrower step-by-step. There are still quite a few authentic stepped-gables in sober or in a more exuberant renaissance style. In the 19th century more stepped-gables were built, but in a neo-renaissance style.

Spout-gable and Trapezium-gable (1620-1720)

On this type of gable the top step is in the shape of a spout. The spout gable was often used on warehouses and on back sides of homes. The trapezium gable (a double spouted gable) occurs mostly in double warehouses.

Brouwersgracht 184

Trapezium-gable Brouwersgracht 208

Elevated neck-gable (1640-1670)

This is a transition between the stepped-gable and the neck-gable. The raised neck-gable has two steps and a classical application of frontons, cornices, and pilasters.

Keizersgracht 319

Neck-gable (1640-1780)

Herengracht 390-392

The neck-gable developed from the stepped-gable and has one step. In many neck-gables there are stone scrolls applied with sculptured or relief figures of persons, animals, frontons and decorations.

Dutch gable (1660-1790)

The scrolls around the bell-shape are of brick. The 17th century Dutch gables have curved-in sides. The 18th century Dutch gables are usually high. The Dutch gables in different Louis-styles are crowned with a crest or a decorative vase.

Keizersgracht 546

Cornice-gable

These are gables with a straight cornice where the centre section is decorated with sculpture-work. Around 1780 many triangular pediment were placed above the middle section of the cornice-gable. In the 19th century there was much use made of wood for finishing the cornice moulding. On the raised-cornice gable (1700-1775), the cornice moulding is made higher to have room for an attic trapdoor and to hide the steep pitched roof behind.

Herengracht 527

Singel 24 - Raised-cornice gable

Architectural styles

Hollands Brich Gothic (1300)

Is a style that reaches back to building in the gothic style. The first gothic brick houses that were built in Amsterdam have all been demolished.
The Agnietenkapel, the Old Church, de Nieuwe Kerk, de Waag and the Schreierstoren all have gothic elements.

Renaissance (1570-1665)

After about 1570 the renaissance period starts, at the same time of the building of brick dwellings. Amsterdam has four renaissance periods:
- **Early renaissance (1540-1600)**
From 1570 the brick-on-edge ornaments come into being. These are decorations along the gable tops in the shape of an S or a C.
Examples:
- gate of the Agnietenkapel (1571)
- gate of the Burgerweeshuis Sint Luciënsteeg (1571)
- gate to the Burgerweeshuis on the Kalverstraat (1581)

- Holland's renaissance (1600- 1615)

Around 1600 each city developed its own architecture style. In Amsterdam the sober Haarlem's renaissance style was mostly used. This style can be recognised by simple stepped-gables with a large number of regular steps. The top step often has a top pilaster with winged scrolls and a small sculpture. Thin small semi-circular relieving arches are above the windows with five blocks of white stone. At the level of the windows there are different layers of soapstone.

Examples:
- Singel 2-2a (1603)
- Nieuwmarkt 20-22 (1605)
- Oudezijds Voorburgwal 14 (1605)
- Kattegat 4-6 (1614)

- Amsterdam's renaissance (1615-1640)

This style is especially designed by the city's architect Hendrick de Keyser. The style can be recognised by stepped-gables with a small number of unequal risers and large steps. Each step has a sculptured stone scroll filling. Between the windows the piers have two pilasters with ornaments. Use of S-shaped relieving arches and many playful decorations, like men's or women's faces are typical. Furthermore there is much use of pediments, balls, and pillars.

Examples:
- Oudezijds Voorburgwal 57 (1615)
- Oudezijds Voorburgwal 18 (1615)
- Herengracht 170-172 (1622)

- Sober Amsterdam's renaissance (1615-1665)

This is a less expensive model of Amsterdam's renaissance. It was used for common homes. It can be recognised by simple stepped-gables with equal small steps, a small sculpture on the top pilaster. The relieving arches are made from three heavy pieces of stone.

Examples:
- Prinsengracht 2-4 (1641)
- Bloemgracht 87, 89, 91 (1642)
- Herengracht 81 (1625)

Holland´s Classicism (1640-1670)

Has a stern symmetrical building style, based on the Roman book of orders. Many Doric, Ionic, Tuscan and Corinthian elements are used. Because of the use of pilasters and pillars the buildings are broad and imposing.

Examples:
- Palace on the Dam (1665)
- Kloveniersburgwal 29 (1662)
- Kloveniersburgwal 95 (1642)

The Austere (sober classicism) style (1665-1700)

No pilasters are used anymore. The gables are bare and austere and can be recognised by the simple brick neck-gable. The filling scrolls are usually lavishly decorated with figures of people and animals. There is usually a decoration applied above the door or the middle window.

Examples:
- Herengracht 168 (1638)
- Herengracht 412 (1664)
- Herengracht 462 (1672)

Louis XIV style (1700-1740)

Herengracht 284

This is a robust style of architecture, especially the cornices with a balustrade on the cornice moulding. It has much baroque decoration and sculpture work.

Examples:
- Herengracht 364-370 (1660)
- Herengracht 284 (1728)
- Single 390 (1700)

Louis XV style (1749-1770)

This style is mainly applied to the Dutch gable. It is a loose asymmetrical building style with many decorations and narrow tall windows.

Keizersgracht 240

Examples:
- Keizersgracht 240 (1750)
- Keizersgracht 546 (1760)
- Reestraat 8 (1763)

Louis XVI style (1770-1800)

Herengracht 527

This is an austere classicism style with sober gables and little ornamentation. Only the cornices are decorated with festoons and crowned with tympanums.
Examples:
- Keizersgracht 324 (1787)
- Muiderpoort (1770)
- Herengracht 527 (1770)

Neo-styles (1815-1900)

This is the use of old styles (gothic, renaissance, and baroque), that leads to neo-gothic, neo-renaissance, and neo-baroque. When these styles are combined, we call it eclecticism.
Examples:
- Neo-gothic, Vondelkerk (1880)
- Neo-renaissance, Stadsschouwburg (1894)
- Neo-baroque, St Nicholas Church (1884)

Eclecticism (1850-1880)

This is a combination of different architecture styles. The styles come back separately in the building or the styles are combined to form a new style.
Examples:
- Rokin 112 (1856)
- Amstel Hotel - Prof. Tulpplein 1 (1867)

Jugendstil or Art nouveau (1890-1905)

Modern whimsical architecture style that is noticeable in its use of smooth bricks, lead glass windows, glazed tiles, and fanciful plant and animal figures in striking colours.
Examples:
- Haarlemmerdijk 39 (1896)
- Raadhuisstraat 23-55 (1899)

Historicizing (about 1910)

This style reaches back to the past. The buildings look older than their age.
Examples:
- Herengracht 206-214 (1918)
- Keizersgracht 555 (1919)

Amsterdam's School (1915-1940)

This style resists the use of neo-styles. The emphasis is on striking but modest decoration of the façades, the masonry is lavish.
Examples:
- Prins Hendrikkade 108-114 (1916)
- Damrak 243 (1903)

Architects

Hendrick de Keyser (1565-1621)

He was one of the most influential master builders in Amsterdam. He developed his own renaissance style that reached back to the classicism. His use of cornice mouldings,pediments, and pilasters led to the Amsterdam renaissance style. Besides being an architect, he was also a stone mason and sculptor.
Examples:
- Zuiderkerk (1611)
- Oudezijds Voorburgwal 57 (1615)
- Westerkerk (1632)

Jacob van Campen (1596-1657)

He was the founder of the Holland's Classicism.
Examples:
- Rembrandthuis (1628)
- Oude Accijnshuis (1638)
- Paleis op de Dam (1665)

Philip Vingboons (1607-1678)
He was a creative designer in classicism. He is also the inventor of the neck-gable (Vingboonsgable) that we come across many times in Amsterdam. Besides dwellings, he also designed 'city palaces'.
Examples:
- Keizersgracht 319 (1639)
- Kloveniersburgwal 95 (1642)
- Herengracht 364-370 (1660)

Justus Vingboons (1620-1698)
The brother of Philip Vingboons also built in the Holland's classicism style.
Examples:
- Kloveniersburgwal 29 (1662)
- Herengracht 390-392 (1665)

Daniel Stalpaert (1615-1676)

He is one of the most influential architects of Amsterdam. He finished the Koninklijk Paleis (1665) and built 's Lands Zeemagazijn, now the Scheepvaartmuseum (Maritime Museum) (1656) and the Oosterkerk (1669).

Adriaan Dortsman (1635-1682)
He designed in the style of Holland's classicism. His speciality was double houses along the canals.
Examples:
- The Round Lutheran Church (1671)
- Keizersgracht 672-674 (1671)
- Herengracht 462 (1672)

Elias Bouman (1636-1686)
He built in the style of Holland's Classicism.
Examples:
- Portuguese Israelite Synagogue (1675)
- Sint Antoniesbreedsstraat 69 (about 1680)

Jacob Otten Husly (1738-1796)
He built especially in the Louis XVI style.
Examples:
- Felix Meritus (1787)
- Herengracht 40 (1790)

Abraham van der Hart (1747-1820)
He was master builder on the austere Louis XVI style.
Examples:
- The Maagdenhuis (1787)
- Prinsengracht 89-133 (1804)

Pierre Cuypers (1827-1921)

He designed mostly in the neo-renaissance and neo-gothic styles.
Examples:
- Central Station (1889)
- Rijksmuseum (1876)

Gerlof Salm (1831-1897) and Abraham Salm (1857-1915)

Abraham Salm

Father and son Salm combined various neo-styles from the past. In this eclectic style they produced a great many buildings that are vital to the image of the city. They also built homes.
Examples:
- Artis Aquarium (1882)
- Keisersgrachtkerk (1888)
- Herengracht 380-382 (1890)

Adolf van Gendt (1835-1901)

He built in the eclecticism style until 1880, and after that mostly in neo-renaissance.
Examples:
- Concertgebouw (1886)
- Raadhuisstraat 23-55 (1899)
- Vondelstraat 140 (1880)

Gerrit van Arkel (1858-1918)

He especially designed homes and office/bank buildings. Before 1894 he mostly used the neo-gothic and neo-renaissance and after 1894 mostly Jugendstil. His buildings can be recognised by the use of asymmetrically placed balconies, bay windows, open towers, and cupolas.
Examples:
- Utrechtsestraat 30 (1894)
- Spui 15-19 (1895)

H.P. Berlage (1856-1934)

Berlage rejected the use of neo-styles and developed his own Berlage-style from which later the Amsterdam's School developed. Berlage was also an important urban developer. Large parts of Amsterdam-South are by his hand.
Examples:
- Kalverstraat 152 (1886)
- Beurs van Berlage (1903)

Joan Melchior van der Mey (1878-1949)

He was an architect in the style of the Amsterdam's School.
Example:
- Scheepvaarthuis

Piet Kramer (1881-1961)

He was one of the leading architects of the Amsterdam's School. Kramer designed more than 400 bridges, including the Magere Brug on the Amstel.

He also assisted J.M. van der Mey in building the Scheepvaarthuis.

M. de Klerk (1884-1923)
He was an architect in the Amsterdam's School. He assisted J.M. van der Mey in building the Scheepvaarthuis and designed housing complexes in the style of the Amsterdam's School for housing corporations.
Examples:
• Spaarndammerplantsoen 140 (1917)
• Vrijheidslaan 2-46/50-78 (1923)

Bridges
Amsterdam is hemmed in by a lot of water. During your stay in Amsterdam you will come across five types of historical bridges.

Plate Bridge

Blauwbrug - Amstel (1884)

These bridges are built since 1860. The bridge is supported by iron or metal carriers. In the 20th century many of these bridges were built in the style of the Amsterdam's School.

Girder Bridge

Kloveniersburgwal (1904)

This is the oldest type of bridge in the city. The bridge is supported by wooden, straight girders, upon which the road surface rests. The girder bridge cannot be opened.

Bridge or sluice

In Amsterdam bridge or sluice mean the same.

Drawbridge
This is a wooden or metal single or double drawbridge. The wooden specimens are usually white and have a typical old-Holland's character. The metal drawbridges are green and have a robust design.

Hoogte Kadijk (1903)

Footbridge

Oudezijds Voorburgwal
(1893)

Footbridges, as the name suggests, are narrow bridges for pedestrians only. Footbridges can be girder or plate bridges.

Arched Bridge

Keizersgracht

The bridge is supported by more or less half circular or ellipse-shaped brick arches on which the road surface lies. An arched bridge cannot be opened.

Arched Bridges - Reguliersgracht

Hofjes (almshouses built around a courtyard garden)

A hofje is a early typical Dutch form of care for the elderly. Hofjes were founded by rich citizens in the 17th, 18th and 19th centuries to provide housing for older men and women. Because of their secluded layout, they are difficult to see from the street. They are square complexes with small houses and a regent's room. In the courtyard there was usually a lantern post and a pump. This is where they bleached and dried their laundry. Nowadays these are courtyard gardens. The entrance to a hofje is usually through a gatehouse where the regent's room was. Most of the hofjes are named after their founder. There are still 200 hofjes left in the Netherlands and 47 of them are in Amsterdam. Most of the hofjes are in the Jordaan. It is possible to see a number of the hofjes (free entry).

The most beautiful hofjes

Begijnhof (1389)

Sint Andrieshofje (1614)
Egelantiersgracht 105-141

Raepenhofje (1648)
Palmgracht 28-38

Karthuizerhof (1650)
Karthuizerstraat t.o. 155

Nieuw Suykerhofje (1755)
Prinsengracht 385-393

Van Brienenhofje (1804)
Prinsengracht 89-133

Begijnhof

Dam

T he name Dam comes from the function it had at the time of the founding of Amsterdam. Between 1205 and 1275 a dam was built at this place on the

river the Amstel. The Dam was the connection between the people of the settlements on both shores of the river. The plaza is rectangular and is (from north to south) 100 metres long and (from west to east) 200 metres wide. Through the centuries the Dam has been drastically changed. Until the 17th century the square was hemmed in by houses and could only be reached by streets and allies.At the beginning of the 20th century the Dam was radically changed. The Nieuwe Kerk, the Koninklijk Paleis (Royal Palace) and the 17th century house at nr. 11 are the only three buildings that date from a former period.

☛ **Royal Palace - J. van Campen & D. Stalpaert/1648**

The building in the style of the Holland's classicism is standing on 13,659 piles, measures 80x57.5 metres and is completely built of sandstone. It is one of the most important monuments in the Netherlands.
The palace was originally built as the city hall and had to mirror the prestige and riches of Amsterdam as economic world power.
The seven undecorated arches at the height of the entrance (Dam side) pertain to the seven provinces that made up the Northern Netherlands.
The centre section, both front and back, has seven windows with pediments. These have bronze statues and marble sculptures from the famous sculptor Quellijn. A statue of Atlas is standing at the back of the building. The two corner pavilions each have three windows. The façades above the first floor are grouped by colossal Corinthian and composite pilasters that support the heavy cornices.
Between the high and the low windows festoons are applied as decoration. The chimneys are decorated with streamers, laurel leaves and flowers. The (open) cupola tower has eight round arches. The pillars are ornamented Corinthian three-quarter columns. The weather vane on top of the cupola has the shape of a cog ship, part of the old city coat of arms of Amsterdam. In the 17th and 18th centuries they could watch from the cupola to see the ships come in on the IJ.
The fronton at the front refers to Amsterdam as a trading city. Between 1648 and 1808 the building was the city hall of Amsterdam.
During the French occupation the city hall functioned as palace for King Louis Napoleon.
In 1813 the palace became city hall of Amsterdam again for a short time. In 1815 it became the official Royal Palace of the Dutch royal family. Presently the palace has a predominantly symbolic function. The king and the royal family make use of it.

First floor:

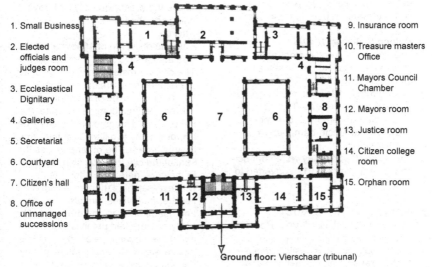

1. Small Business

2. Elected officials and judges room

3. Ecclesiastical Dignitary

4. Galleries

5. Secretariat

6. Courtyard

7. Citizen's hall

8. Office of unmanaged successions

9. Insurance room

10. Treasure masters Office

11. Mayors Council Chamber

12. Mayors room

13. Justice room

14. Citizen college room

15. Orphan room

Ground floor: Vierschaar (tribunal)

Interior:
The palace has lots of marble, sculpture, and paintings. Important halls and rooms in the palace are:
The Burgerzaal (citizen's hall): this is in the middle of the building and is impressive with its statue of Atlas, and the stars of the east and western hemispheres pictures in marble on the floor. There are two courtyards, one on each side of the Burgerzaal. Next to the entrance (on the side of the Dam) is *the Vierschaar* where the highest court of law was established. The statues in the Vierschaar pertain to justice.

The Troonzaal, or former Schepenenzaal, served in the 17th century as courtroom for lesser court cases. Presently it is a reception hall.

The Burgemeesters Kamer (mayor's room) served as a conference room for the four mayors that Amsterdam had in the 17th century.

In *the Oude Raadzaal (old council room)* the big meetings of the four mayors were held in the 17th and 18th centuries. During the French occupation, in 1808, it was a private chamber of King Louis Napoleon.

In *the Justitiekamer (judicial room)* convicts were prepared for the death sentence.

Palace lanterns (1840)

The six gas lanterns in front and behind the royal palace were presented by King William II to the city of Amsterdam in 1843. On the foot of the lanterns there are lions. The crowns on the lanterns are not the emperor's crown of Amsterdam, but just a general crown.

Since July 1, 1844 they were connected with gas, and in 1917 converted to electricity.

☞ Nieuwe Kerk - (1408)

The Nieuwe Kerk is a former Roman Catholic parish church. The church is a multiple buttress basilica with a normal transept and is built in a style combination of French gothic and early renaissance. In January 1645 a

large part of the church was ravaged by a great fire. Afterwards the church was restored by Jacob van Campen in gothic style.

Like more churches in Amsterdam, the Nieuwe Kerk does not have a real tower. The city council on the 17th century did not want the church to tower above the prestigious city hall (royal palace on the Dam).

Interior:
After the great fire of 1645 the interior was also restored in 17th century style. The city of Amsterdam commissioned the famous silversmith Johannes Lutma to make the brass choir gates. He received the commission after the fire of 1645. The gate on the one side is crowned by two lions with the arms of Amsterdam. The other side has the seal of the city (the cog ship) applied to the choir gate. The adornments with eye-catching themes from nature: flowers, fruit, vines, angels, animals and heads of rams and monsters. The richly ornamented pulpit is exceptional. The woodcarvings on the pulpit depict the works of virtuousness, mercy, the last ordeal, and parables from the New Testament.

The oldest part of the church is

around the choir and the ten chapels. Each of the ten chapels have different late gothic characteristics. To the right of the choir is the oldest chapel, the Eggert Chapel, named after the master builder of the Nieuwe Kerk, William Eggert. In the church there are five monuments to sea heroes, one of which is the tomb of Netherlands greatest heroes of the sea, Michiel de Ruyter (1607-1677), is the most known.

The Nieuwe Kerk has a rich tradition of stained-glass windows. The oldest dates from the middle of the 17th century and the newest is from 2005. The two organs are also exceptional. The small portable organ is noteworthy for its graceful style with three small spires. The organ did not perish in the fire of 1645, because it was away for repairs. In 1651 the portable organ was placed back.

Behind the organ there is an orphan gallery. The gallery is named after the orphans from the Burgerweeshuis (citizens' orphanage) (in the Kalverstraat) who attended church in the Nieuwe Kerk. The monumental main organ dates from 1655 and is decorated with likenesses of King David and King Saul.

Presently the Nieuwe Kerk is a place for social and cultural activities and exhibitions. The church also has a constitutional function. According to the Netherlands' Constitution, the king will accept his duties here in the Nieuwe Kerk by taking the oath on the Constitution. King William I did this for the first time in 1814, King Willem-Alexander on April 30, 2013.

The church was completely restored between 1959 and 1980.

Dam about 1544

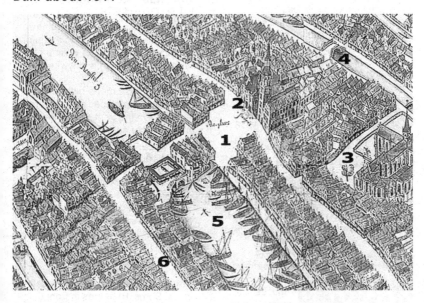

1 Dam
2 Old city hall
3 Nieuwe Kerk
4 The bridge over Nieuwezijds Voorburgwal (now Raadhuisstraat)

5 Amstel (now Damrak)
6 Warmoesstraat

Dam 1 - De Bijenkorf (B.A. Lubbers & J.A. van Straten/1914).
The outside of the building is built from stone. The floors are supported by a socle.The corner pavilions and the centre section have a cornice of half-round pediments. The tower is striking on the middle of the building. In memory of the founder of the Bijenkorf, Simon Philip Goldsmit, the initials S. P. G. are inscribed above the entrances above the coping stones. The symmetrical design and the pediments are typically classicism. The building is a national monument.

Dam 9 - Grand Hotel Krasnapolsky/ Glazen Paleis or Wintertuin (G.B. Salm/1879).
Hotel Krasnapolsky is one of the best known hotels in Amsterdam. Until 1879 Krasnapolsky was a café-restaurant. After rebuilding in 1879 the large hall was changed into the Wintertuin. A high glass cap was attached, supported by an iron roof construction, made with cast iron columns. The Wintertuin has a special atmosphere through its paintings, galleries and real palm trees.

Dam 27 - De Industrieele Groote Club (F. Kuipers/1913-1916).
This is an asymmetrical building in the style of the Amsterdam's School, built for the manufacturers and industrialists of Amsterdam who joined in 1913 in the Sociëteit Industria (industrial association). The building has four different gables. The sandstone bottom structure stands out behind this stores are situated, as well as the tower with its green copper roof. The society's rooms are (still) on the first floor.

Dam 20 - Peek & Cloppenburg (A.J. Jong/1914-1917).

In 1914 fourteen picturesque houses were demolished on the south side of the Dam between the Kalverstraat and the Rokin to make the building of this large clothing store in historical style possible. Around the building fourteen gable stones are cemented in as a memorial to the names of the houses that once stood here.

Dam 16
Sociëteitsgebouw De Groote Club (Th. G. Schill/1914).
The association the Groote Club (founded in 1872) commissioned this building to be built. In 1975 the Industrieele Club and the Groote Club decide to go together as the Industrieele Groote Club at Dam 27. In this building members of the German War Marines found themselves on May 7, 1945. While the people of Amsterdam were celebrating their freedom, the German soldiers opened fire on the crowds from the balcony. There were 22 dead and 120 wounded.

☞ Nationaal Monument - J.J.P. Oud/1956

Since 1956, the National Monument on the Dam is the symbol to the public for respect for the Dutch victims of war or peace missions, anywhere in the world.
The imposing 22 metre high white stone column is placed on a square pedestal. On the front side of the column is a relief depicting four shackled men. Above this relief is a tableau with a woman and a child. On both sides of the column is a stone plateau of a man with crying dogs at his feet.
At the back of the column is a relief with doves flying upward. To the rear of the column a semicircular memorial wall is built in white stone. In the niches of the wall urns are placed with earth.
The memorial is placed on a paving of bricks that goes upwards in concentric circles. Some 10 metres in front of the column a lion is placed on both sides on a circular pedestal.

The National Monument on the Dam

Damrak

The word Damrak is derived from 'rak', a straight stretch of waterway that goes up to the Dam (Damrak). The name dates from the 15th century when there was still an open water connection with the IJ. The houses on the east side were along the water, while the houses on the west side were on the dike (Nieuwendijk). During the 19th century most of the Damrak was filled in and it lost its function as a city harbour. The present Damrak is the last part of open water of the Amstel between the Dam and the IJ. Today the Damrak is a traffic artery between the Dam and the Central Station.

The most important buildings on the Damrak:

☛ 1-5 Victoriahotel - J.F. Henkenhoff/1890

The building is completely built with stone in the eclecticism style and makes a robust impression. The Corinthian half columns bear the imposing cornice. The domed tower and the semi-circular dome in the front immediately attract attention when one walks from the Central Station towards the Damrak.
26-30 Verzekeringsmaatschappij De Utrecht (A.J. Kropholler & J.F. Staal/1905)

This is a combination of a warehouse (nr. 26-27) and an office building (nr. 28-30). The building was inspired by New York sky-scrapers. This eight floor office building is striking because of its handsome combination of black granite and natural stone.
The five statues (J. Mendes da Costa/ 1863-1939) bear reference to economy, love, volatility, wisdom, and vigilance. The statue above the main entrance (nr. 28-30) refers to adoration. The statues all have a relation to the pre-

cariousness of life. But, that there is a possibility to insure against financial setbacks. The owls, the monkeys, and the other flower and animal figures are also from the hand of Mendes da Costa. A small corner tower and a piece of the roof that is covered with green copper catches the eye.

37-38 Is an asymmetric business building (J.W.F. Hartkamp/1903) of stone in art nouveau style. There are many decorations with animal figures.

50 Neck-gable (± 1720) with decorated stone scrolls.

55 Neck gable (± 1750) in Louis XIV-style with stone scrolls with scale motif.

59 Stepped-gable (1632) with Doric pilasters and human heads in the style of the Holland's renaissance. The stack of books refers to Casper Commelin who was a writer and bookseller; he had this house built and lived here.

62 Former bookstore Allert de Lange (G. van Looy/1886). The building is in neo-renaissance style with chequered relieving arches above the windows. The owl in the gable top and the different sculptured objects and texts have to do with the function the building had as a bookstore.

243 The Beurs van Berlage - H.P. Berlage/1903

The Beurs (stock exchange) was built

in the period 1898-1903 and is characterised by its austere style. The three corner statues picture Hugo de Groot (jurist and philosopher), Gijsbrecht van Amstel (founder of the city Amsterdam), and Jan Pietersz. Coen (admiral in the merchant marines 17th century). The statues as well as doors, steps, and window casings are all within the gable. Berlage used this technique to create the idea of unity.

The main entrance on Beursplein consists of three arches with the doors behind. Above the arches is a relief that has three sections: Paradise, The Future, The Spoilt Culture. On the tower under the clock-hands there are two proverbs: 'Beidt Uw Tijd' (Bide Your Time) and 'Duur Uw Uur' (Pluck Your Hour). These proverbs pertain to the mission of the building: take care, but take your chance if it arises. Until 1998 the building served as stock exchange. Today the building is used for exhibitions. The Beurs van Berlage is restored in 2001-2003.

80-81 Former building of the Buitenlandsche Bankvereeniging (G. A. van Arkel/1903).This is an asymmetric building built of brick and sandstone in the style of the sober Holland's neo-renaissance.

83 Cornice-gable (± 1800) in the Louis XVI style with a triangular pediment containing a decorated round window.

85/corner Zoutsteeg Is a richly decorated raised Dutch gable (± 1725) built of stone.

95 This building is built of yellow and red brick. Sadly, because of many renovations hardly anything remains from the original Berlage-design.

98 Is a building (A. J. Kropholler-J. F. Staal/1907) in the style of H. P. Berlage.

Rokin

T he name Rokin is derived from rak, the old name for sailing water. The Rak-in, stands for an inland waterway. The Rokin, just like Damrak, was originally part of the inland waterway between the Amstel and the IJ. The houses on the west side stood with their back gables on the Amstel. In 1572 a quay is built on the west side. On the east side there were mostly cloisters.

The water has only been filled in as recently as the 1930's on the east side when the Rokin got its present character.

Rokin 69

The most important buildings on the Rokin:

18 Stepped-gable (± 1740). The forward leaning gable is much younger than It looks at first sight. The stepped-gable is added at the time of a renovation in 1935 (!). Before that it was a spout-gable.

58 Store building in Jugendstil style (G. A. van Arkel/1898).

On the top floor there are birds-of-prey placed on consoles on either side. The gable has many ornaments. The contrast between the white plastered bricks and the gray stones disappeared in the 1980's.

64 Cornice-gable (± 1720).

In the gable there is a Moor pictured with a bow and arrow and a draped sheet.

69 Office building (G.A. van Arkel/ 1901) commissioned by the Marine Insurance Company Limited in acombination of Jugendstil and Berlage. The building is built of sandstone and hard stone and is asymmetrical. There is an impressive tile mosaic with the firm's name.

72 Schmidts Optische Instrumentenhandel (1918). On the roof's edge there is a monkey with a telescope. The interior and the store are mostly of mahogany wood.

78-82 The Heilige Stede (1912). In the 14th century the Nieuwezijds Kapel stood at this place. In 1912 this space made room for the present building that is not used as a church anymore. Now The Amsterdam Dungeon is housed here.

84 Former restaurant Riche (A. L. van Gendt/1883). In eclecticism style with neo-renaissance and Louis XIV elements.

91 Neck-gable (1664) with an eagle with a coat of arms in its talons in the stone scrolls.

92-96 Hajenius (A.L. van Gendt/1914) The gable, in eclecticism style is of stone covered with sandstone. The bottom is made of granite. Above the entrance there is a sculpted royal coat

Rokin 91

of arms. In the 19th century the Hajénius family was purveyor of smokers' requisites to His Majesty the King and to several other European royal families. The name 'de Rijnstroom' in the gable refers to the first shop of Hajénius in 1826 in hotel De Rijnstroom on the Dam. The socles that support the floors are closed with a cornice. The interior of the shop is also designed by the van Gendt

brothers and is almost completely original.

95 Cornice-gable (1646). The straight cornice is supported by Ionic pilasters.

98 Was originally a cornice-gable, but is renovated in 1926 to a neck-gable.

100 Building in art nouveau style (1910).

102 (C.B. Posthumus Meyjes/ 1902) Former reading museum, built of brick.

109-111 Nederlandsch Tabak Maatschappij (J. London/1920) in a combination of Roman architecture and the style of the Amsterdam's School. In the middle there is a relief of a tobacco vat.

112 Sociëteit Arti et Amicitiae (J.H. Leliman/1855). In 1855 the buildings of Rokin 112-114 combined into one building with a new façade. It was commissioned in 1840 by the artists' association Arti et Amicitiae. In 1893/1894 the building was restored by A.C. Bleys and H.P. Berlage. The eclectic façade is symmetric and has seven windows on each floor. The small pediment has a sandstone winged ox head. The ox is the symbol of the evangelist Luke, the patron saint of the painters. The images are bronze castings from the original pine wood images that are saved, and stand for the art of architecture, sculpture, engraving, and painting.

115 Building (1928) in the style of the Amsterdam's School.

140 Back of former department store Maison de Bonneterie.

154-156 Neck-gable twin (± 1750) with stone scrolls in the style of Louis XIV.

158-160 Warehouse twin (± 1750).

162 Former department store Vroom & Dreesmann.

Spui

T he Spui is one of the most beautiful squares in Amsterdam. Its rich history goes back to the middle ages, when a tributary of the Boerenwetering flowed to the Amstel (now the Rokin). In the space of time this tributary developed into a natural canal between the Singel and the Amstel. Along the Begijnhof was a small quay. At the height of nr.10 (now fashions shop Esprit) warehouses stood at the edge of the water. Across the water the Maagdenhuis (nr. 21) also stood along the water until 1881.

The Spui is filled-in in 1882. Old buildings were demolished and replaced by a number of large shops. In the 1990's the square was reorganised again.

The most important buildings on the Spui:

14-16 Atheneum bookstore (L.G. Mohrmann/1904) in the style of the New Art with a spout gable and bay windows.
18 (corner Heisteeg) Cornice-gable, former Dutch gable (± 1670) with wooden under façade.
20 Dutch gable (± 1670).
22-24 Café Luxembourg, Dutch gable with side house (± 1700) and gable stone 'in de walvisch' (whale).
26 Building in neo-style (± 1885) with bay window and balcony.
28 Stepped-gable in neo-renaissance style with gable stones and lion heads.
30 Low Dutch gable (± 1650) that con-

tinues on to the Singel.
Entrance to the Begijnhof (1907)
The gate lies between the back of the houses of the Begijnhof (all spout-gables). St. Ursula, the patron saint of the Begijnhof, is depicted on the gable stone above the gate.
10 Corner building (Ed Cuypers/ 1892) in neo-renaissance style. The combination of brick, stone, marble and iron gives this building a whimsical aura. The round pilasters at the corners are richly decorated with ornaments. The round-arched windows with wrought iron fence work on the first floor are striking.
The modern projection of zinc with three porches dates from 1988.
Spui/Kalverstraat 152 building

Mercurius van firma Focke & Melzer/ Waterstone English Bookstore (H.P. Berlage/1886) This building is a good example of the early style of Berlage and is characterised by the abundant use of renaissance inspired decorations. Above the diagonally placed entrance there is a bay window with a tower at the top. Above the windows on the ground floor balustrades are applied.

11 Stepped-gable (± 1650) with round top and a cross-wise pavement .

13 In neo-renaissance style with a lion head in a gable stone placed above the entrance to the basement.

15-19 Helios/photographic atelier M. Buttinghausen (G.A. van Arkel/1895). Living quarters/shop designed in the style of art nouveau, richly decorated with flower and plant decorations (sunflowers and seaweed, etc.). The round bay window on the first floor above the entrance is striking and the way the tower is built as well. Over the years the building has been remodeled. In 1900 the design was awarded a bronze medal at the World Fair in Paris.

21 The Maagdenhuis (A. van der Hart/1784).

Former Roman Catholic orphanage for girls. The neo-classicism building has a protruding Ionic cornice made from Bremer sandstone. The cornice contains four rows of five windows. The lower level consists of round-arched windows, of which the middle one is the entrance door. These were the rooms of the regents of the orphanage. The top is crowned with a pediment entablature. In the tympanum are two orphan girls holding a medallion with the Bible scene 'let the children come unto Me'.

Old Amsterdam 1

This walk takes us through the oldest part of Amsterdam. Via the Kloveniers burgwal we walk to the Nieuwmarkt and the Waag. Then we visit the Zeedijk, which is also known as the Chinatown of Amsterdam. Then follow the Oudezijds Kolk and the Gelderse Kade with the only remaining defence tower, the Schreierstoren (1487). Via the Oudezijds Voorburgwal we arrive at the world famous Red Light District of Amsterdam.

Staalstraat

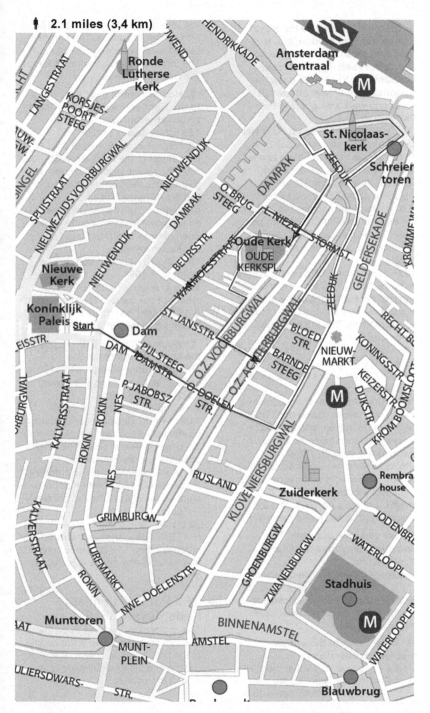

2.1 miles (3,4 km)

Ronde Lutherse Kerk

Amsterdam Centraal

St. Nicolaas-kerk

Schreierstoren

Nieuwe Kerk

Oude Kerk

OUDE KERKSPL.

Koninklijk Paleis

Start

Dam

BLOED STR.

NIEUW-MARKT

BARNDE STEEG

RUSLAND

Zuiderkerk

Rembrandt house

GRIMBURGW.

Stadhuis

Munttoren

MUNT-PLEIN

BINNENAMSTEL

AMSTEL

Blauwbrug

🛉 On the Dam we face the Royal Palace. We turn around, and go right and cross the Dam/Paleisstraat. We keep right and cross the Dam/ the Rokin. We pass the Nationaal Monument on the left hand and walk straight into the Damstraat.

Until 1868 this street was named Halsteeg. After the ally was made broader, the people that lived there chose to call it Damstraat. On the bridge (Varkenssluis) we look left across the water at the St Nicholas Church (1884). Diagonally across the gables the tower of the Old Church can be seen. To the right, on the Oudezijds Voorburgwal, are three beautiful gables:

183 » Neck-gable (1675) with decorated stone scrolls with vases at the corners. On both sides of the attic window are oval windows with sculpted decorations. The top has a half round pediment.

185 » Straight cornice (1675) in late Louis XIV-style with a low neck-gable. This type is not often seen in Amsterdam.

187 » Amsterdam merchant's house (1663) with raised neck-gable. The neck has Corinthian, and the façade Ionian pilasters. Under the windows festoons are applied. The scroll stones have Moors and Indians sitting on and against rolls of tobacco. There is an oval window in the neck with shields and the date 1663. The top is crowned with a half round pediment.

🛉 We continue our walk. The Damstraat becomes the Oude Doelenstraat.

The street dates from the beginning of the 16th century. In the 14th and 15th centuries the archers practiced shooting at the so-called schuttersdoelen (shooting-range).

🛉 We walk on to the bridge (Paulus Broedersluis).

On the bridge we look left at the Red Light District (see later). To the right, on the Oudezijds Achterburgwal 151-

155, are lovely pilaster gables (1643) with a straight cornice. The four oval carved windows are exceptional. The three windows underneath have triangular pediments.

🛉 Now we cross <u>over</u> the bridge to the right and walk on the Oudezijds Achterburgwal.

159 « Waalsekerk (1409)
This church is the former chapel of the cloister of the Brothers of St. Paul. After the reformation the church was given to the Huguenots who had fled from France. The church was expanded in 1661 with a side aisle on the southern side in gothic style. The entrance port (1647) was built in classicism style.
The Waalse Kerk was completely restored in 1991.

161 » The former staff residence (1643) of the church. The neck-gable is added later and dates from the beginning of the 18th century.

🛉 We walk back and turn <u>right</u> on the Oude Hoogstraat.

This street originated around 1490 and as the name says, it is higher (hoog) than the Dam.

2 » Shop/dwelling with stepped-gable (1901). Because of its historical building style (Holland's renaissance) the building seems older. The blocks of sandstone are noticeable.

14-18 » Amsterdam Volkswarenhuis Rotterdam (± 1900), now Kok book-store, in the style of the Amsterdam's School.

22 » Low, narrow Dutch gable (± 1720). This is the narrowest house in Amsterdam. The façade is only 2.02 metres wide (the house is 6 metres deep).

☞ 22 » Poort Walenkerk - H. de Keyser/1616

The centrepiece pictures three lilies. The city coat of arms is in the middle of the half-round pediment. The skulls denote that the funerals were on this side of the church.

Oude Hoogstraat 22

24 » Poort Oost-Indisch Huis (1606)

During opening hours of the University of Amsterdam the courtyard is open to the public.

 We walk through the gate and reach a lovely 17th century courtyard.

This was the courtyard of the former Dutch East India Company (VOC) and gave entry to different offices of the company. This is also where the ship's crew for the East-India trips were hired and discharged. The south façade (H. de Keyser sr./1606) has a trapezium-shaped top gable with ornamental brick-on-edge coping. The S-shaped stone scrolls have flared outsides and a vase balustrade. Above the door is a round window with the date 1606 and the VOC emblem. The west façade (H. de Keyser, jr./ 1635) is on the Oude Hoogstraat side. The façade has a Tuscan port and pilasters. The pilasters are Doric on the underside and Ionic on the top. The gable on the side of the Kloveniersburgwal (left) is taken down in 1890 and rebuilt in the same style.

 We walk back to the Oude Hoogstraat and continue our walk to the Kloveniersburgwal.

The name refers to the Kloveniers (members of the militia) who carried a klover (firing arm) in the 16th century. Above the gables the tower of the Zuiderkerk (1614) rises.

 Before the bridge we turn left on the Kloveniersburgwal.

34 « Cornice-gable (± 1775) with a gables stone that depicts a chest with rolls of linen. Underneath it states: 'De Linnenkist' (the linen chest).

31 » Cornice-gable (± 1715) with decorations under the windows and a beautiful entrance of sandstone.

☞ 29 » Trippenhuis - J. Vingboons/1660

The Trippenhuis has the widest canal-side façade in Amsterdam.

The commissioners were the Trip brothers, merchants in iron and weapons. The Trippenhuis is a commoner's palace that consists of two complete houses behind one shared façade. It is one of the last examples of the Holland's classicism in Amsterdam. The cornice-gable has eight sandstone pilasters that run from two and one-half stories. The family coat of arms is in the pediment entablature (three little trip wooden shoes and canons). The two chimneys are made to look like mortars. The façade is decorated with streamers of fruit, olive and palm branches that stand for peace. In the cornice left it says 'Anno' and right '1662'. One of the brothers, Louys Trip was mayor of Amsterdam three times.

26 « Klein Trippenhuis (1696)
The house is only 2.5 metres wide. The gable is of sandstone and has two pilasters. The cornice is raised and has two portrayals of sphinxes and the date 1696. Under the round attic window there is a festoon with an hourglass. This was the house of the coachman of the large Trippenhuis.

23 » Former stepped-gable (1625) that was changed in the 18th century to spout-Dutch gable.

12 «Spice shop Jacob Hooy en Co.

The Oldenboom family is specialised in herbs & spices for more than 150 years.

6-8 « Twin neck-gable (1722) 'Isaac + Abraham' in Louis XIV style.

🚶 **We walk to the Nieuwmarkt.**
The canal around the Sint Antoniespoort (Waag) (weighing house) was filled-in in 1614. This area around the Waag got the name Nieuwmarkt. The square was completely renovated in the 1980's. We see a combination of old and new constructions. The Waag (1488) is in the middle of the Nieuwmarkt.

De Waag

The Waag (weighing house) (1488) served as city-gate (Sint Antoniespoort) until the end of the 16th century. Around the gate was a moat that was filled-in in 1610 which formed the Nieuwmarkt. Because of the intensive trading activities in the 17th century, the weighing house on the Dam (no longer in existence) became too small. A second weighing house was needed. In 1617 the old city-gate was rebuilt into the Sint Antoniespoort, when the beautiful guild gates were made. The guilds were housed in the upper stories. The emblems of the guilds can still be seen above the gates and underneath you find a carving of Hendrik de Keyser (the mason's guild). In 1692 the building was finished with a dome-shaped room with a tower in the middle. In the Waag you can also visit the room of the masons' and smiths' guild. The inside of the building is also worth your while.

The most beautiful gables on the Nieuwmarkt:

8 Dutch gable (± 1680).
15 Dutch gable (1727) in Louis XIV style.
16 Neck-gable (± 1680).
17-23 'Flesseman' (1927) with elements of Amsterdam's School.
18 Dutch gable (± 1750) in Louis XV style.
20-22 Double stepped-gable in Holland's renaissance; around 1800 divided into two shops. These houses were standing until the filling-in of the canal in 1614. The wooden under-façade dates from 1932.
25 Raised neck-gable (1724).
34-36 Twin neck-gables (±1720) with two horse-back riders in the top.

⚑ We walk to the right around the Waag.
At the height of the Bloedstraat is the Sint Lucasgilde.

Sint Barbaragilde

In this guild the house painters, the artists and the sculptors were united. The relief was made in the atelier of Hendrick de Keyser. A way further on is the gate of the Sint Barbaragilde (the guild of the masons and the stone cutters). The decorations are made by Hendrick de Keyser.

⚑ We walk further and pass the (main) entrance of the Waag with the date 1617.
Next we come to the entrance of the Theatrum Anatomicum. Hippocrates is depicted in the half-round pediment. In the Theatrum the doctors (chirurgijns) lessens in anatomy and Rembrandt van Rijn painted his famous 'the Anatomical Lessen of

dr. Nicolas Tulp'. Next (left) to the Theatrum is the Antoniespoort. Right around the corner is the entrance to the Sint Eloy (the blacksmiths' guild).

⚑ We walk straight on and turn left on the Zeedijk.
The Zeedijk is part of the old harbour quarter of Amsterdam and is one of the oldest parts of the city. This part of the city is known as China Town. Chinese restaurants and oriental shops dominate the look of the street.
116-106 « This is the first traditional Chinese temple in Europe. The prominent dragons on the roof protect the temple and neighbourhood from evil spirits. The temple is higher than the Zeedijk. Inside there is a Buddha that weighs more than 400 kilos. The temple is free to the public. A gift is appreciated.

⚑ We continue on the Zeedijk.
84 « Cornice-gable (1660) with gable stone 'Anno 1660'.
82 « Cornice-gable with gable stone depicting a hunter with dogs and hares, with an under script 'Duynsigt Anno 1725'.
67 » Neck-gable (1715) with an illustration of a 'barrel'.
43 » Dutch gable (± 1650) with medieval timbre frame and gable stone 'Het Kalf' (the calf).
39 » Straight cornice-gable (± 1740) with a lower façade from the beginning of the 19th century. The decoration between the door and upper window points to the grain harvest.
31 » Dutch gable (1686). The curved in sides are ornamented with fruit motifs. The top has a half-round cornice moulding.
22/20 « Dutch gables (± 1725) with decorated stone scrolls.

⚑ At the height of 21 Zeedijk (± 1800) we turn right on the Oudezijdskolk.
The Oudezijdskolk dates from 1425 and was excavated as a sluice to the IJ. Until the end of the 1980's, there were many sailors' cafés here. Nowa-

days we find mostly restaurants here.

13 » Warehouse De Blauwe Hoorn (1720). The hatches for the lifting tackles are placed in separate openings.

7 » Warehouse Keulen (1650) with round arches around the separate attic windows.

☞ 5 » Warehouse Malaga (1617)

This is the oldest warehouse in Amsterdam. The vertical coupling of the attic hatches is striking. Also the window frames are coupled sideways.

3 » Warehouse De Korendrager (1720) with vertically coupled attic hatches and an original lower façade. To the left we see the rear of the St.Nicholas Church (1884). The building of the paint ware house Vettewinkel (1888) is next. The building

view of the Old Church.

⚲ We walk on and reach the Geldersekade.

The quay dates from 1425 and was the harbour area of Amsterdam for centuries. The sailing ships of the VOC departed from here to the Far East and came back with their exotic cargos. Right in front of us is the Schreierstoren.

⚲ We turn left on the Prins Hendrikkade.

This part of the quay was called the Oude Teertuinen (tar gardens); until 1879 where the ships would get their tar coating (until 1645). When the Central Station was built the view of the IJ was lost.

84-85 « Front of the office building Batavia (1918) in the style of the Amsterdam's School.

De Schreierstoren

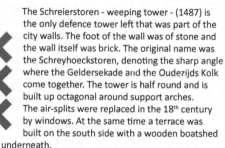

The Schreierstoren - weeping tower - (1487) is the only defence tower left that was part of the city walls. The foot of the wall was of stone and the wall itself was brick. The original name was the Schreyhoeckstoren, denoting the sharp angle where the Geldersekade and the Oudezijds Kolk come together. The tower is half round and is built up octagonal around support arches. The air-splits were replaced in the 18th century by windows. At the same time a terrace was built on the south side with a wooden boatshed underneath.

In 1569 a gable stone is placed in the tower (on the side of the Geldersekade) with a woman and a boat. Traditionally, the story goes that this was the place that the women said good-bye to their men before they set sail to sea. The interior still has the wooden frame with pear-beading from the 15th century.

---

was destroyed by fire in 1975 and only the neo-renaissance gable on this side was saved. There are balls on the even steps and there is a lion on the top. Next we see the backside of the building Batavia (1918) in the style of the Amsterdam's School. When we look back, we have a nice

☞ 74-77 « St Nicholas Church - A.C. Bleys/1884-1887

The church is a transept basilica with three aisles and is built in a combination of neo-baroque and neo-renaissance. The two towers with the rose window with a relief of Christ and the

evangelists are remarkable. The Holy Nicholas, patron saint of the city of Amsterdam, stands in a niche high in the top gable.

Note the eight-sided tower with baroque dome and large cross on top. In 1999 the Nicholas Church was restored.

To the right we see the Central Station. In front of the station we see the *Noord-ZuidHollands Koffiehuis (1911)*

Originally this was the waiting-room for the passengers of the Noord-Zuid-Hollandse Tramweg Maatschappij (tram company). The interior of the coffeehouse has a wooden ceiling and lattice windows with stained-glass Amsterdam coat of arms. On the roof there is a weather vane in the shape of a 17th century merchant's sailing ship.

At the entrance there are replicas of the Jan van der Heijden-lanterns. These oil lanterns lit the city in the 17th century. Today the VVV (tourist office) and a café-restaurant occupy the coffeehouse.

🚶 **We walk straight on to nr. 53 Hotel Prins Hendrik.**
A plaque commemorates the famous jazz-musician Chet Baker (1929-1988), who died here after a fall from a 1st floor window.

🚶 **We walk on to the corner and turn left.**
On the other side (right) we see Damrak. At the corner is theVictoria Hotel. Straight ahead (across the water) is the Beurs van Berlage.

🚶 **We turn left on the Nieuwebrugsteeg.**

🔊 13 « 'In de Lompen' (± 1605)

Has a stepped-gable in the style of the Holland's renaissance top pilaster. The keystones and coping stones are decorated with sculpted heads. Above the lower façade there is a gable stone depicting a sugar bakery with the title: 'In de Lompen', which means sugar loaf. The building has a lean-to building in the Sint Olofspoort.

🚶 **We turn left on the Sint Olofspoort.**
1 » Stepped-gable (1605) in Holland's renaissance style. The building runs through to the Zeedijk and has a lean-to building there.

🚶 **We turn right into the Zeedijk.**

🔊 1 « 't Aepgen' (± 1550)

This is one of the two remaining houses with a wooden façade in Amsterdam (see also 34 Begijnhof). 't Aepgen is a house that is placed sideways, where the ridge of the roof runs in the same direction as the front gable. The side gable is brick. The horizontal wooden boards were renewed around 1800. The lower façade dates from the 19th century. The building was restored in 1987.

🔊 2 a » Sint Olofskapel (1440)

The Sint Olofskapel is built onto the great Sint Olofspoort (city gate). In 1618 this city gate was torn down. Between 1578 and 1586 the chapel was empty and from that time the merchants had a stock market there (until 1602). Since 1602 the Reformed hold their church services there. The chapel is a hall church (three aisles of equal height) in gothic style and has 17th century entrances in renaissance style. The port (H. de Keyser/1645) on the Zeedijk is built of sandstone. The Latin inscription means 'Hope for a better life'. In the pediment there is a skeleton encircled by skulls. Both ports to the Nieuwe

Port Heilige Grafkapel

brugsteeg date from 1620 and 1671. Only at the port to the Zeedijk can we see the 15th century wooden vaulting and a window with the original medieval filling and hewn brick. The other pointed arches have stone frameworks and decorative fillings.

The last church service was held in 1912. Afterwards the chapel got various uses. After a fire in 1966 the building was empty until the restoration in 1991. Presently the building is used as a congress centre.

🚶 **We turn right on the Sint Olofssteeg.**

Nieuwebrugsteeg 8 » Dutch gable (± 1675) with a gable stone depicting a cask. The stairs are placed sideways with an entrance to the basement underneath.

On the left there is a nice view of the Kolksluis and Zeedijk. The rear sides of the houses are on the waterside.

🚶 **We walk straight on to the Oudezijds Voorburgwal.**

8 » Stepped-gable (± 1600) in sober Amsterdam's renaissance with three gable stones.

☞ 14 » Het Wapen van Riga/ Leeuwenburg and Burcht van Leiden (1605)

Stepped-gable, built in the style of the Holland's renaissance for a merchant from Riga. The house has a wooden frame and boards which are used like thin stone walls. The side façade is built out over the beams that are protruding. In the pediment between the

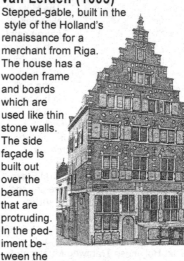

ground floor and the first floor there are lion heads and the coat of arms of Riga (the two keys) with a fortress underneath where a lion head sticks out.

☞ 18 » Int Stodt Van Egmond (1615)

The house is built in the style of Holland's renaissance. Only the middle section is in the original state. The stepped-gable is replaced in 1939 for its present spout-gable. The pilasters that are connected by shields are notable and the stone accolade arches. The keystone is flanked on either side by lovely lion masks. On the middle of the stone the castle of Egmond is depicted.

19 « Wide pilaster gable (1656), with Corinthian pilasters on the second and third floors, while the ground floor and the first floor have Ionic pilasters. There are richly decorated stone scrolls with dolphins. The top has a half round pediment.

40 » The original classicism Dutch gable is renovated in the 18th century into a spout-gable. The attic church is

built above the complete attic area of the house on the Oudezijds Voorburgwal and the house on the Heintje Hoeksteeg. On the front there is no lifting tackle, which is unusual. The hoisting apparatus is on the Heintje Hoeksteeg on the side façade.
The front façade is four windows wide and has a part wooden front with a lintel. In 1661 the house is bought by a stocking merchant Jan Hartman. In 1663 the attic was made suitable for the Roman Catholic Church as a hidden church Het Hert, consecrated to the Holy Nicolaas. In 1739, the Protestants renamed the church into 'Ons Lieve Heer op Zolder' because of the alliteration.
The church is in use as a museum, since 1888.
42 » Dutch gable warehouse D' Vygeboom (1653). There is a fig tree in the crest.
23-25 « Dutch gables (± 1680) with oval windows, festoons and half-round pediments.
45 « Cornice-gable (± 1750) with a raised cornice moulding.

☞ 57 « De Gecroonde Raep - H. de Keyser/1615
The stepped-gable in the style of the Amsterdam's renaissance has large steps with rich sculptured stone scrolls. The coupled pilasters are connected by wall-shields. The heads, masks, the two date stones (1615) and the gable stone 'De Gecroonde Raep' (crowned turnip) are striking. The building is restored in 1985.

Before the Old Church we turn right on the Oudekerksplein.
We are now in the heart of old Amsterdam. The Oudekerksplein and the surrounding area have been already for centuries the Red Light District of the city.
To the left is the monumental gothic Old Church (± 1280).

Red Light District

The Old Church

The church (± 1280) is the oldest brick building in Amsterdam and is built as a hall church (three equally large aisles).

About 1306 the Old Church is consecrated to the Holy Nicolaas, bishop of Myra. Until the reformation (1578) the church was named the Sint Nicholas Church. Thereafter the Old Church is made suitable for the protestant worship service.

Between 1584 and 1611 the church was also used as a place for the stock market. After that the stock-market function was taken over by the Beurs of Hendrick de Keyser on the Rokin. In 1650 the church is renovated to a basilica. The nave is then raised. In later times the side aisles were also raised as high as the nave. The Noorderportaal (north portal) is made from brick and stone and has a richly worked balustrade. The new spire dates from 1565 and is designed in gothic style by Joost Bilthamer. The eight-sided tower has three balustrades. The clock faces are crowned with an entablature. The high rounded arches in the second frame are also crowned with entablatures. The spire is lead-clad wood.

Because of its crooked state, the tower was covered with bricks in 1718 (the original tower is still underneath). The brick foot is 36 metres high; the wooden spire 31 metres. From the Enge Kerksteeg there is a good view of the Noorderportaal and the Heilige Grafkapel.

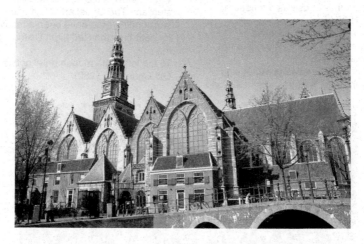

Interior:
The Old Church is a hall church, which is especially obvious from inside. The church is a large hall with a number of side chapels. You can see that the large pillars have cabbage leaves in their capitals; these are unique to churches in Amsterdam. At the time of the great restoration between 1955 and 1979, a large number of frescos were returned to their former state. At the Zuiderportaal (southern portal) is the Sint Sebastian's chapel.

The stairway gives entrance to a dry and fireproof space where the most important documents are kept. The Maria chapel is in the northeast corner of the church. The stained-glass windows dating from 1550 here are special.

The main organ (1726) is built by Christian Vader and is one of the most famous organs in the Netherlands. The organ is crowned with two coats of arms of the city of Amsterdam.

Like many of the historical churches, the Old Church has tombstones on the floor and a few grave monuments. On the tombstone floor the gravestones from the Netherlands composer Sweelinck, the architect Vingboons, and the wife of Rembrandt van Rijn, Saskia van Uylenburgh (1612-1642) can be found.

✝ **We walk on to the Enge Kerksteeg.**
There are two lovely buildings in this alley.
2 (corner house) Oude Kerksplein/ Enge Kerksteeg. This house has a peculiar overhanging side façade and a gable stone with three women figures (representing Faith, Hope, and Love) and Christ carrying the cross.
4 De Verghulde Wan (1634) gilded winnow is built in the style of the sober Amsterdam's renaissance. The stepped-top gable is of stone and has a pilaster on a console. The middle section is stone.
The five gable stones depict a winnow with the title: 'De Verghulde Wan' (centre stone).

✝ **We go back to the Oudekerksplein and pass the Wijde Kerksteeg.**
Oudekerksplein 50 « Building (1658). The Dutch gable is added around 1750. The lower wooden façade is notable, with Ionic pilasters above. Alas the festoons have been removed.

✝ **We walk straight through the Sint Annen Dwarsstraat and turn right on the Sint Annenstraat.**
This street dates from the 15th century and is one of the first city streets of Amsterdam. Here there is a lot of window prostitution as well.

12 « De Gulden Trip (1565)
is the only remaining house with a gable with ornamental brick-on-edge coping in the manner of Hans Vredeman de Vries. It has S-shaped stone scrolls with in and out curving sides. During the restoration in 1993, unique ceiling paintings were exposed. Tile floors were also excavated up from the oldest brick houses in Amsterdam from 1380.
The house next door (no. 10) is also from 1565 and was owned by the same person (a stockings salesman).

✝ **We turn around and walk back**

out of the Sint Annenstraat.
Now we turn right on the Oudezijds Voorburgwal.
100 » Gable (± 1650) in the style of Hendrick de Keyser.
111 « Stepped gable (± 1625). Sadly one step is missing.
115 « Dutch gable (1685) with decorative vases and a half-round pediment with shell motif.
136 » Dutch gable (1733) with a relief above the door where Admiral Tromp is depicted in the battle at Kijkduin.
162 » Dutch gable (± 1750) in Louis XV style with wooden lower façade and coach house.
131 « Eclecticism gable (± 1880) in a combination of neo-classicism and neo-renaissance. The entablatures above the windows are eye-catching.
135 « Neck-gable (± 1725) with an orange tree in the top.

✝ **At the Sint Jansstraat we turn left and cross the footbridge (Sint Jansbrug).**
We walk straight through into the Stoofsteeg, cross the Stoofbrug and turn left on the Oudezijds Achterburgwal.
Now we are in the centre of the Red Light District.

Red Light District

The prostitution is concentrated in a labyrinth of streets and alleys around the Old Church and the Oudezijds Achterburgwal since the 14th century. This neighbourhood is known worldwide under the name Red Light District, because of the red lamps in the windows of the prostitutes. In Amsterdam we also call it the 'walletjes' and 'rosse buurt'. The walletjes refer to the medieval embankments upon which Amsterdam is established and where still nowadays most of the prostitution is situated. The term rosse buurt comes the closest to Red Light District and denotes the reddish glow the red lamps give the area at night. There are also many sex shops and theatres here.

62-60 « Stepped-gable (1610) in the style of the Amsterdam's renaissance.
54 « 'God is mijn Burgh' (1685); former warehouse with spout-gable.
46a « Rear side of 'De Gecroonde Raep'.

🚶 **We walk further and at the end of the Oudezijds Achterburgwal we turn left and walk on the Korte Niezel. Now we come to the Oudezijds Voorburgwal and walk onto the bridge.**
On the bridge (the Liesdelsluis), to the right we see a beautiful part of old Amsterdam and the St Nicholas Church.
On the left there is a beautiful view through to the Old Church.

🚶 **We walk straight on in the Lange Niezel.**
24 « Bolwerck (1646). This raised neck-gable with wooden lower façade and various gable stones stood on the Zwanenburgerstraat (close by the Stopera) until 1978, and it was rebuilt here in 1996.
22 « Dutch gable (± 1587-1650) the original wooden frame can still be seen in many places, since a restoration in 1992.

🚶 **We vervolgen de Lange Niezel en lopen door naar de Wamoesstraat.**
In the 16th century this was one of the most important trading centres of the city. The rich merchants lived in this street. They moved in the 17th century to the newly excavated Herengracht. The Warmoesstraat developed from a residential street into a business street in the 17th century. The warmoesmarkt (vegetable market) was held here until the 19th century. Around 1910 the first part of the Old Church (formerly Kerkstraat) was also added to the Warmoesstraat.

🚶 **We turn left. At the first side street we turn right on the Oudebrugsteeg.**
This alley connected the old and the new sides of the city until 1883 and runs from the other side of the Damrak to the Nieuwendijk.

☞ **1 « Het Oude Accijnshuis - J. van Campen/1638**
In this building taxes were put on grain, beer, wine, peat and coal in the 17th century. The building in the style of Holland's classicism is built in sandstone. The Ionic pilasters run along two stories to the straight cornice. Above the cornice another gable section is built. Above the windows on the first floor there are alternately triangular and semi-circular pediments. On the Oudebrugsteeg there is a narrow gable with two doors in a stone frame. Above both doors there are two lions, that serve as shield bearers carrying the coat of arms of Amsterdam (the old and the new emblems). Above that there are two entablatures.

🚶 **We walk straight on.**
Here we can imagine standing on the oldest bridge in Amsterdam. The bridge was built in the 14th century, but through the filling-in of the Damrak (1883) it can no longer be recognised as such. To the left we see the backside of the Beurs van Berlage.
To the right there is a nice view in the direction of the Central Station.

🚶 **We walk back to the Warmoesstraat and turn right.**
67 Cornice-gable (1686).
At the Enge Kerksteeg («) we have a beautiful view through to the Noorderportaal and the Heilige Grafkapel of the Old Church.

🚶 **We continue on until the Wijde Kerksteeg.**
This is one of the oldest alleys in Amsterdam. The alley was built around 1375 to make it possible to get to the Old Church from the dike that runs along the Amstel. From the alley you have a lovely view of the Old Church.

🚶 **We continue our walk up to the end of the Warmoesstraat.**
We turn right and now we are back on the Dam again.

Beurs van Berlage

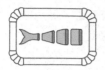

Old Amsterdam 2

V ia the Nes and the Oudezijds Achterburgwal we walk to the 17th century
Zuiderkerk (South church), and the living quarters and atelier of Rembrandt
van Rijn. Then we walk along the warehouses on the Krom Boomstraat and the 17th
century merchants' houses on the Kloveniersburgwal.
Via the Binnengasthuis terrain we arrive back at the Oudezijds Achterburgwal again
for the Agnietenkapel (1631) and the former Admiralty building of the VOC, the
Prinsenhof (1666).

Sint Antoniesluis

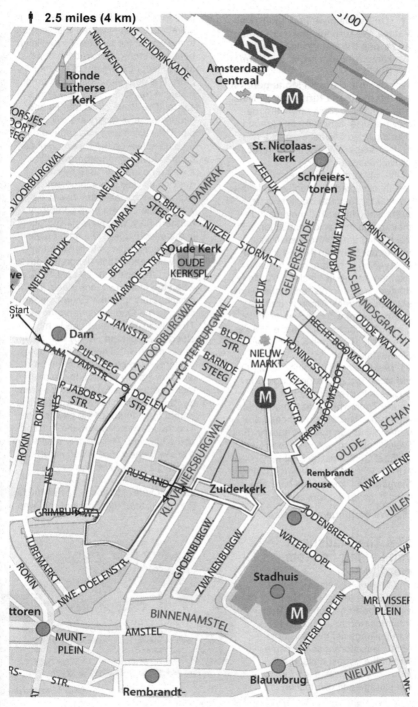

† 2.5 miles (4 km)

⚑ On the Dam we face the Royal Palace. We turn around, turn right and cross the Dam/Paleisstraat. We keep right and cross the Dam/ het Rokin.

We pass the National Monument on the left hand and turn right on Nes. The name Nes comes from the medieval 'nesse', which means ground that is carried downstream by a river, (in this case the Amstel) and forms an alluvial deposit.

In the 14th century this area was mostly occupied by shepherds. In the 15th century several cloisters were established here, and they played their part in the rapid connection with the trading area, Warmoesstraat, further up. Between 1800 and 1890 this was an important cultural entertainment centre in Amsterdam. Many theatres, restaurants, and cafés were established here. Around 1890 the entertainment world moved to other parts of the city centre. In the 1980's Nes again developed a modest area of entertainment.

11-19 « Business building (1912). On the stone façade images depict the business in precious metals of Drijfhout & Zoon which was situated here until 1988. The women's heads are very striking. On the next square (Sint Pietershalsteeg) stands « the Flemish Cultural Centrum, **the Brakke Grond (1979).** In the 15th century the Sint Margaretha Cloister was here and in the 17th century it was an inn.

⚑ We continue on the Nes.

☞ 57 « The Stadsbank van Lening / de lommerd (1614)

The Maria Magdelena Cloister stood here since 1411. On the side of the Enge Lombardsteeg a former storehouse for peat was built against the cloister in 1550. This storehouse became one of the largest buildings in the city and was used for the storage and distribution of peat to the poor. The south wall of this storehouse was fastened with anchors to the wall of the cloister. The building needed a strong construction to be able to carry the weight of the moist peat. The peat storehouse has ornaments in the style of the new renaissance. The stone cross frames and girders in the masonry are still original. The storehouse has spout-gables on both sides, on the Nes as well as on the Oudezijds Voorburgwal side. It was renovated in 1616 by Hendrick de Keyser into a lommerd. The expression 'de lommerd' has to do with people coming from Lombardy, northern Italy, who were pawnbrokers in the middle ages. The gate on the Nes in late gothic style is walled up. The white sandstone decorated gable stone states the date 29 april 1614 when the first pawn took place. The building runs from the Enge Lombardsteeg to the Oudezijds Voorburgwal. There is a gate in the Enge Lombardsteeg of sandstone (1650) with a half-round pediment. There are two horns of plenty lying on the pediment from which coins are flowing. In the pediment there is a relief depicting Willem de Keyser with three women standing before the counter of the pawnshop. The verse lines describe the function of the building. The window above has a stone frame which is decorated with a sandglass and also the two horns of plenty.

On the Oudezijds Voorburgwal 300 is the rear side of the lommerd that was

Enge Lombardsteeg

built on in 1669. The brick gable with a straight cornice does not have a pediment in the upper front section, which was unusual at that time.
The sandstone gate is built in the style of Hendrick de Keyser. By the date in the gate we can tell that it originated in 1550. So the gate was probably reused in 1669. There is Amsterdam's coat of arms in the keystone of the arch. In the pediment above the arch are the verse lines that explain how a pawnshop works. Since the 17th century there has always been a pawnshop established here.

♦ **We walk further and come to the part of the Nes where there are many theatres.**
At the end of the Nes we look to the right in the Langebrugsteeg to see the view of the Rokin.
Nes 89 Already in 1557 this was a large house with a basement, four stories and a saddleback roof.
Since its building many parts of the gables, the oak frame, and the oak cap construction have been saved. There is low lean-to building on the side of the Grimnessesluis.
The store furnishings come from the period 1825-1850, as well as the details of the store front.

♦ **We turn left on the Grimburgwal.**
2 » Dutch gable (± 1750).
4 » Stepped-gable (± 1650).
To the right, across the water, we see a part of the former hospital, the Binnengasthuis. Presently it is used by the University of Amsterdam.

♦ **We walk on and pass the Sleutelbrug.**

Oudezijds Voorburgwal 249 Huis aan de Drie Grachten - House on the three canals - C. Adriaans/1610
The first mention of this double mansion dates from 1407 when it was given by a soap-boiler to a convent of nuns. In 1585 the beer brewery De

Sleutel was established in the building. The Sleutelbrug (bridge) that lies in front of the house thanks its name to the brewery.
In 1610 the house got a stepped-gable in the style of the Haarlem's renaissance. Note the circular arches above the windows. Above the door there is a small entablature.
On both sides of the house there are three gable stones with the inscription 'Fluweelenburgwal', 'Grimburgwal', and 'Oudezijds Agterburgwal' (the three canals). The lovely leaded glass windows give the house an atmospheric aura.

♦ **We walk straight on.**
Oudezijds Achterburgwal 233
The former gate to the Sint Pietersgasthuis. The infirmary was torn down in 1913 and replaced by the (meanwhile partly demolished) Binnengasthuis hospital.
In the half-round pediment stands the coat of arms of Amsterdam with underneath the text 'Gast-Huys'. The emperor's crown is placed on the top. On either side there is an image of a sick man and a sick woman.

♦ **We turn left on the Oudezijds Achterburgwal.**

☞ 227 » De Oudemanhuispoort (1754)

This gate gives entrance to an inner street and the main building of the University of Amsterdam (former Oudemanhuis, home for old men). The gate rests on two Ionic half-pillars. In the half-round pediment there is a relief that represents a pair of glasses (symbol for the old men). The pediment is flanked on both sides by decorative vases.

✝ **We walk through the gate and reach the roofed-over passageway.**
Since 1757 a secondhand book market is held here weekly.
On the left side there is a nice view of the courtyard and the building of the former Oudemannen and Vrouwenhuis (1754). The courtyard can be visited for free during open hours of the university.

✝ **We walk around the courtyard.**
Since 1876 the building is part of the University of Amsterdam and is a rest point in the busy city centre.
The square courtyard has four wings. The gables of the main building are made of brick and stone. In the northern pediment there is Amsterdam's coat of arms. The southern wing (the Oudemanhuispoort) is the covered passageway between the Oudezijds Achterburgwal en Kloveniersburgwal.

✝ **We leave the courtyard and the passageway the same way we came In through the Oudemanhuispoort. We turn right and continue on the Oudezijds Achterburgwal.**
At nr. **213** « we can see the rear side of the Sint Agnituskapel.
201 » Neck-gable (1673) with fes-

toons, Ionic (corner) pilasters and Corinthian (centre) pilasters. It has a high lower façade with two lean-to buildings. A cooper is represented in the gable stone.

✝ **We turn right on Rusland.**
The peculiar street name Rusland (Russia) comes from the Willem Ruuschentuin (1403) that was later changed into Willem Ruijssenandt. His name was adulterated to 'Het Russeland', later to ''t Ruslant' and finally to 'Rusland'.
19-21 « Cornice-gable (1767) with two lower façades with cut-glass windows in the style of Louis XVI. At the end of Rusland the tower of the Zuiderkerk sticks out above the gables.

✝ **We walk to the bridge of the Kloveniersburgwal.**
This beam-bridge looks old because of its wooden pile construction, but it dates from 1904. On the bridge we have a lovely view of the Amstel. Behind the Amstel we see the two green domes of the cinema/theatre Tuschinski.
To the right is the Doelen Hotel.
To the left we see the Waag.

✝ **We walk and go on the Raamgracht.**
The name of this canal has to do with the woolen cloth industry that was established here in the 16th and 17th centuries. The dyed pieces of cloth were dried on 'ramen' (frames).
4 » Building in historical building style (1935) with Dutch gables and entablatures.
To the left we can see the tower of the Zuiderkerk again.
10 » Cornice-gable (± 1850) with round windows in the cornice. The door frame is decorated.

✝ **We cross the bridge of the Groenburgwal and walk on to the end of the Raamgracht.**
To the right we see the rear side of the market of the Waterlooplein. Behind that is the Stopera.

✝ **We turn left over the bridge**

and then left again. **We turn right on the first side street, the Moddermolenstraat. We walk to the Zuiderkerkhof.**

The cemetery was taken into use in 1602. In the 1980's the terrain was reorganised. Note the unique combination of modern and colorful living complexes at the foot of the historic Zuiderkerk. To the left we have a beautiful view of the Zuiderkerk. The mausoleum of Isaac Hartman and his wife Jaapje Hans dr. Roodenburg is built against the church wall.

De Zuiderkerk

The Zuiderkerk (H. de Keyser/1603) is a pseudo-basilica and is the first protestant church to be built in Amsterdam.

The three aisles are separated by two Tuscan pillars. The belt of arches from the side aisles are resting on Tuscan pilasters from the side gable. The tower is finished in 1619 and is characterised by its austere renaissance forms. The tower has a square base made of brick and stone. Above the base an octagon is placed with a pillar on four corners. The tower spire is made of wood covered with lead. The tower of the Zuiderkerk is considered to be the most beautiful tower of Amsterdam. The church is restored between 1976 and 1979.

We leave the Zuiderkerkhof via the Zuiderkerkhofpoortje (N. Stone/ ± 1620).

The gate was the entrance to the graveyard (Zuiderkerkhof) in the 17th century. Above the round arch we see a bier with two skulls and some bones on it. There are two shields of coats of arms lying on a black shroud.

In 1944 the port was taken down and put away at a safe place. In 1985, after the reorganisation of this neighbourhood, the gate was built up again.

Right in front of us on the Sint Antoniesbreestraat 69

☛ Huis De Pinto - E. Bouman/1680

The house is built in the style of Holland's classicism and thanks its name to the De Pinto family. This rich family of bankers and merchants bought the house in 1651. The house behind the façade was built in 1605 and probably had a double stepped-gable. The commissioner to build the house was one of the first leaders of the Dutch East India Company that was set up in 1602, Jan Jansz Carel. It had a broad head building and a narrow side house. The straight sandstone cornice-gable is added around 1680. The house is five windows wide with six bare pilasters. Between the windows marble slabs are attached. A closed balustrade somewhat keeps the 17th century pitched roofs out of sight.

In the 1960's the house was in such deplorable state that it stood on the list to be demolished. Through action taken by the people in the neighbourhood, the house was saved and totally restored. Presently a branch of the public library houses in the building. During opening hours you can visit the building with its authentic interior. On the left hand we see the Waag (1488) again.

We turn right on the Sint Antoniesbreestraat.

The Antoniedijk and the Sint Antoniegasthuis (lepers' house) were in this street until the 17th century. If we look over the bridge (Sint Antoniesluis) we can see the Zwanenburgwal with the Stopera and the market of the Waterlooplein again.

⛷ We walk right through to the Jodenbreestraat.
In this part of the city many of the Jewish Amsterdammers lived until the II World War. In the 1960's and 1970's the street is totally changed because of the metro. Complete blocks of houses were demolished to make

café in this national monument. The terrace has a nice view of the Oude Schans and Montelbaanstoren.

⛷ We cross the square left and walk to the Leprozenpoortje (H. de Keyser/1609).
The gate is built of stone; the pilasters and rounded arches are decorated with block work. The high pediment has a relief with a man and a woman who have leprosy. The city coat of

Rembrandt House

Next to the Rijksmuseum and the Van Gogh Museum, this is the most visited museum in Amsterdam.
In this house Rembrandt van Rijn painted a great deal of his most famous paintings. He bought the house in 1639 and stayed there until 1658. Rembrandt painted his masterworks on the first floor and lived on the ground floor.
In the museum a large collection of the works of the painter can be seen, including more than 250 etchings.
The house was originally built in 1606 as a double mansion with a neck-gable in Holland's (Haarlem's) renaissance style. In 1627 a major revision in the style of Holland's classicism took place. The stepped-gable was replaced by the present cornice-gable with pediment, with a window in the middle with frame-work surrounded with fruit streamers. There is a pediment entablature above house number 4. The second big renovation took place from 1660-1662.
The city of Amsterdam bought the house in 1906 when it was in very poor shape. A complete restoration followed (1907-1911), after which on June 10, 1911 the museum Rembrandt House was opened. In 1998 a new building was built next door. A large collection of drawings and etchings can be seen here. In the original house it can be seen how Rembrandt lived and worked.

space for new buildings.

⛷ We cross the Jodenbreestraat and walk right across the square (Sint Antoniesluis).
If we turn around to look back, we have a good view of the Rembrandt House. On the bridge we look to the right towards the old lock keeper's building.
De Sluyswacht (1695)
In this crooked little house the lock keeper of the city of Amsterdam lived and worked. He worked the locks that were built here in 1602 to replace the dam that stood here. The locks are still in function. Presently there is a

arms with emperor's crown adorns the top. The gate provides entry to a courtyard that is behind the Huis De Pinto. Until 1867 the gate was the entry to the leper's house in the Lazarussteeg. This alley was a side street of the Jodenbreestraat and disappeared after a traffic breakthrough in the 1960's.

⛷ We turn right down the steps and follow the Sint Antoniesluis.
10-8 « Dutch gable twins (± 1750) with six crests and decorated stone scrolls. It has a raised door cornice with three entrance doors and a wide pavement. Straight ahead we can

see the Montelbaanstoren and the science museum NEMO.

🚶 We turn left on the Snoekjesgracht and then turn right across the Snoekjesbrug. We walk (right) along with the curve to the Krom Boomsloot.

73 » Storehouse (± 1650) with a pilaster gable; the spout-gable was added later.
69 » Dutch gable (± 1680) with a wooden lower façade.
61-63 » Storehouses De Tyeger (1723) with two spout-gables. In the gable stone there is a tiger pictured and the date 1723.
59 » Storehouse (± 1723).
53 » Storehouse (1757) with spout-gable.

🚶 We walk on to the Krom Boomsloot 39.
22 « Cornice-gable Armenian Apostolic Church (1714).
The building was a storage place for goods until 1714 when it was turned into a church. The round arched windows were put in on a plastered façade. The steps to the entrance have wrought iron railings in rococo style on sculpted coupling links. In the cornice above the door the Lamb is lying on the Book with the seven seals and the date 1714.
Through the centuries the church has been a place of worship for the Persian Church, the Lutheran Church, the Free Church of Scotland, and the Roman Catholic Church. In 1986 the church returned in Armenian hands.

18-20 « Warehouse Schottenburch (1636)
The double warehouse has a twin spout-gable with curls at the edges of the capping. The warehouse on the right has a top pilaster. The windlass boxes of the hoisting hooks protrude from the gable.

🚶 We continue on the Krom Boomsloot and arrive at the Recht Boomsloot. We <u>cross</u> the bridge left and go further on the Recht Boomsloot.
31 » Warehouse (1650) with spout-gable. The half-round windows and the entrance door are unusual.

🚶 At the height of the Sint Antoniusschool we turn left and cross the footbridge.
14 » A former business in cutting and polishing diamonds (1889).

🚶 We turn in the Brandewijnsteeg.
2, 4 en 6 » Spout-gables (± 1720).

🚶 At the end of the alley we turn right on the Koningsstraat and then left on the Nieuwmarkt.
The Waag is on the right hand.

🚶 We walk straight on into the Sint Antoniebreestraat.
We cross the street so that we can walk on the footpath on the right. We walk on and turn right on the Nieuwe Hoogstraat. Then we turn left on the Zanddwarsstraat.
Now we are walking quite close to the Zuiderkerk.
6B » Dutch gable (1747) with wooden lower façade.

Warehouse Schottenburch (1636)

67

6C » Neck-gable (1747) with small pavement and lean-to buildings.
8 » Coach house (± 1750).
10-12 » Warehouse, coach houses (± 1750).There is a fortress depicted on nr. 12 with the name 'Int huys van Nassau'.

🕯 **At the end of the Zanddwars-straat we come to the Raamgracht again and turn right.**
We walk down the Raamgracht and turn left on the Kloveniersburgwal.
62 Graceful Neck-gable (1658).
The gable has stone scrolls with dolphins. There is a decorative sculpted oval window under the hoisting hook. There are festoons under the windows. The gable stone depicts a man with a fish. The lower façade dates from the 18th century.
58-60 » Neck-gable twins (± 1700) with decorative stone scrolls and a half-round pediment with a shell motif. The hoisting hook is in a carved oval window.
The entranceway of nr. 58 (added later) has two pilasters and an entablature.

☞ 50 » Former church of the Hersteld Evangelische Lutherse Gemeente (1793)
This large building in classicism style currently houses the Compagnie Theatre.
Because the Lutheran church did not belong to the Reformed 'state church', it was not permitted to have a tower with bells. The building has two wings with Ionic ports and a centre section that juts out with Ionic pilasters and round arched windows.
The pediment entablature has Bible symbols, like an open Bible, the challis, the altar, the Law (Ten Commandments) and the good news. The main entrance is on the Spinhuissteeg.

🕯 **We turn right and cross the bridge. Then we go right on the Kloveniersburgwal. We turn left the Spinhuissteeg.**
On the right is the main entrance to the former church of the Hersteld Evangelische Lutherse Gemeente.
18-16 « Neck-gable 't Friese Wapen (1728).
3 » Wide Dutch gable (± 1750) with sculpted side pieces and a large crest.
4 » Former Sint Augustinus Church (1848) with Ionic pilasters and round arched windows and a changed lower façade.

☞ 1 » The Spinhuis and the Spinhuispoort (1645) - H. de Keyser/1607

The gate is made of stone and has connected pillars and round arched windows, and as a crown the city coat of arms. In the sculpture work two women are depicted who are punished with whips. The date 1645 is above it. Above that there is a verse by P.C. Hoofd.
The Spinhuis was used as a workhouse for among others prostitutes and beggars. After 1782 the building had various functions. Now it is a branch of the University of Amsterdam.

🕯 **We walk back and turn right on the Kloveniersburgwal.**

☞ 77 « House Bambeeck - P. Vingboons/1650
This is a double mansion in the style of Holland's classicism. The house has a centre section that juts out with

a pediment entablature. On the ground floor and mezzanine there are Doric pilasters, on the second and third floors Ionic pilasters. It is remarkable that there is also a pilaster in the middle through which the doorway is placed to the right side.

87-89 « The former building of the Maatschappij van de Werkende Stand (1883), now the Doelenzaal.
The gable is a combination of neo-renaissance (first floor) and Holland's renaissance (second floor). The first floor has three connected round arched windows. The top of the windows depict the tools of a smith, carpenter, and mason.

► 95 « Vincentius- or poppenhuis - P. Vingboons/1642

The original name of this house is the Gulden Steur (golden sturgeon). The commissioner was Joan Poppen, where the nickname poppenhuis (dollhouse) comes from. The house is built in the style of Holland's classicism. The sandstone cornice-gable has six Corinthian pilasters and a large pediment entablature. The high sideways roof has ornamented chimneys. The former servants' entry is the present entry to the house. The high stoop in front of house was removed in 1904.

A little further we pass the rear of the **Oudemanhuispoort (A. van der Hart/1785)** to the right.

The gate with two Tuscan pillars is of stone. On the headpiece there is a sculpture depicting Mildness, Poverty, and Old-age.

99 « Cornice-gable (± 1740) with figures of women and an ornamental vase on the top.
82 » The Gasthuisapotheek (1887). The building in renaissance style was the pharmacy of the former Binnengasthuis hospital (take note of the statues).
84 » The laboratory for Artsenijbereidkunde (preparation of medicine) (1897) with entrance.
At the crossing we see the Doelen Hotel straight ahead.

⚑ We turn right through the gate (1913) and walk on the Vendelstraat. Now we come on the terrain of the former Binnengasthuis hospital.
This terrain has a long tradition in the care of the sick. In the middle ages there was a nun's convent here where the sick were nursed. In 1586 the convent was expanded with a hospital. Around 1635 the 'regular' sick stayed within the city walls (Binnengasthuis) (binnen=within), while plague sufferers were placed outside (Buitengasthuis) (buiten=outside) the city. During the 19th and 20th century modern buildings are added on the grounds. In 1981 the Binnengasthuis became part of the Amsterdams Medisch Centrum (AMC) in Amsterdam-Zuidoost. The grounds of the Binnengasthuis as this area is still called in popular speech, is now a combination of old (1870-1913) and

new (from 1981) buildings. The buildings dating from 1870-1930 are national monuments.
On the left is the former Tweede Chirurgische Kliniek (1899). On the right the former Klinisch Ziekenhuis (1890). Between the two wings lies the university restaurant Atrium. The restaurant has a glass construction for a roof.

We turn right on the Binnen-gasthuisstraat.

☞ 9 » Administration office Binnengasthuis - J.M. van der Mey/1912

The office is built in the style of the Amsterdam's School. On the side of the water, on the Oudezijds Achterburgwal there is a sculpture of a baby in the top.

We walk on to the bridge and arrive at the Oudezijds Achterburgwal.

235-237 » Former waiting room of the city's and private pharmacy (A.N. Godefroy/1875).
233 » The Gasthuispoort (see page 63).

We cross the bridge and turn left. Now we are at the Grimburgwal and in front of the Sleutelbrug we turn right on the Oudezijds Voorburgwal.
Again we pass nr. 249 The House on the three canals.

☞ 316 « Double mansion 'de Ladder Jacobs' - P. Vingboons/1655

This time Vingboons did not use the neck-gable, but a straight cornice-gable. The protruding centre section has Tuscan and Ionic pilasters with pediment entablature. There are festoons above the windows on the first floor. Between the middle windows there is a gable stone with the figure of a resting pilgrim and two angels.
239 » Transition from stepped-gable to neck-gable (P. Vingboons/1634) with pilasters and narrow middle windows and wider side windows.
237 » Merchant's house with cornice-gable (1736) in Louis XIV-style. The richly decorated top includes a balustrade

☞ 231 » The Agnietenkapel (1631)

Chapel of the former Agnieten Cloister that stood here from 1397 to the 17th century. After the reformation the city became the owner. In 1632 the chapel is organised as Atheneum Illustre. The gate is built in 1571 and only in 1631 is it moved to the chapel and given the inscription 1631. Note the round arch with the lion heads. The city coat of arms of Amsterdam is above the gate and decoration with the date 1631.
The chapel is completely restored in 1921 and functions since 1988 as museum of the University of Amsterdam.

At nr. 225 we pass the Makelaarsbruggetje.
This footbridge has a late 19th century character with piles of cast iron, a balustrade of wrought iron, and a wooden bridge-surface. The bridge was built on a private initiative and served as a shortcut for brokers in tobacco who had to go the Nes on Fridays.
302 « Wide Dutch gable (1680) with decorated edges and a crest.
215-217 » Double cornice-gable (± 1750) in Louis XIV-style.
Here we can see the rear of the Stadsbank van Lening.
To the left is a footbridge (1926) with a wrought iron balustrade and wooden bridge surface.
On the opposite side of the street is
« The gate of De Brakke Grond

(1624)
The name De Brakke Grond originated in the middle ages.
The ground here was brackish because of the sweet water of the Amstel River and the salt water of the Zuider Sea. The Sint Margaretha Klooster formerly stood on this spot. The round arched gate is built of stone. On the centrepiece it says 'De Brakke Grond' surrounded by two lion heads. In the middle above the door-opening between larger lion heads it says 'Anno 1624'. It is thought to be designed by Hendrick de Keyser. The winged angel heads in the pilasters were an often used motif in the beginning of the 17th century.
197 » The former city hall (1808-1988) of Amsterdam. Between 1924 and 1926 the City Hall, on the side where we are now walking past, got an addition of four stories in the style of the Amsterdam's School.

ᵼ **We walk on to nr. 197.**
Poort van café The Grand.
This gate is also built in the style of the Amsterdam's School. But, when we go through the gate we find ourselves in back in the 17th century.

◄ Prinsenhof (1661)

Between 1411 and 1575 the Sint Ceciliaklooster stood on this spot. After the reformation the cloister became the property of the city of Amsterdam. A part of the cloister was renovated into the Prinsenhof, a guesthouse of honoured guests. Guests here were among others, William of Orange, Prince Mauritz, and Prince William II with his wife the Queen of England. From 1597 to 1795 the Admiralty (Council in charge of the fleet of battleships) was also based here. In 1662 the Admiralty got its own building.
During the French occupation (1806-1813) by Napoleon, the French viceroy Louis Napoleon furnished the city hall on the Dam as a palace. The city council moved in 1808 to the Prinsenhof. Between 1808 and 1988 the Prinsenhof was the city hall of Amsterdam.
The wide classicistic façade with pediment entablature rests on Ionic pilasters. In pediment the coat of arms of the Admiralty and the Holland's lion are used. To the right of the lion stands Mars the god of war, the sons of Neptune, and a few ship's canons. On the left side the Lady of Justice is standing, the sea god Neptune, and attributes of shipping and trade. If we look left we can see the spire of the (former) cloister chapel.

ᵼ **We walk back to the Oudezijds Voorburgwal.**
274 ^ The former meat hall (1779). The oxen heads in the spout-gable allude to the function that the building had as meat hall.

ᵼ **We continue on the Oudezijds Voorburgwal.**
Opposite 193 « there is a *urinal* (1926) in the style of the Amsterdam's School.
246 « Neck-gables (1683) has a ribbon with the date, gable stones, decorated scroll stones, decorated entablatures and festoons.
Ahead of us is the tower of the Old Church.

187 » Raised neck-gable (1663). The neck has Corinthian pilasters, the façade Ionic. Under the windows there are festoons. In the scroll stones there are Moors and Indians sitting on and against bales of tobacco. There is an oval window framed by shields with the date 1663 underneath. The façade has a half-round cornice.

185 » Straight cornice moulding (1680) with a low neck-gable. This type of gable is rare in Amsterdam.

183 » Neck-gable (± 1750) with decorated scroll stones, corner vases, and two windows decorated with sculpture-work.

🚶 **We turn left and cross the bridge (Varkenssluis).**
On the bridge we can see the St Nicholas Church to the right.

🚶 **We go in the Damstraat and follow it until we come out at the Dam again.**

Urinal in the style of the Amsterdam's School

72

Oudezijds Voorburgwal 231 - The gate of the former Agnieten Cloister

 # The Amstel

T his walk takes us along the river Amstel. In the 11th and 12th centuries the first settlements were made along the shores that finally resulted in the founding of the city Amsterdam. Via Rokin (filled-in section of the Amstel in 1913) we walk along the Amstel. Exceptional things here are: the Huis met de Bloedvlekken (1671), the Magere Brug (Skinny Bridge), Royal Theatre Carré, and the former home for the elderly Amstelhof (now the Hermitage Amsterdam).

Magere brug

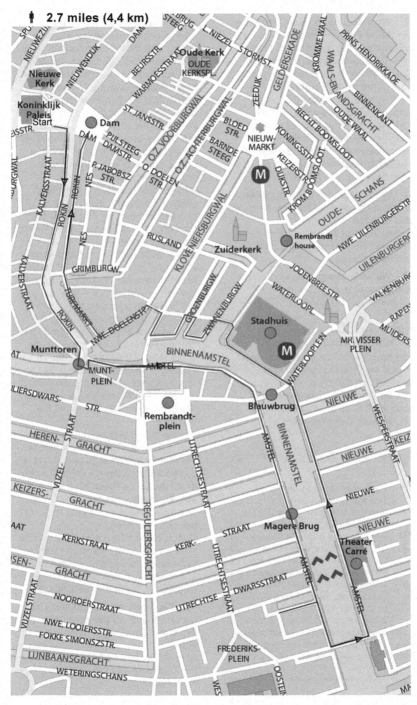

2.7 miles (4,4 km)

🕯 **We stand on the Dam and face the Royal Palace.** We turn around and walk in the direction of Madame Tussauds and turn right on Rokin. We walk through Rokin and now come to the Muntplein.

2 « Insurance company De Nederlanden (H.P. Berlage/ 1895). The building is not in its original state of 1895 (impressionistic style), but is extensively renovated by Berlage in 1910. The result is an austere rectangular building.

🕯 **We walk under the Munttoren, cross at the pedestrian crossing and turn left.**
corner Amstel 2 Dwelling/shop (A.L. van Gendt/1892) in the style of neo-renaissance.

🕯 **We walk straight on and cross at the pedestrian crossing.**
On the other side is the

☞ Hotel de L'Europe - W. Hamer/1897

The hotel in neo-renaissance style is built of mountain stone and red brick and rests on 620 piles.
Director Alfred Hitchcock used this hotel in 1939 as the location for his film 'Foreign Correspondent'.

De Amstel

The river Amstel is 31 kilometres long and flows from Uithoorn to the centre of Amsterdam. Originally the river flowed out into the IJ. Because the last part of Rokin was filled-in (1936), the Amstel stops at Rokin. Under Rokin and the Dam are pipes that allow the water of the Amstel to flow to the IJ via Rokin. The first section of the street along the river is still called Amstel.

Along this part of the Amstel there are many houseboats. On both sides of the river are beautiful and imposing 17th and 18th century mansions.

🕯 **We turn right on Amstel.**
14 » Elevated pilaster neck-gable (1661) 'Het Wapen van Londen'. The house is built of sandstone and brick. The scroll stones are decorated. Next to the attic window are two sculpted windows.In the gable are the coat of arms of London and the date 1661. At Amstel nr. 30 we can see (left) the Doelen Hotel and the Waag. The green bridge is a so-called balance bridge (1896) that we often see in Amsterdam.

34 » Warehouse (1733) with Dutch gable in Louis XIV style. A turkey can be seen in the gable that refers to the brewery De Calkoen (= turkey) which was on this spot.

54 » Stepped-gable (1629) of sandstone and brick in the style of sober Amsterdam's renaissance. The gable has men's and women's heads.
In the Halvemaansteeg the house has a notched roof, top gable, covered windlass box and hoisting trap doors.

56-58 » A small side-winged theatre in the style of the baroque theatre building. The cornice-gable is five windows wide. On the ground floor there are five rounded arch windows, of which the middle one forms the entrance.
It is the oldest theatre in Amsterdam, built in 1785 as Theatre Français sur l' Erwtemarkt. The style of building is copied from the small French theatres along the Seine River. King Willem I and Napoleon were regular visitors. The theatre functioned as a lecture hall or for debates.
During World War II it was the bicycle shed for the Amsterdamsche Bank. The Kleine Komedie has 500 seats and presently functions as a stage for established talent and new talent.

🕯 **The pavement stops here so we cross over to the other side of the street (Amstel), the right hand side.**
At nr. 84 we have a beautiful view « of the Zuiderkerk. To the right is the City Hall and Stopera.

88-98 » Gateway of the Swigtershofje (1746)

The rococo gateway is of stone, but now it is covered with white paint. In the half-round pediment the horn of plenty is depicted, filled with grain and fruit.

106 » Pilaster neck-gable (1659) with four decorated scroll stones, a half-round pediment, and sculpted square around the hoisting hook. It has a high wooden under façade and stoop.

134-136 » Corner house with a Dutch gable (± 1780) in Louis XVI-style.

172-174 » Pilaster-gable (± 1690). Note the pediment entablature that is supported by five Ionic pilasters. There is a shield and festoons in the entablature. Under that there are four little windows with sculpted frames. The two scroll stones are decorated and are above the second story.

180 » Stepped gable (1616) in the style of Holland's renaissance, with decorative blocks and a top pilaster. Underneath a woman's head is added.

186 » Dutch gable (± 1720) in Louis XVI-style. With a richly decorated top.

190 » Cornice gable (± 1730) with decorated door frame and a double stoop. On the roof there are three dormer windows.

⚲ We cross Amstelstraat and continue to follow the Amstel. We pass the intersection Amstel/

Blauwbrug

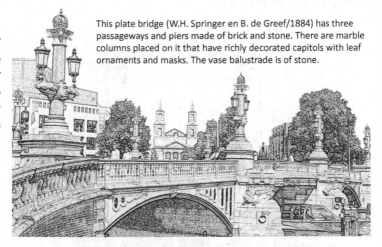

This plate bridge (W.H. Springer en B. de Greef/1884) has three passageways and piers made of brick and stone. There are marble columns placed on it that have richly decorated capitols with leaf ornaments and masks. The vase balustrade is of stone.

On the columns are lantern poles shaped like the bow of a ship and above the lanterns the imperial crown of Austria. The bridge is a monument and is restored in 1999.

Herengracht (Hendrick Jacobsz Staetsbrug 1773, arched bridge).
To the left we look over the Amstel and see the Walter Suskindbrug with next the Amstelhof (see later).

☞ 216 » Huis met de Bloed-vlekken - House with the Blood Spots - A. Dortsman/1671

This double mansion in austere Holland's classicism has a sandstone cornice-gable and a straight cornice moulding with balustrade. In the middle the balustrade is circularly indented to make room for a coat of arms shield. The entrance has two columns on which a balcony rests. In the door frame the date can be read in Roman numerals.

The story of The House with the Blood Spots is handed down traditionally. Coenraad van Beuningen (1622-1693) was a wellknown and rich resident of this house. He became insane in the last few years of his life. He wrote his name, the name of his wife, three master ships, Hebrew letters, and cabbalistic signs on the sand stone gable with his own blood. If we look closely we can still see the signs.

218 » Wide cornice-gable in Louis XIV-style (± 1725). With decorated girders, double stoop and a basement. The door and the windows on the first story are richly decorated.
220 » Cornice-gable (± 1725) with decorated middle elevation, decorated date shield, and two mythical figures on the top.

🕴 **We walk on straight and we reach the junction Amstel/Keizersgracht.**
On the bridge (Lucas Jansz. Sinck-brug) we have a beautiful view (left) of the Amstel and the Nieuwe Keizersgracht.

🕴 **We continue along the Amstel.**
Left, at the Kerkstraat lies Amsterdam's most famous bridge.

☞ Magere Brug (1934)

The name Magere Brug (skinny bridge) refers to the first bridge that was here around 1670. It was a 'small' or 'skinny' bridge used only for pedestrians.
The Magere Brug has nine passageways for boats and at night it is fairylike with hundreds of lights.

Magere brug

284 » Corner house on the Prinsengracht (W. van Brederode/1670). It formed a twin with the long gone nr. 282.

🧍 **We continue walking and pass the Prinsengracht (Frans Hendriksz Oetgensbrug).**
On the left side of the bridge we have a good view of the Amstel locks (1675) and next the Royal Theatre Carré (see later).

🧍 **We pass the Hendrick de Keyserbrug and turn right on the Achtergracht.**
34 « Dutch gable (1680) with a high stoop
32-30-28 « Neck-gable triplets (± 1670) with four stoops, decorated scroll stones and half-round pediments. Next-door thirteen warehouses -De Zon and January-December (± 1750) with spout-gable.

🧍 **We walk back and follow the Amstel.**
316-318 » Wide Dutch gable (± 1700) has wooden under façade and basement.
332-338 » Former neck-gable quadruplets (± 1710). The scroll stones are decorated. Nr.332 has sculpted oval windows, nr. 332 and 334 have half-round pediments, 336 a pediment entablature, and 338 is renovated to a cornice-gable.

🧍 **We continue walking and turn left on Sarphatistraat.**

☞ Hoge Sluisbrug - W. Springer/1883
This is a plate bridge in Parisian style with ten openings for boats. The decorative pieces are if cast iron with a city coat of arms.
Note the obelisks of stone with decorated lamp holders and lovely lamps. On the bridge there is an especially beautiful view from both sides of Amsterdam. On the left are the locks of the Amstel and to the right of the locks is the Royal Theatre Carré. A little further on we see the Magere Brug, the Stopera and the tower of the Zuiderkerk. We turn around, then on the right side is the Rembrandttoren and to the right of that the tower of the former city archives.
At the end of the bridge is the

☞ » Amstelhotel - C. Oudshoorn/1867
The use of red and yellow brick is eyecatching. Originally the eclecticism style building was three stories high. In 1899 floor was added. The cornice moulding above the third floor shows what the original height was. The hotel has 79 rooms and suites.

Amstelhotel

↑ Across the bridge we turn left again on the Amstel.
At the height of nr. 135 we can see the Amstelsluizen (locks) in close-up.

☞ 115 » Royal Theatre Carré - J. van Rossum & W. Vuyk/ 1887

This is a circus theatre in eclecticism style commissioned by the German circus director Oscar Carré. Originally only circus and revue shows were given in this building. From 1920 on Carré turned slowly into a general theatre. Cabaret, music, and dance are now the major numbers on the programme.

The front façade is neo-classicism and has four layers. The protruding middle section is supported by pilasters. There are sixteen windows on both sides and the lowest windows are crowned with small pediment entablatures. The centre section rests on Ionic pillars with a balcony in the middle. The gable is decorated with a clown's heads and horses. In the pediment entablature two lions and a crown are depicted. The roofing structure has a steel construction and is boarded with wood. The span width is 37 metres.

During the renovation of 2004 paintings were found from different periods.

↑ We walk further to the bridge of the Nieuwe Prinsengracht (Jan Vinckbrug).
Nieuwe Prinsengracht 3-7 » Warehouse Le Papillon (1732).
83-85-87 » Neck-gables (1736) in Louis XIV style.

↑ We continue on Amstel and at the height of the Nieuwe Kerkstraat we can see the Magere Brug again. We cross the Nieuwe Keizersgracht (Dirk van Nimwegenbrug).

☞ 51 » Hermitage aan de Amstel - H.J. van Petersom/ 1681

The foundation rests on 1,432 piles. The Amstelhof is built in the style of classicism and has a long symmetric front façade. The entrance in the middle, surrounded by four decorated Ionic pilasters and a pediment, is not a real entrance. This pseudo entrance was placed there for aesthetic reasons. The façade on the side of the Amstel is 76 metres long and has 31 windows. The two doors at the fourth windows (left and right) are real entrances. Because the city of Amsterdam (1681) donated a large piece of land, the orphanage Amstelhof could be built. It was later expanded to include the care of old women and (in 1719) old men as well. With a capacity of 400 people, it was the largest home in the Netherlands for almost two hundred years.

In the spring of 2007 the last residents moved. Since June 2009 the site has been home to Hermitage Amsterdam.

↑ We walk past the Amstelhof and turn right on the Nieuwe Herengracht.

☞ 14 » Hermitage aan de Amstel

In 1888 the Deanery built a rest home for old, married couples beside Amstelhof: Neerlandia. This is where the Russian Hermitage (Amsterdam) is established since 2004. Following a renovation, the building was transformed into a museum in which visitors were introduced to selections from the Hermitage collection in Russia.

☞ 18 » The Corvershof (1723)

The Corvershof is for welfare work of the Nederlands Hervormde Gemeente (Dutch reformed congregation). The middle section of the front façade is richly decorated in Louis XIV style and is crowned with a half-round pediment that depicts the care of the needy. Above the middle window are the family coat of arms of Jan Corver and his wife Sara Maria Trip. The Corvershof

Hermitage aan de Amstel

was built thanks to a legacy from the couple.

20 » The Bestedelingenhuis (1790)

Here needy Amsterdammers, that didn't fit in anywhere else in the regular Reformed institutions, could find a home. The text in the gable refers to Johanna van Mekeren-Bontekoning. Because of her legacy this house could be built.

⸙ We walk back to the Amstel, turn right and reach the Walter Suskindbrug.
On the bridge we can see the Hortus Botanicus to the right.

⸙ We continue walking and come to the Amstelstraat. We cross the Amstelstraat and walk on the Waterlooplein. We continue to follow the Amstel.
The Stopera is on the right.

⸙ We walk on to the Zwanenburgwal.
Right in front of us is the market of the Waterlooplein (Mon-Sun).

⸙ We turn left and cross the bridge (B. Bijvoetsluis) and then left on the Zwanenburgwal.
290-288 » Dutch gable (± 1710) with coach house.

⸙ We walk further. The Zwanenburgwal turns (after the curve) into the Staalkade.
3 » Warehouse (± 1680) De Wildeman with spout-gable.

⸙ We turn right on the Groenburgwal.
69 » High neck-gable (± 1740) with decorated scroll stones and a decorated half-round pediment.
59 » Elevated cornice-gable (± 1720) with a richly decorated half-round cornice moulding and three vases.

⸙ We turn left.
When standing on the bridge and looking to the right, we have a beautiful view of the Zuiderkerk. This is one of the best vantage points in the city for taking photographs.
Right ahead we see the monumental house Staalstraat 7 (see page 135).

⸙ We cross the bridge and turn left on the Grimburgwal.
52 » Warehouse (± 1680) has a spout-gable.

⸙ We walk on. The Grimburgwal now turns into the 's Gravelandseveer. Then we turn right on Kloveniersburgwal.
To the left we see the rear of the Doelen Hotel. Note the cupola tower with clock and on each side two statues of marksmen (Kloveniers).

⸙ We turn left and cross the green balance bridge (1896). To the right is the Waag. We turn left on Nieuwe Doelenstraat. We cross the street and continue on the right side. Now we come to the Amstel again.
To the right are Rokin and the Muntplein with the Munttoren.

ᛏ **Before the bridge we turn right on the Oude Turfmarkt (Peat Market).**
The name refers to the peat market that was held here between 1550 and 1643.

147 » House in neo-renaissance style (A. Salm/1884). This house formed a twin with nr. 145, but 1884 it was replaced by this house.

☞ 145 » Pilaster neck-gable - P. Vingboons/1643

It's decorated with festoons, Roman numeral date ribbon, decorated attic windows and crowned with pediment entablature.

141 » Warehouse with a Dutch gable (± 1775).

129 » Archaeological Museum Allard Pierson, formerly the Nederlandsche Bank (W.A. Froger/ 1869) The building in neo-classicism style is made of Oberkircheren Bentheimer-sandstone. In the façade there are two figures of women, one steam locomotive, and a sailing ship denoting international trade.

91 » Neck-gable (1664) built of sandstone. In the scroll stones we see eagles with a weapon in their talons.

ᛏ **We walk through to the Grimnessesluis.**
To the right we have a beautiful view of the rear of the buildings of the Langebrugsteeg and Nes 89 (the white house with shutters). Past the tree we see the House on the Three Canals and behind that the gate of the former Binnengasthuis hospital. To the left is a statue of the former Queen Wilhelmina (1880-1962) on horseback. Just a little further on we see (left) the tower of the Enge Kapelsteeg.

ᛏ **We continue.**
On the right side we pass the mill of the Diamond Factory. The Oude Turfmarkt passes into the Rokin.

ᛏ **We walk on and pass under the Beurspoortje (1916). Now we are back at the Dam again.**

Waterlooplein Market

Munttoren (1620)

East Centre City

This walk takes us via the Prins Hendrikkade to the East Centre City. We walk past the science museum NEMO and the Netherlands Scheepvaartmuseum (Maritime museum) in the direction of the Eastern Islands. Via the Kattenburgergracht and the Sarphatistraat we come to the largest habituated warehouse complex in Amsterdam, the Entrepotdok.

Scheepvaartmuseum (Maritime museum) - D. Stalpaert/1665

♙ 4.8 miles (7,7 km)

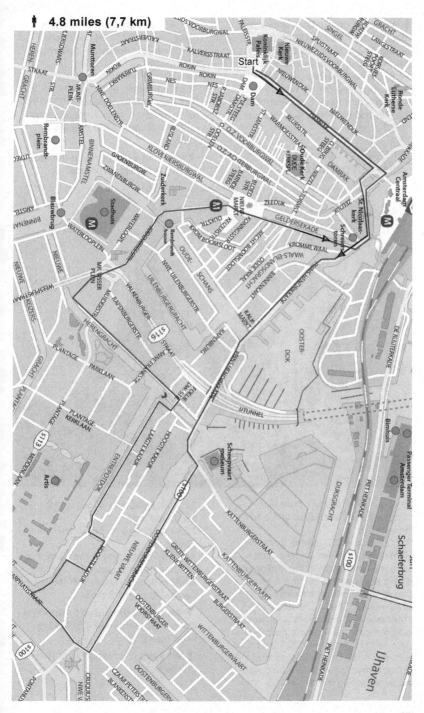

♟ We stand on the Dam and walk past the Bijenkorf to Damrak. On the right side, we pass the Beursplein with the Beurs building and the Beurs van Berlage. Past the Oudebrugsteeg (right) we see the rear gables of the Warmoesstraat. The Central Station is straight ahead of us.

☞ **Central Station - P.J.H. Cuypers/1889**

♟ At the traffic lights we turn right on the Prins Hendrikkade.
« *Noord-ZuidHollands Koffiehuis* (See page 53).
53 » Hotel Prins Hendrik.
The plaque tells us that the famous jazz musician Chet Baker (1929-1988) fell to his death from an open window on the first floor of this building in 1988.

♟ We follow the curve in the road on the Prins Hendrikkade.

Design in old-Holland's style in a combination of late gothic and early renaissance.
The building is 360 metres long and 30 metres deep. Two towers accentuate the centre part of the station. It is also worth noting that the arch capping Is 45 metres broad with a height of 25 metres. The two towers on either side of the arch are supposed to accentuate the station's quality of 'gateway to the city'. In 1922 a second arch was built. On the east side of the station a royal pavilion is added with the royal waiting room.

72 » Neck-gable (± 1750) with a decorated top.
73 » Parsonage of the St. Nicholas Church.
74-77 » Front porch of the St. Nicholas Church (see page 52).
84-85 » Building Batavia in the style of the Amsterdam's School.

♟ We follow the curve to the right.
Corner Gelderskade » Schreierstoren (see page 52).

♟ We keep following Prins Hendrikkade.

101 » Stepped-gable (± 1650) in sober Amsterdam's renaissance style with two lion masks and a gable stone.

🚶 At nr. 103 we cross the street and walk on the wide pavement. We pass the Kraansluis.

108-114 The Scheepvaart-huis - A.L van Gendt & J.M. van der Mey/1913

Until 1981 several shipping companies were established in this building in the style of the Amsterdam's School. Almost all of the decorations refer to the shipping past of Amsterdam. The building is made of brick in combination with granite and marble. Note that the main entrance has the shape of the keel of a ship. Above that is a half-tower that is lined with slate. Presently a hotel is established here.

🚶 We continue walking and turn right on Buiten Bantammerstraat. From here we have a beautiful view of the rear façade of the Scheepvaart-huis.

3 « Neck-gable (1652) with pilasters, decorated scroll stones, a pediment entablature on top. The lower façade is of wood, with a basement.

5 « Stepped-gable (1652) with pilasters, high wooden lower-façade and basement.

7 & 9 « Dutch gables (± 1680) with high wooden lower-façade and basement.

🚶 We walk back and follow the Prins Hendrikkade.

To the left we have a beautiful view of the Binnen-IJ and the science museum NEMO.

129 » Cornice-gable (± 1725) in Louis XV-style. With straight cornice moulding and crest.

131 » Cornice-gable (± 1650) home of the famous admiral and sea hero Michiel de Ruyter (1607-1676). The relief shows the bust of De Ruyter.

133 » Cornice-gable (1727) in Louis XIV-style. Of sandstone with richly worked cornice moulding with two

horn-blowing tritons, Mercury's staff and two corner vases.

134 » Cornice-gable (± 1750) with a richly worked high cornice moulding with in the middle a cloverleaf trapdoor.

☞ Montelbaanstoren (1516)

This tower along with a wide defence moat (now the Oude Schans) is built as a defensive works. After the city's expansion in 1591 the tower was lowered and got the function of guard house and storage building.

In 1606 the tower is made higher and was equipped with a bell and timepiece. This renovation and wooden spire is designed by Hendrick de Keyser and is called 'the crazy Jan' by the people. The tower got this nickname because the clock showed a different time on four sides and the bell rang at the strangest moments. Above the bells pediment entablatures are placed. The upper two sections

are open and are separated by a balustrade. The spire is wooden and covered with lead. A pirate serves as a weathervane on the top of the spire is. In 1610 the tower almost collapsed because it started leaning towards one side. Then a new foundation and wall was placed around it.
Since 1878 the city water office is housed in the Montelsbaantoren.

↟ We walk further to the 's-Gravenhekje (hekje = small gate).
The name of this side-street dates from the 18th century, when wood-buyer De Graaf had a lumberyard here. According to city ordinances the lumberyard was only allowed to be closed with a gate.
The name of De Graaf was coupled with hek, so that the compound name 's-Gravenhekje was made.

☞ 's-Gravenhekje 1 - corner Prins Hendrikkade, the West-India House (1641)
was a former storehouse of the West-India-Company (WIC).
The two trapezium shaped top gables rise above the quadruple ware-house. The gables are connected by an inserted pediment entablature. Festoons and the emblem of WIC can be seen in the pediment. The framed oval windows and the gable stones in the top gables are lovely.

↟ We continue on the Prins Hen-
drikkade.
171 » Cornice-gable (1754) in Louis XV style with a ship and a globe in the gable top.
176 » Two warehouses De Oude Werf (± 1610) of the Verenigde Oost-India Compagnie Amsterdam (VOCA).
Until 1661 the company's wharf was located behind the warehouses, which was accessible via the gateway that is on the right side of the warehouses.

↟ We continue on the Prins Hendrikkade.

☞ 189-190/Schippersgracht 1-3 the training school for sea-manship W. Springer/1880
The style of the building goes back to the beginning of the 17th century.
The neo-renaissance gable on the Prins Hendrikkade is symmetric and higher than the side gable on the Schippersgracht. The stepped-gables and the relief with the representation of shipping are noticeable. Until 1971 the institute for training for the mer-chant marines was established in this building. Now it is a housing institute of the College of Higher Education Amsterdam.

↟ At the traffic lights we turn left and cross the Prins Hendrikkade.
We turn right and then immediately left to reach the entrance of NEMO. We turn right and walk up the steps to NEMO.

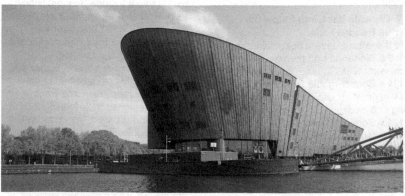

NEMO

NEMO - R. Piano/1997

The green copper curved building stands above the IJ tunnel. The tunnel tube is the foundation for the building that has the shape of a ship. On the roof terrace there is a terrific view across Amsterdam. Between July 1st and September 1st the roof terrace is changed into a beach terrace. Brightly coloured beach chairs, water, sand, olive trees, ice-cream, a giant chess-board, and exotic snacks make for a sea-side atmosphere.

🚶 **We walk back to the Prins Hendrikkade, turn left and pass the Kortjewantsbrug.**

To the left we can see the Maritime Museum (Scheepvaartmuseum) and the replica of the East-India sailing ship 'the Amsterdam'.

Scheepvaartmuseum - D. Stalpaert/1656

a-symmetrical. The original ware-house function is clear by the rows of shutters. The four outside façades are almost identical. In the pediments there are sculptured figures.

The woman's figure on the side of the entrance stands for the Ruler of the seas. On the two side gables male figures carry goods which provide for the fleet. Among other things, we see: ropes, a canon, a canon undercar-riage, and a keg of gunpowder.

On the side of the Binnen-IJ we see Neptune arm-in-arm with the country's Ruler of the seas. Around them the sea gods are carrying the goods that the Virgin of Amsterdam takes into reception.

In 1791 the building was ravaged by fire, only the walls remained. At the time of rebuilding which lasted until 1793, the walls were plastered with sandstone. After 1795 the building

This building is in the style of Holland's classicism and is the largest still remaining warehouse from the 17th century. The square building has four wings around a beautiful courtyard. The wing on the Kattenburgerplein has less depth than the other three wings which makes the building

came into use as a depot for the navy. In 1822 a bell tower was added to the façade that juts out on the east side. Since 1973 the building is used as storehouse of the Maritime Museum. In front of the museum is a replica of East-India sailing ship. The ship sank during a storm off the English coast

in 1749. From 1985 to 1990 four hundred volunteers worked on the replica. Since 1991 'the Amsterdam' is moored at the Maritime Museum.
A visit to 'the Amsterdam' is included in the price of the ticket to the museum.

🚶 **We turn right and cross at the pedestrian crossing.**
Then we turn left and cross the pedestrian crossing and walk straight on.
Kadijksplein 18 Zeemanshuis - A.N. Godefroy/1856 in eclecticism style. At the time of a renovation the lovely gable crown was removed which mutilated the building.

🚶 **We walk straight on, cross the bridge and turn right on Kattenburgergracht.**
9 « Stepped-gable (1663) with two sculpted oval windows, two date stones, and a high wooden under façade.
11« Spout-gable (1663) with high wooden under façade, carved joists and a basement.
13 « Dutch gable (1663) with two sculpted oval windows, gable stone, high wooden under façade, and basement.

🚶 **We walk further on the Wittenburgergracht.**
3-71 « Warehouse De Paerl (1662), former beer and vinegar brewery. The beer was mostly delivered to the ships of the VOC.
77-95 « Former Roman Catholic Church St. Anna (1900). Only the front façade is left from this neo-gothic church. In the pedestrian tunnel the pointed arches can be seen.

☞ **« Oosterkerk - D. Stalpaert & A. Dortsman/1671**
This is a cruciform church with two crossing aisles and four corner areas. There is an octagonal dome in the middle with a tower on top. This building style comes from Solomon's Temple. The interior is plastered white and is sober. The pulpit dates from the

time of building.

🚶 **We walk straight on.**
To the right on the other side of the water we see the shipyard Kromhout (see later).
Now the Wittenburgergracht goes over into the Oostenburgergracht.
75 « Werktheater - M.F. Duintjer/1952.

☞ **77 « VOC-warehouse (1661)**
Entrance hall of the former Company's rope yard, the rope factory of the VOC. To the right was the storehouse of the Admiralty. The coat of arms of the Amsterdam's chapter of the VOC (AVOC) with two crossed anchors is in the gable.
Today only the entrance hall exists anymore and serves as a warehouse for rope and hemp.

🚶 **At the traffic lights we turn right.**

☞ **« Mill 'De Gooyer' (± 1814)**

This octagonal corn windmill with wooden beams has a thatched roof. It is the highest wooden windmill in the Netherlands and is one of the six remaining windmills in the city. 'De Gooyer' can not be visited.

☗ **We walk straight into the Sarphatistraat.**

☛ Oranje Nassau Kazerne -barracks- A. van der Hart/ 1810

This neo-classicism barrack is 276 metres long and 16 metres wide. It is built during the French occupation of the Netherlands (1806-1813) by order of Louis Napoleon. After the defeat of the French (1813), Netherlands became a monarchy in 1815. The barracks received the name Oranje Nassau Kazerne. The French emperor's coat of arms in the pediment entablature was replaced by the coat of arms of the Prince of Orange.
In 1990 the barracks were changed into tenement houses, the front façade was preserved in its original state.

☗ **We walk along the barracks. Past the park we turn right on the Entrepotdok.**

☛ » Aquarius - L. van der Pol/ 2001

This is a combination of old and new. The retaining wall of the former coal depot of the power station is saved. Above the retaining wall caps of wood and glass are placed. Note the enormous glass façades and sun-rooms. To the left are the new feeding buildings of Artis Zoo and the African Savannah (1999). Before the savannah was created, the terrain belonged to the railway until 1950. Until 1997 it was no-man's-land.

☗ **We continue walking until we reach the Geschutswerf.**
Until 1835, the wharf of the artillery of the navy was established on this terrain.

In front of us are the renovated

☛ Kalenderpanden - C.W.M. Kleijn/1838

The Kalenderpanden are built between 1838 and 1840 as an expansion of the warehouses of the Entrepot. The Kalenderpanden have five stories. The months of the year are designated on the gables. For nearly 75 years the state entrepôt (government bonded warehouses) is situated in the Entrepotdok. From 1899 to 2000 the warehouses were rented to private enterprises as warehouses. Since 2002 apartments were built in the warehouse.

☗ **We turn right on Geschutswerf and then left on the Hoogte Kadijk.**
147 » Museum/ships' wharf 't Kromhout (1760).
The wharf is the last shipyard still in use in East Centre City under this name since 1760. The iron roofing structures from 1888 are remarkable. One of the roofing structures covers a forty metre long slipway. The shipyard also oriented itself towards the development of steam engines. In 1904 the owner Goedkoop constructed a four stroke paraffin motor with sparkplug ignition which laid a basis for the internal combustion engine.
The museum 't Kromhout is located on the terrain. At the present repairs are still made on ships here.

☗ **In front of the green bascule bridge we turn left and walk down the steps.**
Straight ahead we see the restaurant of the Artis zoo.
De twee cheetah's (1999)
The restaurant is on the former shunting terrain of the Entrepotdok that was added to Artis zoo in 1995. Natural kinds of wood are used in the building. In combination with various stone formations and numerous large windows the restaurant has a large and spacious atmosphere. Inside there is a magnificent view of the African Savannah next door and a part

of the historic zoological gardens. On the other side there is a lovely view of the monumental buildings of the Entrepotdok.

🕯 We turn right and pass the Entrepotdoksluis and the Laagte Kadijk and arrive at the Entrepotdok.
This part of the Entrepotdok consists of 84 monumental warehouses that were built in the 19th century as depots for transhipment of goods from far countries. At nr. 73 (Vlissingen) the crane is a reminder of the origin of Entrepotdok as a transfer warehouse for goods. Customs did not have to be paid on the goods that were shipped on to another country.
Each warehouse has the name of a Dutch or Belgium city. The names of these cities are on name boards on the gables. The alphabetic order has no reference to the date of the buildings.Muiden to Weesp are built after 1829, Winschoten - Zierikzee are built before 1750.
In 1710 the first warehouse was built on the Rapenburgergracht (now Entrepotdok) as a storehouse for the Dutch East India Company (VOC).
In 1980 the warehouses are restored and renovated into apartments. Now, with over six hundred apartments the Entrepotdok is the largest occupied warehouse complex in Amsterdam.

🕯 We continue on the Entrepotdok. To the left we pass the Nijlpaardenbrug.
The dome behind the bridge is the Planetarium of the Artis zoo.
At the end of the Entrepotdok we pass the entrance gateway to the Entrepotdok on the right hand.

☞ Entrepotdok (1829)
10-3 » Former sheds of the Entrepotdok (1885).
1 ^ Former Entrepotdok administration office (J. de Greef/1830). This monumental building is presently a dwelling.

🕯 We turn right and walk through the neo-classicism Entrepotdok

entrance gateway (J. de Greef/ 1830).
Now we arrive at Kadijksplein.

☞ 4 Coffee house of the Volksbond (1840)

In the 19th century and a better part of the 20th century this coffee house was for the workers. This lovely building has been nominated for demolition several times. Because of squatting in the 1980s the building is saved. Now a restaurant is established in this authentic building.
Again we can see the Maritime Museum straight ahead of us and the replica of the 'Amsterdam'.

🕯 We turn left and cross the Scharrebiersluis.
Scharrebier is a thin (cheap) beer variety that was drunk by the skippers and sailors and sold especially here.

🕯 We turn left here to the Rapenburgerplein.
9/corner Rapenburg 105-103 » Former Dutch-Jewish Hospital (1804). On the side façade there is

a gable stone with a pelican feeding her young. This is the Jewish symbol for care.

83 ^ Café De Druif.
This café opened its doors in 1631 as a public house and Dutch gin distillery and was popular with many sailors who found themselves in this area. Note the lean-to building that juts out from the basement which runs across two façades.

ꝑ We walk straight through to the Nieuwe Herengracht.
At the level of nr. 255 we have a beautiful view of the Entrepotdok and of the locks that connect the Nieuwe Herengracht with the IJ.
187 « Cornice-gable (± 1750) with sunflowers and wreaths on the girders. This is part of a Dutch gable quintuple.
181, 183, 185 « Elevated neck-gable triplets (± 1750) with decorated scroll stones and in half-round pediment relief figures of Greek gods.

ꝑ We pass the Anne Frankstraat.
The street is named after Anne Frank (see Prinsengracht 263), writer of the world famous diary.
In this street there are many new buildings, that were built here in the 1980s.

ꝑ We continue on the Nieuwe Herengracht.

▸ 103 » Double mansion (1751)
Sandstone cornice-gable is in Louis XV style. The transom above the door is decorated with grapevines. The doorframe is richly decorated as well as are the windows of the first story. The cornice is supported by decorated joists. The decorated rococo stoop gate is considered to be the most beautiful in Amsterdam.
To the left we see the Wertheimpark.

ꝑ We pass the Hortusbrug, turn left across the Muiderstraat via the tram rails and continue again on the Nieuwe Herengracht.

« **Hothouses of the Hortus Botanicus (1992).**
63 » Dutch gable (± 1700) with basement, festoon around the attic window and a half-round pediment decorated with flower motifs.
61 » Dutch gable (± 1670) with half-round pediment and festoons around the attic window and hoisting hook.

ꝑ We turn right on the Jonas Daniël Meyerplein.
7 » Out-buildings and synagogue.
To the left we see the rear of the statue 'the Dockworker' (see page 136).

ꝑ At the corner we turn right on Mr. Visserplein. We walk straight on and cross the street at the traffic lights. We turn left and walk along the building of the Dutch Film and Television Academy.
We cross the Valkenburgerstraat at the traffic lights and walk straight into the Jodenbreestraat.
4 « The Rembrandthouse + museum (see page 66).

ꝑ We pass the bridge (Sint Antoniesluis) and into the Sint Antoniebreestraat.
69 » Huis De Pinto (see page 65).
To the right is the gateway to the Zuiderkerkhof and we can see the Zuiderkerk (see page 65).

ꝑ We continue on the Sint Antoniebreestraat and walk on until the Nieuwmarkt. Now we continue straight on and pass the Waag to the left. We walk until we get to the Gelderskade.
The quay was excavated at the end of the 15th century and had the function of a defensive moat until the 17th century. Until the 17th century there was city wall of Amsterdam on the west side of the city. The houses on this side are built after the city wall was torn down and therefore the houses are not as old as the houses on the east side. Many gable stones refer to the tobacco industry that was established here in previous centuries.
3 Three window wide Dutch gable

(± 1775). It is interesting that this house is still on its old foundation.

8 Amsterdam's merchant's house Het Tabaksvat (1622/1775).
It was a spout-gable until it was renovated with a cornice-gable in the style of Louis XVI in 1775. Note the richly decorated rococo door frame with the inscription 'Tabaksvat'. The shop interior is still in the original 18th century state.

55 Cornice-gable (1775) with the portrayal of Neptune in the cornice and three crests.

56 Dutch gable (1732) in Louis XIV style.

82 Neck-gable (1644) with Doric pilasters. In the neck there are three round windows, where from one the hoisting hook sticks out. The pediment entablature is crowned with a vase.
It has decorated scroll stones and a wooden lower façade.

84 In this store building from the 17th century the oldest pharmacy in the Netherlands was established. The interior dates from 1875 and is original.

☞ 97 High stepped-gable (1610)

in sober Haarlem's renaissance style. Above the wooden lower façade there are golden lion masks. Two gable stones, and above the first and second stories are a man's and a woman's head. Above the side gable there is a dormer with a hoisting hook and trapdoors.

107 Corner house (1634) with a high pilaster Dutch gable and a wooden lower façade.
There is a lean-to building on the side of the Rechtboomsloot.

🕴 **We walk along the Geldersekade and turn left. We pass the Schreierstoren. We walk further on the Prins Hendrikkade.**
To the left is the St. Nicholas Church. The Central Station is to the right with the Noord-Zuid-Hollands Koffiehuis.

🕴 **We continue on the Prins Hendrikkade and we curve to the right. At the traffic lights we turn left on Damrak. We follow Damrak until we get to the Dam again.**

Gelderse Kade 97

Noord-Zuid-Hollands koffiehuis and the Central Station

The Nine Streets

The nine streets (Negen Straatjes) run straight through the ring of canals of Amsterdam and are cross-connections between the Heren-, Keizers- and Prinsengracht. There are more than 190 small shops and restaurants.
The streets have a past of rich history and traditional trades. The street names remind us of this.

Reestraat

1.9 miles (3,1 km)

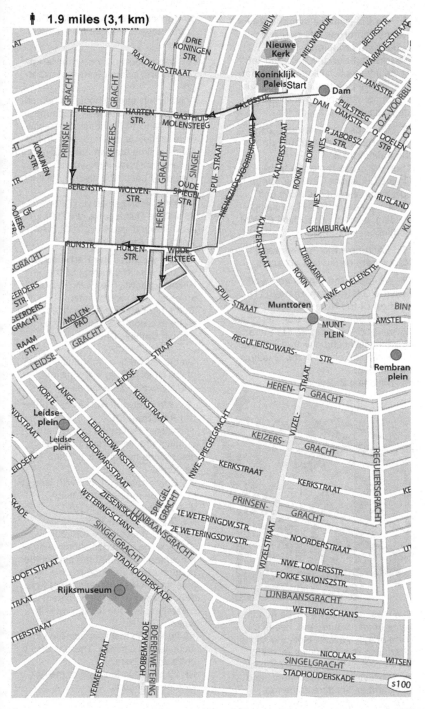

On the Dam we face the Royal Palace and cross left over the pedestrian crossing.
We turn right on the Paleisstraat.
At the intersection Nieuwezijds Voorburgwal we look to the right and see the former main post office, now the shopping centre Magna Plaza.

We cross the Nieuwezijds Voorburgwal and continue on the Paleisstraat.
Then we cross the Spuistraat.
On the Spuistraat left is the Bungehuis (bros. Van Gendt/1932) and to the right on nr. 172-174 a bank building, now Kas-Associatie (F.W.M. Poggenbeek/1908).

We follow the Paleisstraat.
Now we are on the ring of canals.

We pass the Singel and walk into the Gasthuismolensteeg (1), the first of the Nine Streets.
This alley bordered the city wall in the 15th and 16th centuries where there was a hospital and a windmill. There are a few nice shops in the Gasthuismolensteeg.
7 « Nationaal Brilmuseum.

The museum reviews seven hundred years of art, culture, and development of eye-glasses. Note the two protruding shop-windows (± 1875).
9 « Raised neck-gable (± 1750) with Doric pilasters, elevated steps, and pediment entablature in the top.

18-corner Herengracht 243 » De Transvaalse Boer (see Herengracht 243).

We walk on, cross the Herengracht and come on Hartenstraat (2).
Actually this street should be named Hertenstraat (hert=deer), because in the 15th and 16th centuries deerskins were tanned and traded here. In the space of time the name was corrupted into Hartenstraat. Here you also immediately notice the diversity of shops and restaurants.
2 en 4 » Neck-gables (± 1750).
16 » Wide Dutch gable (± 1750).
29 « Stepped-gable (± 1700) in Amsterdamse renaissance.

As we leave the Hartenstraat, we arrive on the bridge of the Keizersgracht. The view on both sides is very worthwhile.
To the right on Keizersgracht 218-220 is the neo-gothic Syrian-orthodox and Roman Catholic Church.

On the left we have a beautiful view of the canal with its many historic mansions along the canal.

We continue further and enter the Reestraat (3).
This street also refers to the leather tanning and hides trade that was established here in the 17th and 18th centuries.
2 » Dutch gable (± 1750) with lean-to building on the Keizersgracht.
4 » Cornice-gable (± 1750).
6 » Dutch gable (± 1750).
8 » Dutch gable in (1620) Louis XV-styleThe authentic shop/house is renovated in 1763. At the time of the restoration on 1980 the marble pillars (see also in the shop windows) from 1880 were kept. In the pediment with crest there is a roe resting with the legend 'Ree Rust'.
18-20 » Shop that is specialised in incense and candles. There is also a doll's doctor here.
Nr. 20 is built in the style of the Amsterdam's School.

19 « Elevated Dutch gable (1772) in Louis XV-style. With gable stone 'niet Sonder Arbeid 1772' (not without labour).
At the end of the street (left on the corner) we can have a cup of coffee in an authentic Amsterdam's koffiehuis.

⚑ **Now we reach the Prinsengracht and turn left in front of the bridge. We walk straight on and turn left on the Berenstraat (4).**
On this street in the 15th and 16th centuries bearskins were tanned and traded. Now there are mostly bookshops and restaurants here.
37-39 » Neck-gable (± 1750) with decorated scroll stones and a half-round pediment with a shell motif.
24 « Neck-gable (± 1750) with fruit motifs on the scroll stones and in the top an entablature.

► 7 » The former nursery school Amsterdam Welvaren P.J. Hamer/1864

The building with a spout-gable, designed in neo-gothic style, has many English elements. There is a relief above the door with the sailing ship Amsterdams Welvaren that reminds us that this building was originally a nursery school. Also there is a sailing ship in the top. The initials (JW) are at various places on the façade of the English Quaker James Warder, whose legacy made it possible to found and build this school.

⚑ **We leave the Berenstraat and walk straight on into the Wolvenstraat (5).**
The hides of wolves were tanned and traded here. At the beginning of the street there are new buildings, but also a number of historic buildings have been saved.
29 » Neck-gable (± 1750) with decorated scroll stones and a decorated half-round pediment. The lower wooden façade is lovely.
17 » Dutch gable (± 1725) in Louis XV-style. Also with a lower façade of wood.
1 » Side gable of the building Herengracht 300 with a wide lean-to building.

⚑ **We leave the Wolvenstraat and come to the Herengracht. We walk straight into the Oude Spiegelstraat (6).**
The street is named after the influential Spiegel family, manufacturers of soap.
11-9 » Neck-gable twins (± 1750) with decorated scroll stones and half-round pediments.
3 » Cornice-gable (± 1780) with a straight cornice, decorated girders and at the top a dormer window with a hoisting hook. Between nr.1 and 1a is a wide lean-to building that belongs to nr. 1a.

⚑ **When we leave the Oude Spiegelstraat, we turn right on the Singel.**
Straight ahead appears the Roman Catholic Church De Krijtberg.

⚑ **We turn right on the Wijde Heisteeg (7).**
The street is named after the corner house 'Het Hayblok' that stood here in the 16th century. During the expansion of the alley the house was demolished. It is a quiet street with a few unusual shops, like a croissanterie, a

delicatessen, and a flower shop.
5 « Neck-gable (± 1700) with on the gable stone 'de bakkerij' (the bakery).
4 en 6 » Twin neck-gables (± 1775) with decorated scroll stones and a filled half-round pediment. The upper window placement (one larger window in the centre and smaller ones on the outside) is typical for the 18th century.

🚶 **We leave the Wijde Heisteeg and reach the Herengracht. We walk further and go into the Huidenstraat (8).**
In earlier centuries this is where the trade in hides is concentrated. There is a choice of shops here.
12 » Pie shop/lunchroom Pompadour with a wide assortment of tarts, chocolate, and coffee.
1 « Narrow cornice-gable (± 1800) with a later gable stone 't Haasje'.
4 » Neck-gable (1740) in Louis XIV-style. with decorated scroll stones and the date 1740 on the half-round pediment.
6 » Neck-gable (± 1775) in Louis XIV-style.
8 en 10 » Dutch gables (± 1750).
19 « Wide Dutch gable (1761) with coach house. Nowadays the coach house serves as a store.

🚶 **We walk further to the Keizersgracht.**
In the distance (right) we can see the monumental Felix Meritis. Behind that is the tower of the Westerkerk.

🚶 **We continue walking and turn in the Runstraat (9).**
The name of the street refers to run (run=tanning bark) (finely ground oak bark) that was used in the tanning of hides. Besides the many restaurants, there are a few amusing shops to be found.
2 » Elevated neck-gable (± 1750) with decorated scroll pieces and a decorated half-round pediment.
24 » Dutch gable (± 1700) with a small crest on the top.
26 » Small Dutch gable (± 1730).
30 » Neck-gable (± 1730) in Louis XIV-style.

29 « Low Dutch gable (± 1740).
31 « Neck-gable (± 1740).
33 « Neck-gable (1746) in Louis XIV-style. With wooden lower façade, decorated girders and a shell motif in the pediment.

🚶 **We leave the Nine Streets and turn left on the Prinsengracht. After a short walk on the Prinsengracht we turn left on the first side-street, the Molenpad.**
In the 16th century this path was outside of the city and led to one of the windmills that was built on the city wall. After the Molenpad came to be within the city walls, it is the only one of the 16th century paths that leads to and from Amsterdam to keep its name 'pad' (path).
15-17 » The former Agatha Deken-school (1883). The building in eclecticism style is a national monument.
16-10 « Building (± 1920) in the style of the Amsterdam's School.
3-7 » Former warehouse (±1750).

🚶 **At the end of the Molenpad we turn right on the Keizersgracht and then left across the bridge.**
From the bridge we can look (right) and see the Leidsestraat. To the left is the Westertoren.

🚶 **We walk on and go up the Leidsegracht.**
This canal was excavated in 1664 because of the city expansion. Almost all of the gables are from the period 1664-1700.
At the end of the Leidsegracht straight in front of us we can see the back of the Roman Catholic Church De Krijtberg.

🚶 **We turn left on the Herengracht. At the level of the Huidenstraat we turn right across the bridge and right again on the Herengracht.**
On the other side we have a good view of the Bijbels Museum (Cromhouthuizen) and the NIOD.
Note the view at nr. 395 (Beulingsluis) for a beautiful sight of the Singel.

⚑ We walk on and turn left on the Beulingstraat.
27 » Neck-gable (1649) in Holland's classicism. With pilasters running up to the top, crowned with a half-round pediment. Has a high wooden lower façade with pavement.
25 » Neck-gable (1653) in the style of the Holland's classicism, with wooden lower façade and pavement. The gable has pilasters, festoons, date, carved oval windows, decorated scrolls and in the top an entablature.
5-7 » Warehouse (± 1700) with a trapezium-gable and coach house.
1 » Dutch gable (± 1700) De Gulden Ketel has a small attic trapdoor and hoisting hook.

⚑ At the end we turn left on the Singel. When we reach 412 we turn right and cross the Singel (Heibrug) and walk straight through the Heisteeg. Now we arrive at the Spuistraat.
303 « Elevated neck-gable (1693) with two sculpted oval window frames, decorated scroll stones and two bands with the date. The half-round pediment has a shell motif.

⚑ We cross the Spuistraat, walk across the Spui and turn left on Nieuwezijds Voorburgwal.
381-383 » Eclectic stepped-gables (1880) decorated with figures from the Bible, neo-renaissance-elements, and two high pavements. In the centre there is a bay window with a balustrade.
328 « Building in the style of the Amsterdam's School (1925).
316 « High neck-gable (1725) with decorated scroll stones. In the half-round pediment a mulberry tree and the date 1725 are depicted. Underneath the words: 'D' Moerbijeboom'. The pavement is placed sideways.
293 » Parsonage Sint-Jozefskerk/ De Papegaai (1914).
225 » Former building of the newspaper De Telegraaf (J.F. Staal/1930). Is a style combination of New Realism and Amsterdam's School.

The 47 metre high advertising pillar is obvious. The Telegraaf was situated here until 1974. The building is a national monument.
276 « Cornice-gable (± 1760) with a gable stone Berlin. The cornice is supported by three sculpted girders. There are two windows in the cornice.
274 « Pilaster neck-gable (± 1750) with four decorated scroll stones and two sculpted oval windows next to the attic window. Between the attic window and attic trapdoor is a gable stone and a festoon around the hoisting hook. There is a half-round pediment at the top.
264 « Neck-gable (1688) with two attic trapdoors, streamer with the date, decorated scroll stones with two corner vases and a half-round pediment in the top. Beneath the windows of the second and third stories are festoons with fruit motifs. The door frame has two Ionic pilasters. The pavement is placed sideways.
171 » Neck-gable (1684). The scroll stones have lions.
The gable stone has the inscription 'Coddeman' referring to the former owner Codde.
242 « Neck-gable (1725) in Louis XV-style. The scroll stones are decorated with a crest. The half-round fronton has a shell motif. No hoisting hook.
234-240 « Former industrial building (Ed. Cuypers/1903) of the newspaper Algemeen Handelsblad in a combination of neo-styles and a sober Jugendstil.
159 » Dutch gable (1725) with a vase at the top and under that a gable stone depicting three flowers with a crown and the text: 'de drie gecroonde bloemen'.

⚑ We turn right on Paleisstraat, via the pedestrian crossway, cross the Nieuwezijds Voorburgwal, and turn right on the Paleisstraat. Now we have arrived back at the Dam.

The Jordaan

This walk takes us through the neighbourhood of the former 17th century working class, the Jordaan. The swampy area west of the Prinsengracht was filled in and a labyrinth of streets and canals developed.

The Jordaan is about 65 hectares large and is hemmed in by the Leidsegracht, the Prinsengracht, the Brouwersgracht and the Lijnbaansgracht.

The Westerkerk.

ⵣ 2.6 miles (4,2 km)

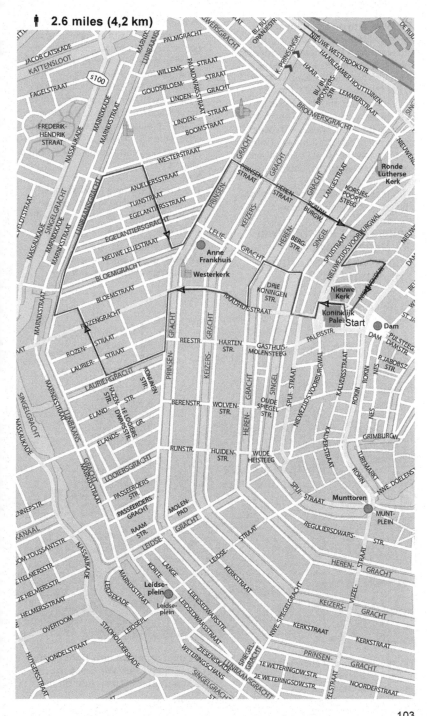

🚶 **We stand on the Dam facing the Royal Palace. We turn right and walk past the Nieuwe Kerk and enter the Mozes en Aaronstraat.**

The churchyard of the Nieuwe Kerk was in this street. In 1655 the cemetery was moved and the Mozes en Aaronstraat was laid out. The street refers to the Bible figures of Moses as symbol of secular authority (former city hall, now the Royal Palace), and Aaron as the symbol of church authority (the Nieuwe Kerk).

In front of us is the former main post office, now the Magna Plaza.

☞ ## Nieuwezijds Voorburgwal 182 Magna Plaza - former main post office C.H. Peters/ 1899

roof are a large number of dormer windows, each with its own stepped-gable. Note the many ornaments in stone and the two towers which gave it the nickname 'Perenburg'.

From 1899-1987 this was the main post office of Amsterdam. Only the ground floor was open to the public. In 1991 the building was restored and renovated. On August 27 1992, the building is opened as Shopping centre Magna Plaza.

Next to the right is
Die Port van Cleve (I. Gosschalk/ 1870). The building in neo-renaissance style has a lovely interior with Delft's Blue tile tableau.

🚶 **We steken de Nieuwezijds VoorWe cross the Nieuwezijds Voorburgwal and turn left.**

It is built in a combination of neo-styles with the accent on neo-renaissance. Along the edge of the

At the corner we turn right on the Raadhuisstraat. We cross the Spuistraat and turn right on the Singel.

To the left via the alley we have a beautiful view of House Bartolotti (see page 170).
Behind it is the tower of the Westerkerk.

🚶 **We continue walking to the bridge.**

Torensluis (1648)

During the summer season this lovely bridge is full of terraces. The Torensluis is an arched bridge with four arches. The bridge is proportionally wide because the Jan Roodenpoort (H. de Keyser/1616) stood on the right hand side. The tower served as a jail. The cells were under the tower. These still exist (to the left under the bridge) and are kept in original state. Also, the jailer's house (right side under the bridge) has been preserved in its original state.
The tower was demolished in 1829 due to the danger of collapsing. From the bridge you can still see where the tower stood exactly.

🚶 **We turn left and cross the Torensluis.**

To the right is a statue of the Dutch writer Eduard Douwes Dekker (1820-1887), better known under his nom de plume Multatuli.

🚶 **We walk straight on into the Oude Leliestraat.**

8 » Dutch gable (1846).
11 « Laundry service Sneeuwwit.

🚶 **We walk straight on, cross the bridge and turn left on the Herengracht. We continue walking until we get to the Raadhuisstraat and turn right.**

Here was the Warmoesgracht until 1896, a connecting canal between the Herengracht and the Singel. The canal was filled in to make parts of the (western) city more accessible for the transportation of goods.

➤ **« Winkelgalerij - shopping arcade - A.L. van Gendt/ 1899**

The shopping arcade is commissioned by the Life Insurance Company Utrecht in a combination of art nouveau, Jugendstil and neo-renaissance. There are many animal designs on the building and it is richly decorated with sculpture works. The façade and the thoroughfare of the arcade curve along with the Raadhuisstraat. The shops of the arcade run on both sides from the Keizersgracht to the Herengracht.
The middle section has an open balustrade of stone. This is different from the side sections which have wrought iron (art nouveau) balustrades.
At several places on the façade the letter 'U' is used. This refers to the Life Insurance Company Utrecht which had the arcade built.
30-32 » (corner of Herengracht 184) Dwelling/shop building (H.P. Berlage/ 1897) of red stone with bay windows and a corner tower with an elephant underneath.
42 » Store (1900) in art nouveau style with a half-round bay windows.
44 » Store (F.M.J. Caron/1904) in art nouveau style with half-round bay windows.
46-50 » building of furniture store 't Binnenhuis (J. F. Staal/1907). The architect was clearly inspired by Berlage.
52-54 » Dwelling/shop (G. van Arkel/ 1902) in a combination of red brick and stone. In the arches green glazed brick is used. The bay windows and the windows are eye-catching. Like most of the designs by van Arkel, his name can be found on the building, this time on the bay window on the corner.
The Westerkerk is in front of us.
From the bridge (Niek Engelsch-man) across the Keizersgracht we can see the triangular homo monument to the right in the water of the Keizersgracht.

☞ **Homomonument - K. Daan/ 1987**

The monument is set up as a memorial to the homosexual men and women who were repressed and persecuted in the past on the grounds of their sexual preference.

⚑ We walk straight ahead and reach the Westermarkt.
The square existed in the beginning of the 17ᵗʰ century, but after the completion of the Westerkerk it got more stature. The churchyard of the Westerkerk was on this side from 1620-1655. As we approach the church, we see two gateways with images of skulls in a half-round pediment.
Between the gateways a high lean-to is built (pothuis 3 > nr. 64).

```
┌─────── The Jordaan ───┐
```

Besides the working class people from Amsterdam, many protestant refugees from France (Huguenots) settled in this working-class area. According to the story, the name Jordaan comes from French Jardin (=garden). The name also could have been derived from the Biblical river Jordan, or the river Jordanne in the Auvergne, France. That is the area in France where many of the refugees came from. In the 18ᵗʰ and 19ᵗʰ centuries the standard of living got worse in this section of the city.
Because of the large population and poor social facilities the Jordaan developed into an area of poverty. Because of the water in the canals and the absence of sewers illness had a free reign. The city council decided to fill in the canals (among others the Lindegracht and the Westerstraat) and start building new houses.
Until the 20ᵗʰ century the Jordaan remained a working-class neighbourhood, where a typical Jordaan's culture developed. The cafés and the Jordaan's music are famous.
Since 1975 the Jordaan made a radical change. From an impoverished working-class area it developed into a greatly desired living area.

⚑ We follow the Westermarkt.
At the corner (right) Westermarkt-Prinsengracht we pass a bronze statue (M.S. Andriessen/1977) of Anne Frank. The statue reminds us of the Jewish girl Anne Frank who was in hiding from 1942-1944 in the Achterhuis on the Prinsengracht 263 with her family.

⚑ We continue walking and cross the Prinsengracht. The Westermarkt becomes the Rozengracht.
This was the most important canal in the Jordaan. The Rozengracht is filled in to make a broader road to the western part of the city.

⚑ At the level of Café de Oude Wester (right hand) we turn left and cross the Rozengracht. We walk straight on the Prinsengracht. At the third side street, <u>before</u> the bridge we turn right on the Lauriergracht. At the second side street we turn right on the Tweede Laurierdwarsstraat.
64 « Wide Dutch gable (± 1680) with crest.
60, 58 « Low Dutch gables (± 1650).
37 » Café Rooie Nelis is a typical Jordaans café.

⚑ We pass the Laurierstraat and continue walking.
8 « Dutch gable (1720) with a lamb in the top.

⚑ We walk straight into the Tweede Rozendwarsstraat.
14-18 « Dutch gable twins (± 1680).

⚑ We walk further to the Rozengracht.
To the right on the other side is the former Roman Catholic Church *De Zaaier (1927)*. The church is built in Roman style, but has a sober aura. The gable is symmetric and has a square steeple. The front façade is completely absorbed in the street wall. The building served as a church until 1971. Now it is used as a mosque. To the left at Rozengracht nr. 160 is a house with a low Dutch gable (1680) with a crest and a pavement on the Akoleienstraat. This house dates from when there was still water in the canal.

♟ We cross the Rozengracht and walk straight into the Akoleienstraat. At the end we turn left on the Bloemstraat.

During the period of city sanitation in the 1960's and 1970's many historic buildings were demolished and replaced by new houses.

188 » Warehouse with a Dutch gable (± 1775).

187 « Dutch gable (1765) has a gable stone above the entrance.

191 « School voor Haveloozen (school for poor people) (1854).

♟ We turn right on the Lijnbaansgracht.

Rope was made here in the 17th and 18th century for the ships in the ropeyards. The rope was stretched on the rope-walk (=lijnbaan). These were long stretches of land, usually at the edge of a city, where the rope-yarn was stretched and twisted to make rope.

♟ We continue walking and pass the Bloemgracht on the right hand.

On the bridge we look to the left at the building with a tower. This is the *Police Station bureau Marnixtraat (B. de Greef en W. Springer/1888)*. The building was built in eclecticism style and is standing where the Raampoortje was demolished in 1844.

♟ We continue on Lijnbaansgracht, pass the Nieuwe Leliestraat and arrive at the Egelantiersgracht. We walk further and pass the Egelantierstraat.

At the height of the Tuinstraat is a footbridge (1921) with torsion balustrades and asphalted wooden walking surface. Left, on the side of the Westerkade, we can see the back of a block of workers' houses (B. de Greef/1878). The nine houses with stair wells have a dormer window and a spout-gable.

♟ We continue straight on, past the Anjeliersstraat and turn right on the Westerstraat.

This street was made when in 1861

the canal the Anjeliersgracht was filled in. After filling in the canal, many historic houses were replaced by new houses. Again in the 1980's many new houses were built.

266 « Neck-Dutch-gable (± 1750) with decorated scroll stones.

♟ We turn right on the Tweede Anjeliersdwarsstraat.

1 « Low Dutch gable (± 1650).

♟ We walk straight into the Tweede Tuindwarsstraat.

12 » Neck-gable (about 1680) with two sculpted oval windows.

In front of us we can see the Westerkerk again.

♟ We walk until the Tweede Egelantierdwarsstraat.

In this narrow street there are a few small shops, restaurants and cafés.

6 » Neck-gable (± 1680) with a galloping unicorn in the half-round pediment.

22 » Dutch gable (1727) 'D. Bykurf'.

♟ We walk on to the Hilletjesbrug (plate bridge/1921).

From here we have a beautiful view of the Egelantiersgracht.

♟ We continue and enter the Eerste Leliedwarsstraat.

15 « stepped-gable (1644) with sandstone blocks and a gable stone 'De Moerjan' (De Moriaan = black moor).

16 » Theo Thyssen Museum.

♟ We turn left on the Bloemgracht.

Across the water on the other side of the Prinsengracht 263 is the Anne Frank House.

To the right there is a good view of the Westerkerk.

♟ We turn left on the Prinsengracht and walk until the Pansemertbrug.

☛ ^ Egelantiersgracht 12

Pieter Hoppe started his jenever (Dutch gin) distillery here in 1780. When it is nice weather there is a terrace along the canal.

Egelantiersgracht 12

🚶 **We continue on the Prinsengracht. At the level of nr. 48 we turn right and cross the bridge (Prinsensluis). We walk straight into the Prinsenstraat.**
12 « Neck-gable (1775). It is interesting that this is the only still existing neck-gable in Louis XVI style in Amsterdam. On the top there is a pediment entablature with a beehive with festoons around it. The scroll stones are decorated with rosettes.

🚶 **We have arrived at the Keizersgracht. We cross the plate bridge (1891) and walk straight into the Herenstraat.**
This street also has houses with neck- and Dutch gables. Special are:
40/corner Keizersgracht 95 « Dutch gable (1686) crowned with a half-round pediment. The scroll stones and oval windows are decorated with flower motifs.
36 « Eclecticism-gable (± 1850).
13 » Wide Dutch gable (± 1680) with gable stone with tobacco rolls.

🚶 **We cross the Herengracht and walk straight into the Blauwburgwal.**

☞ 22 « Dutch gable (1669)
This is the only remaining elevated Dutch gable in Amsterdam. The gable has an extra step with scroll stones. There are decorative vases on the scroll stones. It has oval windows and a lean-to building on the side of the Herengracht.

3 » High neck-gable (1648) in Holland's classicism, crowned with a pediment entablature.
5 » Spout-gable (1648) with gable stone 'D' vliegende vo'.

🚶 **We cross the Singel (Lijnbaansbrug).**
On the bridge we see « the dome of the Ronde Lutherse Kerk.

🚶 **We walk straight on the Lijnbaanssteeg.**
10 « Cornice-gable (± 1650) with a stoop on the Oude Nieuwstraat and a long lean-to building.

🚶 **We leave the Lijnbaanssteeg and come to the Spuistraat.**
53 » Stepped gable (1633) in the style of the sober Amsterdam's renaissance. It has a gable stone with the inscription 'In 't vlygende kalf'.

🚶 **We cross the Spuistraat and straight into the Korte Lijnbaanssteeg. At the end we cross the Nieuwezijds Voorburgwal and turn right.**
65 ^ Has an elevated neck-gable (± 1700) with decorated scroll stones and a half-round pediment with shell motif. Around the hoisting hook there is a festoon. Stoop is placed sideways.
69 « Print shop/offices 't Kasteel van Aemstel (A.J. Joling/1905). This is a combination of sober neo-renaissance and the style of H.P. Berlage. The gable is asymmetric and has a closed in balcony above the bay window.

☞ 75 « 't Makelaers Comptoir (1633)
Stepped-gable in the style of the Holland's renaissance. In this house the guild for brokers was situated. The chartered agents were the middlemen the sale of moveable and immoveable goods. The asymmetric building is built of red brick and is decorated with white bands and decorations. The richly decorated stepped-gable, with scroll stones, brick-on-edge coping and decorative vases is crowned

with a pediment entablature. Entrance is gained via the stoop and Ionic gateway that is crowned with a half-round pediment. Above the pediment is a decorative shield with the date 1633.
97/99 « Cornice-gable (1675). The two stoops are interrupted by a lean-to building.

🚶 **We turn left on the Sint Nicolaasstraat.**

51 (t/m 75) » Dutch gable (1626) with the original sculpted gable stone 'De Barck'.
49 » Dutch gable (± 1630).
88-90 « Neck-gable (± 1700)

with gable stone ''t Sernaemse koffievat'.
22 « Narrow neck-gable (± 1650) with a pediment entablature.
16 « Stepped-gable (± 1630) in Holland's renaissance style with two hoisting hooks and a broad wooden lower façade.
14/12 « Spout-gable (1932) in the style of the Amsterdam's School.

🚶 **We continue walking until we reach the Nieuwendijk. We turn right and follow the Nieuwendijk until we get back to the Dam again.**

Blauwburgwal 22

The Haarlemmer neighbourhood

T his walk starts on the Nieuwendijk, one of the oldest and busiest shopping streets of Amsterdam. Via the Nieuwendijk we walk to the Haarlemmerstraat and the Haarlemmerdijk; a bustling and lively area with many small shops. After the Haarlemmerdijk we visit the Westelijke Eilanden, a trio of artificial islands that were built in the 17th century and form a world unto themselves. Via the lovely Brouwersgracht and the Kattengat we walk back to the Dam.

Haarlemmerstraat

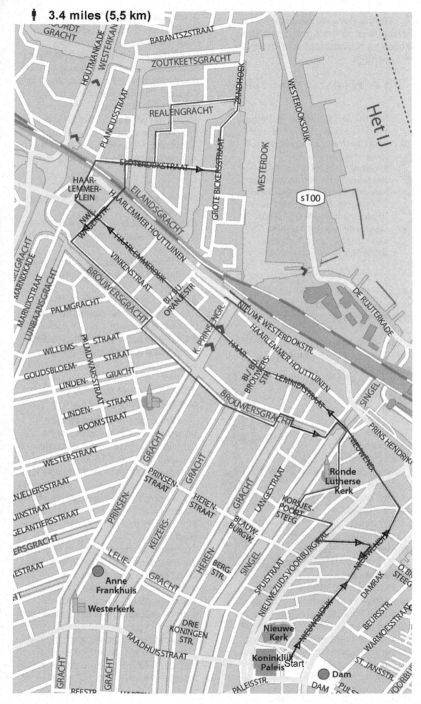

⚡ On the Dam we face the Royal Palace, turn to the right, cross the Mozes en Aaronstraat and enter the Nieuwendijk.

┌ The Nieuwendijk ┐

The Nieuwendijk belongs to the oldest part of Amsterdam and is built in 1170 as a dike along the western shore of the Amstel.
Recent diggings show that fishermen and farmers and craftsmen settled here around 1250. The Nieuwendijk is the oldest shopping street in Amsterdam, with a variety of shops. Besides the many shops there are also many 16th and 17th century gables that are worthwhile.

183 » Pastry bakery Van der Linde (since 1937) you can get home-made (cream) ice-cream the whole year-round.
Opposite the Nieuwe Nieuwstraat:
161 » Elevated neck-gable (1649) with pilasters and decorated scroll stones. The top cornice has a tablature. The house has a decorated hoisting crane, a hoisting trapdoor, an attic window, and two decorated oval windows.
113 » Elevated stepped-gable (1635) in sober Amsterdam's renaissance style. Above the hoisting crane there is a pilaster to the top. Under the hoisting crane there are two hoisting trapdoors. At the lower hoisting trapdoor there are two windows. Above the middle window on the first floor there is a gable stone with a galloping horse and rider.
93-91 » Dwelling/shop building (1886)

in eclecticism style.
89 » Dwelling/shop building (G.A. van Arkel/1887) built in a combination of neo-gothic and Italian neo-renaissance. The classic cornice-gable was built for photography studio Greiner. The decorations pertain to the art of photography.
Above the window on the first floor is the city coat of arms of Amsterdam.
Above the window on the second floor is a pediment entablature with a shell design
74 « Dutch gable (± 1730) with inward curving scroll stones and a crest in the top.
65 » Neck-gable (± 1775) with decorated scroll stones and a crest on the rounded top.
63 » Dutch gable (± 1775) with cluster design and on the top a half-round pediment.
61 » Neck-gable (± 1725) with decorated scroll stones. Above the hoisting crane is a figure of a black horse.
68 « Dutch gable (± 1740) with decorated scroll stones. In the half-round pediment there is a bird of prey on a fortress.
53 » Dutch gable (± 1625) with decorated scroll stones and a crest.

⚡ We cross the Nieuwezijds Voorburgwal/Martelaarsgracht.
On this spot there was a city gate between 1350 and 1506. The Martelaarsgracht dates from 1350 and was originally a water outlet through which the water from the Nieuwezijds Voorburgwal flowed out into the IJ. In the 19th century this water outlet was filled-in.
The name Martelaarsgracht refers to the house 'de Martelaar' (martyr) that stood here in the 16th century.
corner » 26 Neck-gable D' Stam Jesse (± 1750) with a half-round cornice moulding and decorated scroll stones.
50 « (corner Martelaarsgracht) The 'House with nine Golden Diamonds' (1723) has three vases in the top and the family coat of arms 'nine diamonds'.

⊹ We follow the Nieuwendijk.
30/corner Engelsesteeg «
Stepped-gable Het Duyffgen (1630) in
sober Amsterdam's renaissance. Note
the sandstone decorating blocks and
the sculpted dove above the middle
window on the first floor. The stoop is
on the Engelsesteeg.
24 « A stepped-gable in Holland's renaissance (1611) with lion masks and
a sculptured bull's head in the cornice
above the under façade.
18 « High Dutch gable (± 1650).
8 « Neck-gable (± 1700) with a
decorated hoisting crane and scroll
stones, two corner vases and two
gable stones.
5 » Simple spout-gable (1656).

**⊹ Now we reach the end and
cross the Prins Hendrikkade and
walk straight on to the Haarlemmersluis.**
The sluice regulates the water level
between the inside waters of the city
and the IJ. The first sluice (locks) was
built in 1601 and was replaced by the
present one in 1681.
On the spot of the sluice a city gate
stood between 1400 and 1600 (also
called the first Haarlemmerpoort).
Behind the Haarlemmersluis to the left
is the Ronde Lutherse Kerk.
If we turn to the right, we can see the
Central Station behind us.

**⊹ We walk on and pass the Sin-
gel and then walk into the Haarlemmerstraat (shipping area).**
The Haarlemmerstraat used to be the
route between Amsterdam and Haarlem. The street runs from the Singel
and halfway across the Haarlemmerdijk, that runs into the Haarlemmer-
plein/Brouwersgracht.
In earlier centuries the Haarlemmer
neighbourhood was a western suburb
of Amsterdam. There were many
craftsmen established on this street.
We still find many small craftsmen's
businesses here.
1 « Dwelling/shop (1630). The Dutch
gable was built on in 1685 and has
decorative vases on either side

capped with a half-round pediment.
The building has a stoop on the side
of the Singel and a lovely lean-to
building. The house is built on three
basement layers and one of them is
connected via a tunnel under the road
to the Singel.
59 « Neck-gable (± 1740) with a stork
in the gable stone.
At the level of Haarlemmerstraat nr.
65 (Wieringenstraat) we can see the
Herengracht to the left.

☞ 75 « West-Indisch Huis
-The West-India House-
The West-Indisch Huis stand on the
spot where the Haarlemmerpoort
stood that was demolished in 1617.
Until 1623 it was used as a meat-hall
and barrack of the Amsterdam's militia
and since 1623 as the seat of the
Gentlemen of Nine of the West-
Indische Compagnie (WIC). In the
company hall the Gentlemen decided
to build on the island of Manhattan
(now New York) the fort Nieuw Amsterdam. Also the pirate treasures of
Piet Heijn (the silver float) were stored
in this house.
After the WIC left the building served
as a hotel, an orphanage, and a business building. In 1825 it became the
property of the Reformed Evangelical
Lutheran Congregation.
The house is built in the style of the
Holland's classicism. The front façade
on the side on the Haarlemmerstraat
dates from 1825 and consists of a
plastered façade with seven windows.
The gable is capped with a triangular
pediment, in which the symbol of the
Lutheran church, a swan with spread
wings, is depicted.
79 « Former stepped-gable (± 1615),
now a Dutch gable in the sober style
of Amsterdam's renaissance. The lion
masks are remarkable.
83 « A lovely art nouveau dwelling/
shop (1906) with Jugend-stil façade
made with yellow brick and stone. On
the second story the bay window is
supported by an arch in the shape
of a horseshoe. The arch reaches to

the top of the store façade. The bay window is jutted out and has stone arched shapes.

105 « Neck-gable (± 1770), with a scale-motif on the centre window. Around the hoisting crane there are decorations that run out into the half-round pediment. There is a vase in the top and on both sides decorated scroll stones.

110 » Neck-gable (1675) with figures of horses in the scroll stones and decorated oval windows and a hoisting crane.

☞ 124-126 » Roman Catholic Posthoornkerk - P.H.J. Cuypers/1860

This neo-gothic church has two high spires which can be well seen from other parts of the city.

The flying buttresses, the pointed arch windows and the imposing neo-gothic entranceway are lovely. The church is presently used for other purposes (exhibitions).

🕯 **We pass the bridge (Eenhoorn-sluis) of the Korte Prinsengracht.** The sluice dates from the 17th century and served as a sailing route for the flat-bottomed boats that brought goods from the IJ to the city. On the bridge we have (left) a beautiful view across the Prinsengracht with the Westertoren in the background.

🕯 **The Haarlemmerstraat now runs into the Haarlemmerdijk.**

2 » Neck-gable (1729) in Louis XIV-style. With in the top a representation of the vineyard 'De Wynberg'.

20 » Neck-gable (± 1750) in Louis XV-style. With a picture of 'In de swarte koe' (black cow) in the top.

☞ 39 House in Jugendstil - F.M.J. Caron/1896

This is one of the few real Jugendstil houses in Amsterdam. The commissioner, firm Roeraarde, established a store with fish and fruits here in 1896. The fish trade was expressed by the

wall anchors that were designed as writhing eels. The figure of a fisher was applied later. The tile tableaus above the store façade show figures of an octopus with two fish and a seal with different fish. In the hardstone lower façade there are two curved lines with the name of the firm between two dragons. Above the first floor that is plastered and decorated with flowers and lines is a red band painted on with the words 'visch & fruithandel' and fish motifs. The second floor is decorated with lines and flowers. The top floor has a trapdoor with a stone windlass box to the left. The roof balustrade has two narrow arches. The flag mast is designed especially for this building and is to the utter left of the gable. The building is asymmetric and has a tower that is topped off by a pavilion roof.

43 « Dwelling/shop (F.M.J. Caron/1900) also in Jugendstil.
45 « Neck-gable (± 1720) in Louis XIV-style. With sculpted scroll stones, decorative vases, and a three-master in the pediment.
49 « Stepped-gable (± 1650) in Amsterdamse renaissance.
119-121 « Low Dutch gables (± 1775) in Louis XV-style. With crest and decorated scroll stones.
124 » Stepped-gable (± 1630) with a ball on the top step.
147 « Neck-gable (1729) in Louis XIV-style. With decorated scroll stones and a sun and date in the half-round pediment.
161 « Cinema The Movies. It is the oldest local cinema still in use. The Movies has a grand art-deco interior and shows mostly quality films.

We walk out Haarlemmerdijk and come to the Haarlemmerplein. The square was made at the time of the city expansion of 1610. Goods from outside of the city were packed over into small carts and transported to other parts of the city. From 1615 to 1837 the fourth Haarlemmerpoort stood here, designed by Hendrick de Keyser. The gate was replaced by the present

Haarlemmerpoort - B. de Greef/1840

The gateway is a continuation of the Haarlemmerdijk and is called Haarlemmerpoort in the vernacular.
The gateway is an architectural mixture of Greek and Roman (temple) building styles and rests on eight sandstone Corinthian pillars. On both sides are gatehouse buildings with half-round additions. In the gate there is an inscription that refers to the official name: Willemspoort. The poort is namely opened one day before the investiture of King William II.
The gate was originally built for the charging of city excise taxes and later served as a police station and fire station. From 1866 the gate was

regularly threatened to be torn down. Since 1984 it serves as a home.

At the Haarlemmerpoort we turn right. We walk <u>under</u> the railroad bridge. At the <u>first</u> street we turn right on the Sloterdijkstraat straat. We cross the Sloterdijkbrug and are now on the Prinseneiland. This is the smallest of the three islands. In the 18th century there were mostly warehouses here.

Westelijke Eilanden

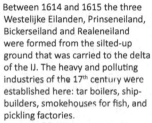

Between 1614 and 1615 the three Westelijke Eilanden, Prinseneiland, Bickerseiland and Realeneiland were formed from the silted-up ground that was carried to the delta of the IJ. The heavy and polluting industries of the 17th century were established here: tar boilers, shipbuilders, smokehouses for fish, and pickling factories.
Around 1800 there were 125 warehouses on the islands. Houses were also built for the workers. The Westelijke Eilanden developed into an important living- and working area. Until long after the II World War this is an industrial area. After the crisis in the shipbuilding in the 1970's many warehouses and factories were demolished. Through the efforts of the inhabitants, a part of the original atmosphere has been saved. There is no question of stench and pollution anymore; the Westelijke Eilanden are presently an oasis of rest.

79-85 « Quadruple warehouse Vrede (1720).
77 « Roode Pakhuis (Red warehouse) (1680).

We walk straight on to the Galgenstraat.
Before 1795 there was a view of the Volewijk (on the other side of the IJ) where the bodies of the condemned were displayed on the gallows.
8 « Low Dutch gable (1680).

⚑ **We pass the Galgenbrug and walk to the Bickerseiland.**

Bickerseiland

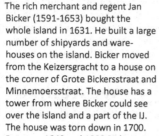

The rich merchant and regent Jan Bicker (1591-1653) bought the whole island in 1631. He built a large number of shipyards and warehouses on the island. Bicker moved from the Keizersgracht to a house on the corner of Grote Bickersstraat and Minnemoersstraat. The house has a tower from where Bicker could see over the island and a part of the IJ. The house was torn down in 1700.

Between 1640 and 1890 Bickerseiland was one of the largest centres for shipbuilding in Amsterdam. In the 1960's a number of large office complexes are built. To accommodate this construction a number of historic buildings are demolished. To prohibit the demolition of the historic warehouses the inhabitants formed an action group, that finally stopped the demolition. The neighbourhood was reorganised into a predominantly residential area. Presently Bickerseiland is a loved spot to live and work.

⚑ **We turn left on the second side-street which is Grote Bickersstraat. We cross the Drieharingenbrug and walk on the Realeneiland.** The narrow bridge connects Prinseneiland with Realeneiland and was a wooden boat-bridge in early days. The name of the bridge derives from the gable stone of the house with the three chimneys that stands on Vierwindenstraat. The name Realeneiland comes from Reynier Reael (1588-1648), an influential alderman and merchant, owner of lots of land and houses on the island.

⚑ **We walk straight on to the Zandhoek.** In the 17th century a sand market was held here along the quay. The sand was used as ballast for the sailing ships. The lovely merchants' houses and the (sailing) yachts in the marina give a good impression of how Am-

sterdam looked in the 17th century.
3 « Dutch gable (± 1680) with gable stone with the Dutch lion and the text 'De Eendragt'.
4 « Dutch gable (± 1775) in Louis XV-style. With three gable stones of St. Peter, Noah's Ark, and St. John.
6 « Stepped-gable (1657) 'H, Wapen van Essendelft' in sober Amsterdam's renaissance with a picture of the limping horse from the coat of arms from the village of Assendelft.
7 « Dutch gable 'De hooge boom' (1657) in Louis XV-style. Depicting a tall tree, named after the first owner, Captain Cornelis Hoogeboom.
10 « Spout-gable (1650), the birthplace of Amsterdam's famous photographer Jacob Olie (1843-1905). Olie was one of the first photographers to take pictures of the society of Amsterdam at the end of the 19th century. The spout gable is brought back to the form of the 17th century in the 19th century.
11 « Spout-gable (± 1650) with gable stone 'Int anker'.
12 « Stepped-gable (± 1650) in sober Amsterdam's renaissance. With a gable stone depicting a barge with the inscription 'Noyt gedogt'.
14 « Stepped-gable (1680) in sober Amsterdam's renaissance. For several centuries this building was decorated with a spout-gable.
In 1990 this was restored into a 17th centrury step-gable. In the gable there is a gable stone depicting a coin with the legend 'in den Gouden Reael'.

⚑ **We turn around and walk back to the beginning of the Zandhoek. In front of the bridge we turn right on Realengracht.**
22-36 » Double warehouse De Lepelaar (1650).
104 » Double warehouse (1670) with trapezium-gable.
108-178 » quadruple warehouse De Real (1660). At the end is a house on the Vierwindenstraat 1-3 (1781) that is five windows broad. In the pediment above the front door there is a portrayal of three herrings that refers to

the earlier house, 'De dry gekroonde haringen', that stood here until 1779.

🚶 **We turn left and cross the Drieharingenbrug and turn left again to the Prinseneiland.**
49-51 » Warehouse Insulinde (1629).
39 » Warehouse (1725).

🚶 **We cross the bridge and turn left on the Nieuwe Teertuinen. We pass under the railroad bridge (Tussen de Bogen) and cross the Haarlemmer Houttuinen. We walk straight into the Kleine Houtstraat, cross the Haarlemmerdijk and walk straight into the Nieuwe Wagenstraat. We continue straight on and now come to the Brouwersgracht.**
On this canal, built between 1614 and 1620, there were predominantly beer brewers, tanneries, tar boilers, and whale-oil processing businesses. The canal lies northwest of the city and therefore it was the connecting canal between the IJ, the river Spaarne and the central harbour. There are many warehouses along the canal to show that Amsterdam was a staple market in the 17th century. The goods that were shipped to Amsterdam were stored in the warehouses and from there distributed to other parts of the city.

🚶 **We turn left on the Brouwersgracht.**
On both sides there are warehouses with spout-gables.
288 « Warehouse (± 1670) with trapezium-gable.
286 « Warehouse (± 1670) with spout-gable.
274-270 « Three warehouses (± 1725) with spout-gables and two statues in the top.
268 « Warehouse (± 1680) Grote Swaen with stepped-gable.
266 « Warehouse (± 1680) Kleine Swaen with spout-gable.
256-252 « Warehouse and double warehouse with spout-gables (1684).

250-248 « Twin warehouse (± 1685) with spout-gables.
244 « Warehouse (± 1685) with spout-gable.
240-236 « Warehouses (± 1685) with spout-gables.

☛ 218 Vingboons neck-gable 'Het Geloof' (1650)
Miniature Vingboons neck-gable is in Holland's classicism.
Along with nr. 220 (left, renovated in the 18th century into a Dutch gable) and nr. 222 (demolished) the building formed neck-gable triplets 'Het Geloof, De Hoop en De Liefde' (faith, hope and love).
The Doric pilasters run up to the neck. There are decorated scroll stones on both sides. The cornice has a tablature. Notice the three decorated oval windows in the front façade and an oval window in the side façade. There is a stoop on both the front- and side façades. There is also an lean-to building on the side.

🚶 **We turn right crossing the Oranjebrug and then left again on the Brouwersgracht.**
At the height of Brouwersgracht 131 we look towards the other side:

☛ 204-212 « Warehouses (1640)
On both sides of the narrow warehouse with spout-gable are two broad warehouses with trapezium-gables. They have the inscriptions 'Het Grote Hert', 'Het Goede Hert', 'Het Kleine Hert', and the 'Grote Groene Hert'.

Oranjebrug

On the roof there is a green deer (=hert). On the narrow warehouse is a green deer on the spout-gable with the inscription 'Het vijfde groene hert'. Formerly there was a beer brewery in this warehouse.

⚑ We walk further.
At the height of the Goudsbloemstraat there are more interesting warehouses on the other side on the Brouwersgracht.

☞ 184-194 « Warehouses with spout-gables (± 1700)

This warehouse group is an example of the Amsterdam's warehouse architecture that we see on this canal, but also regularly come across elsewhere in the city. On the shutters 'Grauwe Valk', 'De David', and 'Koning David' are printed.

⚑ We continue on to the Lindengracht.
This canal was filled-in at the end of the 19th century.
On Saturdays goods market is held here.
174-178 « Double warehouse 't Slaghuis (± 1625) with a trapezium-gable. The coat of arms of Amsterdam is in the top with the emperor's crown.

⚑ We continue walking until the Prinsengracht.

☞ Lekkeresluis
From this arched bridge (1754) we see one of the most beautiful parts of Amsterdam.

⚑ We walk further and follow the Brouwersgracht.
101 »Dutch gable (± 1630) with wooden lower façade and gable stone.
99 » Neck-gable (1711) in Louis XIV-style. With the figure of a wolf in the half-round pediment.
79-83 » Double Dutch gable (± 1700) in Louis XV-style, with a crest.
75-77 » Warehouse (1631) with trapezium-gable and gable stone with crown.
118 « Warehouse (1635) with trape-

zium-gable and gable stone with the emperor's crown.

⚑ We cross the Keizersgracht on the Pastoorsbrug and walk straight on.
86 « Neck-gable (± 1680) with richly decorated scroll stones and corner-vases.
45 » Dutch gable (1616) with two former rounded arch windows and a high wooden lower façade and tall window.
corner Herenmarkt « Stepped-gable (1620) with in the top and neck small decorated scroll stones.
39 » Dutch gable (1630) with rounded arch windows.

⚑ At the Herengracht we turn left. We cross the bridge and turn right on the Brouwersgracht again.
corner Herenmarkt 27-25 « Dutch gable (± 1680) with wooden lower façade and basement. The stoop and entrance are on the Herenmarkt.

☞ 56 « Store corner house (1744)
with a Dutch gable in Louis XIV style. Take note of the indented starting blocks, the half-round pediment with the date 1744 and the decorative vase on the top. The upstairs houses can be reached via the side façade. The stairwell has decorated windows that still date from the time of building. The lean-to building runs along the entire side façade.

⚑ We turn right and cross over on the Melkmeisjesbrug and turn left again on the Brouwersgracht.
Now we have a good view of Brouwersgracht 56.
On the other side:
54 « Dutch gable (1750) in Louis XV-style. With crest and wooden lower façade.
52 « Dutch gable (1740) with a gable stone with a rococo frame with an old-Holland's chair and a Louis chair and the legend 'Nooyt Volmaakt'. The gable stone with the date 1759 was added later.

50 « Dutch gable (1775) in Louis XV-style with three crests.
48 « Neck-gable (± 1675) with dolphins in the scroll stones. Decorations are around the hoisting crane and in the pediment.
46 « Decorated Dutch gable (1720) with crest. There is a wooden staircase with a lean-to building behind it on the side façade.
44 « Dutch gable (1680) with half-round pediment and two sculpted oval windows. Fruit motifs run around the gable.
40 « Neck-gable (1700) in Louis XIV-style. With richly decorated scroll stones, a half-round pediment and a large crest.
20 « Low Dutch gable (1620).
9-7 » Two warehouses (1650) with spout-gables.

🚶 **At the end of the Brouwersgracht we turn left on the Singel. We walk on and then we turn right across the Haarlemmersluis. We turn right on the Stromarkt.**
Until about 1630 there was a trade in straw and the tanners conditioned their leather in barrels.

🚶 **We turn left and follow the Stromarkt.**
5 « Neck-gable (1687) with small decorated scroll stones a half-round pediment and a festoon around the hoisting crane. Two sculptured oval windows, date streamer and a wooden lower façade.

◄ 9 « 't Wape van Venetiën (1645)

This house, in Louis XIV-style, is restored, but still has the characteristics of the original gable. The wooden cornice moulding and the decorated crest are striking. The gable has a few traits that pertain to the spice trader Hendrick Beerenburg, who developed and distilled the famous herbal bitters in this building. The lion in the top denotes St. Mark, the patron saint of Venice.
The letters HB refer to Hendrick

Beerenburg. In the top of the gable there is a bear in a fortress (beer= bear, burg=fortress). In the Netherlands 'Beerenburg' is still a much sold herbal bitter.
15 « Dutch gable (± 1670) with half-round pediment, two festoons, stones with the date, and a high lower façade.

🚶 **We turn left into Gouwenaarssteeg.**
23-25 » Stepped-gable (± 1620) in sober Amsterdam's renaissance, with pilasters between the attic trapdoor and the top. Furthermore, a gable stone and a high wooden lower façade.

🚶 **We go back and continue on the Stromarkt.**
37 « Neck-gable (1752) with decorated scroll stones.In the decorated cornice around the neck are the date and three crests. Above the door is the image of a salmon.
4d » Stepped-gable (± 1620) in sober Amsterdam's renaissance style, has a ball on the top
6 » Corner house (± 1620).

🚶 **We walk straight on and arrive at the Kattengat.**

Kattengat 4-6

Kattengat

Until 1850 there was a canal here. The saying was that the canal hole was so narrow that no cat (kat=cat, gat=hole) could walk through. In the previous century, a few historical buildings (stepped-gables and warehouses) used to be at the place where the Renaissance hotel (left side) is now. Luckily the two stepped-gables (de Gouden en Silveren Spiegel/ 1614) in Holland's renaissance on nr. 4-6 (right) are saved. The houses are built for the soap maker, Laurens Jansz. Spiegel. The soap-boiling factory of Spiegel was situated in the warehouse on Koggestraat 5 (see later).
The façades are built of red brick, while the bands and arches are in yellow brick. On the top are decorative vases. The wooden lower façade is not original and was added during an extensive renovation in 1931.

To the right we see the parsonage and rear of the Ronde Lutherse Kerk.

⚲ **We cross the Kattengat and go right at the fork Teerketelsteeg/ Koggestraat. We walk in the Koggestraat.**
In this street there was a connecting canal until 1873 between the Kattengat and the Singel. The warehouses stood directly on the waterside until 1875. The canal is filled-in in 1875.
2 » Double warehouse Leeuw en Leeuwin (± 1725) with spout-gable.
4-6 » Double warehouse De Hinde en Het Hert (± 1750).
7 « Warehouse (± 1710) with rounded-arch windows. In the shields there are pictures of a rampant lion and a bear.
1 « Double warehouse (± 1720) with spout-gable.
3 « Warehouse (1718) with spout-gable.
8-10 » Warehouses (± 1740) with rounded-arch windows and spout-gables.
12 » Warehouse (± 1740) with spout-gable.
5 « Double warehouse (± 1630) with trapezium-top gable. This warehouse is where in the 17th century Laurens Jansz. Spiegel had his soap-making factory. (See Kattengat 4-6). In the gable stone there is the representation of a hand. This was the symbol of soap makers in the 17th century.

⚲ **We walk back and turn right on Teerketelsteeg.**
In the second half of the 16th century there was a tar-boiling factory here. The tar was boiled in kettles.
To the right we see a few warehouses that we saw earlier from the Koggestraat. The double warehouse with the crowned hand is the front of the soap maker's warehouse of Laurens Jansz. Spiegel. To the left is the side façade of the Roman Catholic Dominicuskerk.

⚲ **We walk on and turn left on Korte Korsjespoortsteeg.**
To the left between closely built buildings is the neo-gothic

☞ **Roman Catholic Dominicuskerk - P.J.H. Cuypers/1884**
Architect Cuypers was able to get hold of a small piece of building ground. That is the reason why the church has a broad nave and narrow side aisles. It is interesting to note that the church does not have a steeple because the city did not give permission for that. In 1996 the church is completely restored.

⚲ **We continue walking and cross Spuistraat. We walk straight into Korte Kolksteeg and come out at Nieuwezijds Voorburgwal. We turn right and cross the pedestrian crossing (at the level of Nieuwezijds Voorburgwal 50). We walk straight into the Nieuwezijds Kolk.**
Until the end of the 15th century the water from the Spui flowed into the Amstel at this point. After being filled-in a livestock and grain market was held here. The trade in grain had its zenith here in the 17th and 18th centuries.

11» Elevated neck-gable (± 1675) in Holland's classicism. With Corinthian and Ionic pilasters and three decorated oval windows. The festoons are decorated with snail shells and other shells. Under the high stoop is a basement.

► 28 « Korenmetershuis (1620)

At the location of the Korenmetershuis (house of one who officially measures grain) the grain guild was established. Between 1558 and 1620 a larger guild house stood here. The Korenmetershuis is built in the style of the sober Amsterdam's renaissance and is built of red brick. The front façade is on the Kolksteeg, because during the construction the Nieuwezijdskolk was not yet filled-in. It has a high sideways roof with many windows and high chimneys. At the entrance there is a double stoop and a relief with grain measurer's tools. At the top of the entrance is the city coat of arms with the Amsterdam's emperor's crown. The side gables have spout-gables.

🚶 **We walk straight into Kolksteeg.**

12 « Neck-gable (± 1725) with decorated scroll stones and vases. Mooy, one of the oldest cafés is established in this building in 1726. The gable stone, ''t Heydel Berchsvadt' (1726), is placed here in 1940.

3 » Stepped-gable (1690) with a high lower façade. This is also one of the oldest cafés in Amsterdam. De Wildeman opened its doors in 1690. In the bar many different kinds of beer are served.

🚶 **We walk further and turn right on the Nieuwendijk. We walk all the way out until we reach the Dam again.**

Brouwersgracht

Around the Kalverstraat

This walk offers much variety. We walk through the Kalverstraat, visit the courtyard of the Amsterdam Museum, and become acquainted with the entertainment area around the Rembrandtplein. We experience the atmosphere of a few of the canals of Amsterdam and walk through the famous floating flower market on the Singel.

Begijnhof

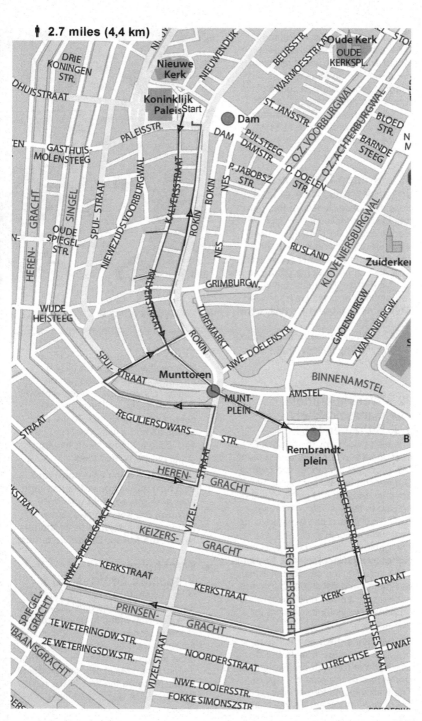

2.7 miles (4,4 km)

123

We face the Royal Palace, turn left, cross the Dam/Paleisstraat and enter the Kalverstraat. We are now in the busiest shopping street of Amsterdam. Because of the illuminated advertising the beautiful historic gables are less noticeable. Still it is worth your while to cast a glance upwards now and then.

58 » Roman Catholic St. Jozefskerk G. Moele/1848

Here the house De Papegaai (parrot) was remodelled in 1650 into a hidden church. In 1848 the house was demolished and the present neo-gothic three aisled church was built. The church has the official name Heilige Petrus en Paulus, but in the vernacular it is called De Papegaai. The church can be visited daily from 10AM-4PM.

80-82 » Dutch gables (± 1750) in Louis XV-style. The houses are coupled together by a communal extension.

92 » Weeshuispoort - Orphanage gateway - J.J. Bilhamer/1581

The inscription is by the famous Dutch poet Joost van den Vondel and reads: 'We grow fast in number and burden. Our second fathers complain. Aye, do not pass through this gateway without helping to carry a little'. The relief is a copy. The original can be seen in the Amsterdam Museum.

The gable above the gateway is made higher by architect Pieter de Keyser in 1642 including the city coat of arms, pediment, and a festoon. In the side gable there are two reliefs where the orphans are asking the visitors for a donation.

We pass through the Weeshuispoort and are now in the Doric portico. We turn left and walk past the pillars to the east courtyard.

The walkway and former boys' school are built in renaissance style. Note the

Weeshuipoort (158

pillar walkway. The brick basket arches with stone bases rest on Tuscan pillars. Between the windows there are Doric wall pilasters with carved console stones. To the right are stairs and a walkway (1762) with 120 lockers where the orphan boys could put away their tools.

We leave the east courtyard and turn left.We pass the passageway and <u>immediately</u> turn right through the second passageway. Now we are just outside of the terrain of the former Burgerweeshuis.

Weeshuispoortje - Vredeman de Vries/1571

(Sint Luciënsteeg 27). This gateway gave entrance to the girls' playground. The gateway with a rounded-arch is made of stone and has geometric figures in its grooved pilasters. In 1634 the gate is moved from the Stadtimmertuinen (city carpentry gardens) to this place. At the time of the move the date 1634 was added. In 1924

124

the wall was decorated with old gable stones.

✝ **We return through the passageway to the former Burgerweeshuis.**
There is an original water pump (1774) to the left.

✝ **We turn right and now we are on the orphanage square (former girls' place).**
To the right we pass the entrance to the Amsterdam Historical Museum.

✝ **We cross over the square and leave the courtyard via the door (crowned with an entablature with a relief).**
Outside showcase « with a collection of armour (1580) from the Amsterdamse Schutterij (city's militia).

✝ **We walk further, pass the black entry gate and turn left.**
We enter in the ^ *Schuttersgalerij* (entrance free). In the 17th century at this place there was a section of the Begijn canal. In the gallery there are sixteen paintings of the militia and the regents. From 1500-1650 the members often had themselves painted. At the beginning of the 17th century the paintings become more impressive. The three wooden statues (1650) are representing David, Goliath and his shield bearer.

✝ **We leave the Schuttersgalerij, turn right and leave the former Burgerweeshuis via the Doric portico. We turn right on the Kalverstraat.**

81-85 « Façade of the Nieuwezijdskapel (1903)

It is easy to see that this was once a chapel by the two towers at both ends of the building. This chapel stands on the place of the Heilige Stede Kapel (1345) (miracle of Amsterdam) and continues on to the Rokin. Because of the stores and the bustling in the street you hardly notice the chapel. When we walk past the building and turn <u>left</u> on the Enge Kapelsteeg, we

get a better view (left) of the rear of the chapel with its two towers and a bell tower in the middle.

✝ **We return to the Kalverstraat and turn left. We walk further and turn right on the Begijnsteeg. We walk to the gate (1574) that gives entrance to the Begijnhof.**
There is a figure of St. Ursula, the patron saint of the Beguines of Amsterdam. Even though the date 1574 is given, the gateway underwent a number of restorations and is not in the original state anymore (see also the text 'renov anno 1907').

✝ **We enter the Begijnhof.**

┌─ The Begijnhof ─┐

The Begijnhof is the only courtyard enclosure dating from the middle ages right in the centre of Amsterdam. The occupants, the Beguines, lived like nuns, but were not nuns. They had more freedom and were allowed to marry. The Begijnhof was not a convent, but an ascetic and philanthropic community of women. It is not clear when the Begijnhof was exactly founded. In a charter from 1389 the courtyard community was mentioned for the first time. The medieval Begijnhof was completely surrounded by water, and the only entrance was the gate at the Begijnsteeg. The houses from the middle ages have almost all disappeared. The courtyard is still at street level of the Middle Ages, almost one metre lower than the street level of Amsterdam now. The last Beguine, Sister Antonia, died on May 26, 1971, at the age of 84 years.

Openings hours:
The Begijnhof and the Begijnhofkapel are open daily from 9AM-5PM and are accessible via the gate on the Gedempte Begijnensloot.
The occupants appreciate it if visits do not take place in large groups and as few photos as possible are taken.

1 Dutch gable (± 1750) two windows wide.
2-3 Spout-gables (1590).
4 Dutch gable (± 1750) one window wide.
5 Dutch gable (± 1710).
6 Dutch gable (± 1750) with connecting piece.
7 Dutch gable (1775) with high pavement.
8 Stepped-gable (± 1475) in sober Amsterdam's renaissance.
9 Low Dutch gable (± 1750).
10 Spout-gable (± 1750).
11 Dutch gable (1673) gable stone with Sint Willibrord.
12 Spout-gable (± 1750).
14 Side façade with spout-gable; the entrance is on the terrain of the Amsterdam Museum (± 1750).
15, 16, 17 Three houses under one roof placed sideways.
18 House with a wooden frame from the middle ages.
19-20 Neck-gable twin (1721) in Louis XIV-style, with a wooden lower façade. On the gable stone (thought to come from the sculptor's workshop of Hendrick de Keyser) are the figures of Joseph, Mary, and Jesus.
21 Spout-gable (± 1750).
22 Neck-gable (1736) in Louis XIV-style.
23 Neck-gable (1660) in Holland's classicism with John the Baptist as an angel.
24 Spout-gable (1670) gable stone with Saint Ursula (1640).
25 Spout-gable (1670) with the Latin inscription 'Iniuria ulciscenda oblivione' (injustice must be revenged by being forgotten).
26 Dutch gable Huis Bethanie in Louis XV style, with stairs placed sideways (± 1750).
27 Dutch-gable (1775) in Louis XIV style, the gable stone is striking with a crown with Mary and Jesus and the inscription underneath 'S Maria'.
28 Spout-gable (1680).

☞ 29 Chapel of the Beguinage of St John the Evangelist and St Ursula - P. Vingboons/1671

In the 17th century the Roman Catholics were not allowed to openly practice their religion. The celebration of the Holy Communion was tolerated in so-called hidden churches. When the original chapel (the present English Church) fell into the hands of the English Presbyterians, the two houses opposite were turned into a hidden church and in 1671 was dedicated to St. John the Evangelist and St Ursula. The chapel has three aisles and the wider side aisles have lofts that rest on wooden Tuscan pillars. The front façade has pointed arched windows with stained-glass windows dating from the 19th century. The chapel is one of the few hidden churches that is still used as a church.

☞ English Church (± 1452)

Until 1607 the English Church was the chapel of the Begijnhof. In that year the Beguine community had to turn over their church to English Presbyterian refugees in Netherlands. The church is built of brick and in 1650 a side aisle was built on the south side. The church has a typical English interior with a brass pulpit lectern that was donated in 1689 by the King-stadtholder William III and Queen Mary Stuart. The pulpit made of oak from the end of the 17th century and the organ cabinet from 1753 in rococo style are eye-catching.
33 Neck-gable Huis Poelenburg (1744) in Louis XIV-style.

☞ 34 Wooden House (±1530)

This is the oldest wooden house in the Netherlands. Since a restoration in 1888 it is no longer authentic, it received side façades of brick.
35 Spout-gable with a wooden frame.
36 Dutch gable (± 1750).
37 Gate building (1917) with passage to the Spui.

Wooden House

38, 39, 40, 41, 43, 45 Dutch gables (± 1750).

42, 44, 46 Spout-gables (± 1750).

🚶 We leave the Begijnhof through the gateway where we came in and turn right on the Gedempte Begijnensloot. We turn left on the first street the Rozenboomsteeg. We walk through this alley and turn right on the Kalverstraat. We pass the Spui and have a view (left) across the Rokin.

152 » Corner Kalverstraat/ Spui, Waterstone English Bookstore - H.P. Berlage & Ph. Sanders/1886

This building is a good example of Berlage in his early period and is characterised by exuberant decorations inspired by the classics.

143 « Dutch gable (± 1750) in Louis XV style, with a half-round pediment with a calf on the top. The calf refers to earlier times when the calves market was held in the Kalverstraat until 1629.

179 « (corner Olieslagersteeg). Richly decorated Dutch gable (± 1720) in stone. The top gable is placed on a brick façade.

190 » Corner Kalverstraat/Heiligenweg, 't Moortje (1891) with a mixture of historic styles.

183 « Former department store Maison de Bonneterie (1889).
Until 1905 'Maison' was established at nr. 183 and sold almost only textiles. In 1907 the buildings on Kalverstraat 179-183 and Rokin 138-142 were combined and changed into a large department store in the style of Louis XVI. By the use of stone and wooden cornice mouldings the building has a classic aura.

200 » Shop building (G.A. van Arkel/ 1893) in a combination of neo-gothic, neo-renaissance, and Jugendstil. The original store-front is completely gone. The balcony on the second story is supported by two buttresses and has a wrought iron balustrade. Next to the balcony sunflowers, a rooster, and an owl denote Jugendstil. The stone scrolls are decorated with women's figures.

212-222 » Shoppingcentre de Kalvertoren (1997).

201 « Former department store Vroom & Dreesmann (1912).
Department store Vroom & Dreesmann (1912).
Because of various renovations in 1932, 1957, 1982, and 1995 the original gable is almost completely lost. The gable of the Rokin side shows many characteristics of the Amsterdam's School style.

🚶 We leave the Kalverstraat and come to the Muntplein.

This square is dominated by the Munttoren (1620). Originally the Regulierspoort (1480) stood on this spot. This gate was part of the old medieval city wall. It had two towers with a gatehouse in between. The gate lost its function after the city's expansion in 1585. In 1613 the wall to the right of the gate was demolished and on the left side a guardhouse was built in 1616. In 1618 the city gate was lost by fire. Hereafter only the western tower was rebuilt. The guardhouse was saved from the fire. The hall on the first floor served as a guild room for a long time. In 1674 it was renovated as an inn. The tower spire is designed in 1619 by Hendrick de Keyser. The eight-sided upper building with an open spire contains an hour piece with four clock faces and a carillon. There is a weathervane on top of the spire in the shape of a gilded ox as a reference to the calves' market in the Kalverstraat. In 1672 Amsterdam got the temporary right to mint money. In the guardhouse money was minted. Since that time the tower and the adjoining square was named Munt and Muntplein (mint and mint square). In 1887 the guard house was replaced by the present building in neo-renaissance style. At the time of the renovation in 1938/1939 the under walkway is made.
The Munt has one of the five carillons in Amsterdam. Originally the carillon consisted of 27 bells, now 38. Every quarter of an hour a mechanism sets the bells off. A carillonneur plays the carillon on special days.

⚲ We walk under the Munttoren and cross the Munt square on the left side. On the other side is the Hotel De L'Europe. We pass right through to the Reguliersbreestraat. This street was here since 1593 and was the thoroughfare from the Regulierspoort (see afterwards at Rembrandtplein) to the bridge across the Singel. Not much is left from the historical street. All the houses date from the late 18th century.
4 » Neck-gable (± 1775) with sculpted scroll stones.

☛ 26-28 » Theatre/cinema Tuschinski - L. de Jong/1921

This is an extraordinary building architecturally as well as decoratively. The façade has glazed tiles, ceramic sculptures, and wrought iron lamps and decorations. On the corners there are two green towers. The art deco interior with the ceiling paintings, lamps, and carpets gives the visitor the feeling to be in a special world. The large hall in art deco style is worth a visit.

31 « Cineac (J. Duiker/1934). In this former cinema short continuous news films were shown. The building in the style of the New Realism is made in glass and steel. The hall is placed diagonally so as to use the available room optimally. In 1994/1996 the building was restored.

Theatre/cinema Tuschinski

39 « Neck-gable with pediment, crest, and a woman's head. The pediment has the picture of a kettle and the name of the house: 'D'Melk Ketel'.
44-46 » Neck-gable twins (± 1775). The pediment shows galloping horses.

🚶 **We walk on and reach the Rembrandtplein.**
This square was first called the Botermarkt (butter market). In the 17th century the Regulierspoort was here, one of the city gates that gave entrance to Amsterdam. Because of the expansion of the city in 1662, the gatehouse got the function of weighing house in 1668. Among other things, butter was traded here. Around 1870 the butter market moved to the Amstelveld. The weighing house was demolished in 1874.

Impressive buildings on the Rembrandtplein:

1 « Former police station Rembrandtplein (1874). The half-round building has pilasters on the top story. A dormer window is built in the Halvemaansteeg.
3 « Dutch gable (± 1775) in rococo style with three crests. The building runs through in the Halvemaansteeg and has three round windows, one of which has been bricked-over. To the right is the Rembrandt public garden. In the middle of this garden there is a statue of Rembrandt van Rijn (L. Royer/1852).
15-23 « Grand café De Kroon (G.A. van Arkel/1898). The building has the typical characteristics of the Jugendstil. The peaked roof with a dome-like cornice with a dormer window behind is notable.
24 opposite » Café/hotel Schiller (M. Lippits & N. Scholte/1892), in historic building style, built with brick and stone with elements of Jugendstil.
20 opposite » Cornice-gable (± 1775) with a raised cornice with the image of a sailing ship. The corners each have an ornamental vase.

27-29 « Hotel Het Gouden Hoofd (1890) in a combination of neo-renaissance and modern styles. Note the diagonally placed bay window with tower and many decorations that give the building a graceful appearance.

🚶 **We walk on further and curve of with the pavement to the right.**
47 « Former building of the AMRO Bank (H.P. Berlage/1932). The tower with clock and the protruding walkway in the Utrechtsestraat are striking. The building was thoroughly renovated in 1969, many Berlage elements were lost.

🚶 **We walk straight on into the Utrechtsestraat.**
The street is named after the city of Utrecht and used to run to the Utrechtsepoort.
On the bridge of the Herengracht we look to the left at the Amstel and the Walter Suskindbrug (white drawbridge).
30 » Dwelling/shop (G.A. van Arkel/1894) in a mixture of neo-gothic and neo-renaissance. The gable is made of brick and lots of stone. The transom in the show window has leaded glass. On both sides of the store façade are richly decorated half-pillars, with a shield and many geometric motifs. On the window piers on the first floor there are gable stones with a portrait on a round frame. The top gable and the top floor are richly decorated.
45 en 51 « Two gables (1897) The lower façade of 51 is made of mahogany and the design resembles nr. 30.
48-corner Keizersgracht » Dwelling/shop (± 1890) in art nouveau style with bay window and tower.

🚶 **We pass the Keizersgracht.**
50 « Concerto; since the 1950's one of the most important record/CD shops in Netherlands.
91 « corner Utrechtsestraat-Kerkstraat dwelling/shop (A.L. van Gendt/1879) in neo-renaissance style.
94-96 » Stepped-gables (± 1650).

111 « Dutch gable (± 1680) with decorated gable, gable stone, two bricked-up oval windows, and a half-round pediment.

🚶 We leave the Utrechtsestraat and turn right on the Prinsengracht. We walk straight on to the Amstelveld.

To the right under the walkway (Spiegelhof) we see many more lovely (antique) shops.

🚶 At the end we turn right on the Herengracht and walk to the Vijzelstraat.
On the right hand is the building

Amstelkerk

At the time of the city expansion of 1660 the idea was that the Amstelveld would grow into a large church square. The Amstelkerk (D. Stalpaert/1670) is a wooden church building that is temporarily built on the Amstelveld. The plan was that a brick (strict Dutch reformed) church would replace it. Due to of lack of financial means the city council at that time changed their plans and the temporary church is still standing on the Amstelveld. From 1840-1842 the church was renovated in neo-gothic style with wooden arches. The addition (on the Reguliersgracht) and the caretaker's home date from 1673. During the restoration in 1988-1990 the interior is renovated as a multifunctional centre.

🚶 We walk on to the bridge of the Reguliersgracht.
On the bridge we have a nice view of the different arched bridges.

🚶 We walk on, cross the Vijzelstraat and continue on the Prinsengracht. We walk further and come to the Nieuwe Spiegelstraat.
To the left we can see the Rijksmuseum.

🚶 We turn right on the Nieuwe Spiegelstraat.
In the street which is known as the 'Spiegelkwartier', there are a great number of art and antique shops.
The houses (neck-, spout-, and Dutch gables) dating from the end of the 17th century.
54 « Dwelling/shop in the style of de Amsterdamse School (± 1920).

🚶 We walk further, pass the Kerkstraat and walk over the bridge of the Herengracht for the last part of the Nieuwe Spiegelstraat.

of the former Nederlandsche Handel-Maatschappij, De Bazel (see page 176).

🚶 We turn left on the Vijzelstraat.
In 1917 this street was made wider. A great number of buildings were demolished to make space for the new buildings.

🚶 We walk straight on and come to the Muntplein.
In front of the bridge we turn left on the Singel.

👉 Singel/flower market
Already since 1862 plants and flowers are sold on these floating barges. water. The market has a large choice of flowers, plants, and souvenirs.

🚶 At the end of the flower market we arrive at the Koningsplein.
1 « Shop (1890), was originally built in neo-renaissance, but in 1925 is renovated in art-deco style. The building is a peculiar mixture of styles.

2 » Shop (A. Jacot/1899) built of Oberkirchner sandstone. Note the large shop-windows that give a sense of spaciousness.
Due to a number of renovations, unfortunately the shop is no longer in the original state.

⚲ We turn right and cross the Heilige Wegsluisbrug. Then we turn left on the Singel
423-425 » Militiabuilding former tack or bus-barn (see page 163).
421 » Doelengebouw (see page 163).

⚲ We keep walking straight on and arrive at the Spui. We follow the curve to the right.
On this square there is a second-hand book market on Fridays and on Sundays there is an art market.

⚲ We walk on and cross the Kalverstraat, follow the Spui and arrive on Rokin. We turn left on Rokin. We walk straight on and have arrived back at the Dam.

Rembrandtplein

The Plantage

This walk takes us to the former 19th century city park area the Plantage. In the middle of the 19th century spacious city parks and Artis zoo were laid out, after French example.

At the end of the 19th century houses were built in the city parks. In spite of the housing, the Plantage still keeps its spacious atmosphere. Starting in the old city centre (the Oudezijds Achterburgwal) we walk via the former Jewish neighbourhood (Waterlooplein) to the Plantage.

Entrance Artis

♟ 3.3 miles (5,3 km)

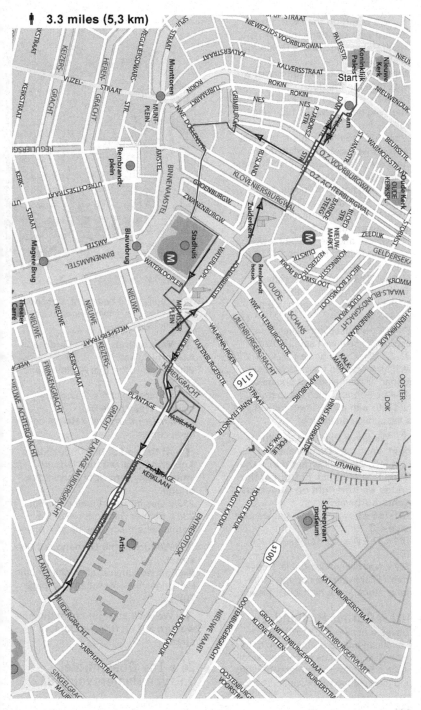

‖ We stand on the Dam; turn around with our back towards the Royal Palace and cross Rokin and the Dam.
Behind the National Monument we walk into the Pijlsteeg.
The alley is named after Dirc Pijlen, who lived here between 1383 and 1394.
Until 1578 there were many brothels here. As we pass the sliding doors, there are a few lovely historic houses on the left hand side.
31 « Public house of liqueur distillery Wijnand Fockink. This Dutch gable (1689) is the only remaining 17th century house in the Pijlsteeg.
The interior and the wooden lower façade date from the period 1775-1800 and are still completely original. The gable is decorated with fruit motifs. The date 1689 is on the gable stone. The top has a flat cornice.
33 « Warehouse/Dutch gin distillery (1720) with spout-gable.
35-37-39 « Dutch gable (1720) with high wooden lower façade and topped with a half-round pediment.
43-41 » Former Dutch gable twins (± 1750) with a high lower façade and a flat cornice on the top.

‖ We leave Pijlsteeg and turn right. We cross Damstraat and turn left. We walk straight into the Oude Doelenstraat. In front of the bridge we turn right on Oudezijds Achterburgwal.
151-155 « Lovely pilaster gables (see page 48).
159 « The Waalse Kerk (see page 48).
187 « Narrow cornice-gable 'Huysman' (1727) with top cornice, large gable stone and a high lower façade.

☞ **197 « Corner Rusland 2**
Elevated neck-gable (1673) has Corinthian pilasters running up to the neck. The gable has decorated scroll stones, festoons, streamer with date, and gable stone with cooper. The top

has a half-round pediment with shell motifs. There are two lean-to buildings on both sides.

‖ **We continue on the Oudezijds Achterburgwal.**
200 » Rear of the Sint Agnietenkapel (1470).
227 « Entrance of the Oudemanhuispoort (see page 64).
Corner Grimburgwal » House on the three canals.

‖ At the end of the Oudezijds Achterburgwal we turn left and immediately turn right across the bridge.
233 « Gasthuispoort (see page 63).
235 « Former waiting room of the hospital pharmacy (see page 70).

‖ **We turn in the Binnengasthuisstraat.**
9 « Former administration office of the Binnengasthuis (hospital) (see page 70).

‖ **We walk straight on, at the end we turn left on Nieuwe Doelenstraat.**

☞ **24 » The Doelenhotel - J.F. van Hamersveld/1882**

The tower Swych Utrecht (1482) stood here until 1882. The tower served as part of the defence works. After 1522 it had the function of practice room for the association of marksmen. This association was portrayed on the world famous painting 'The Night Watch' (1642) by Rembrandt van Rijn. The Night Watch hung in the large Doelen hall until 1715.

In 1822 use was made of the foundations and part of the wall work from the old Doelenzaal for the building of the Doelen Hotel. The Hotel is built in the style of the neo-renaissance. On the façade on the Kloveniersburgwal a gable stone (1883) is placed that refers to the tower Swych Utrecht. On the side of the Amstel the building has a three-sided cupola addition with a clock-face.

🏃 At the Kloveniersburgwal we turn right and cross the green (balance) bridge.

On the bridge we see the Waag (1488) on the left and on the right we see the Amstel.

🏃 We walk straight into Staalstraat.

◄ 7 « The former Saaihal - P. de Keyser/1641

The building is built in the style of the Amsterdam's renaissance and was the boardroom of the staalmeesters. The staalmeesters (staal=sample) inspected samples of the rolls of material that were stored elsewhere in the complex.

The famous painting by Rembrandt van Rijn 'De Staalmeesters' (1661) hung here for a long time until it was moved to the Rijksmuseum.

9 « Dutch gable (± 1775) with a side-gable protruding on a corbel.

🏃 We continue walking and cross the Groenburgwal.

To the left we see the Zuiderkerk that is often photographed from here.

🏃 We follow the Staalstraat, cross the bridge B. Bijvoetbrug and turn left on the Zwanenburgwal.

☞ 2 » The Stopera (1986)

This combination of city hall and music theatre is called Stopera by the people. The glass façade is eye-catching, it gives a panoramic view over the river the Amstel. In the building the city council, the city aldermen, the city civilservants, De Nederlandse Opera, and the National Ballet are established here.

This is also the domain of the second-hand market of the

☞ Waterlooplein (market)

(from Monday to Saturday).

The Waterloo square was formed after the filling-in of the Leprozengracht and Houtgracht.

Up to World War II the market was run by Jewish Amsterdammers who traded in second-hand goods. When the metro was built here in the 1970's, many houses were demolished and new housing was developed.

🏃 We walk straight on, turn right and walk past the Stopera

☞ « Mozes en Aäronkerk church Sint Anthonius van Padua - T.F Suys/1841

On the spot where this church now stands stood the houses Moyses & Aaron in the 17th century that functioned as a Franciscan hidden church. The two 17th century gable stones in the rear façade are a reminder.

The church is built in the style of neo-classicism. At the entrance there is a statue of St. Francis. The pediment entablature is supported by four Ionian pilasters. In the entablature bread and wine are portrayed with the figure of Christ above.

🏃 We walk straight on, turn right

☞ 213-219 The Stadsturfhuizen (1610)

In these buildings the 17th century

'social services' were established that cared for those at home who had no work. In the winter the council of wardens doled out peat for fuel to the poor.

211 « Former Oudezijds Huiszitten Aalmoezeniershuis - W. de Keijser/ 1654

The classicism building has a protruding middle section and a pediment tablature. The council of wardens held their meetings here. The peat was stored in the peat warehouses next door.
In the middle there is a classicism double warehouse with trapezium-gable and a balustrade. The warehouses on both sides have spout-gables.

We turn right and then go left into the Turfsteeg.
The Turfgracht canal was here until 17th century when it was filled-in.

We turn left on Nieuwe Amstelstraat.
To the left we see the rear of the warehouses of the former Oudezijds Huiszitten Aalmoezeniershuis.
Via the classicism gateway with Tuscan pilasters (topped with a pediment tablature that has the old city coat of arms of Amsterdam) one could enter the courtyard where the peat was doled out to the poor in the 17th century .

1 » Jewish Historical Museum

The museum is situated in a complex of four restored High-German synagogues:
● the Grote Synagoge (1671),
● Obbene Sjoel (1685),
● the Dritt Sjoel (1700)
● the Nieuwe Synagoge (1752).
In World War II the buildings were damaged and the interiors were stolen. During the restoration the complex was brought back to its original state as much as possible. The four buildings are connected by glass, steel and concrete.

We leave Nieuwe Amstelstraat and cross the Jonas Daniël Meyerplein.
Visible on the right side of the Jonas Daniel Meyerplein, is the statue of the Dokwerker (Dock worker).

Dock Worker - M. Andriessen/ 1952

The bronze statue is a memorial to the February Strike of February 25, 1941, that was held by mostly communist labourers, in protest of the arrests of 425 Jewish Amsterdammers by the German occupiers.

We walk straight on to the Mr. Visserplein.
On the other side is the Dutch Film and Television Academy (1999). The building is mostly of green glass.

The Portuguese Synagogue

3 » The Portuguese Synagogue - E. Bouman/ 1675

The synagogue is one of Amsterdam's most important monuments. It is the first large synagogue in West-Europe built by the Sephardic Jews. These Jews fled Spain and Portugal because they were persecuted by the Inquisition in the 16th century. In the beginning of the 17th century they got permission from the Amsterdam's city aldermen to build a synagogue.
The classicistic building is square and built of brick. The gable consists of stone cornice with balustrade and decorative vases. Above the rounded-arch windows square windows are placed.
The front façade (on the Muiderstraat > see later) has a stone portico in Doric style. The synagogue was surrounded by service buildings, where the entrance to the museum and one of the most important Jewish libraries (collection Ets Haim) in the world is housed.In comparison with the other synagogues, the interior is exceptional because it got through the II World War unscathed.

 We turn right on Muiderstraat.

From here we have an even better view of the imposing synagogue.

☞ » Doric entranceway of the synagogue (± 1850)

The mainframe rests on two Ionic pillars and is crowned with a pediment entablature with the portrayal of a pelican feeding its young. It is the symbol of the Portuguese Jewish Congregation.
During this walk we will come across this symbol several more times.

 We follow Muiderstraat.
8, 10 en 12 « Three neck-gables (± 1750) with decorated scroll stones and a half-rounded pediment.
Nr. 12 has two decorated windows on both sides of the attic window.

 We walk straight on, pass the Hortusbrug and enter Plantage Middenlaan. We have arrived in the Plantage.

☞ 2 » The Hortus Botanicus (1682)

This was the trainings institute for physicians in the 17th century. It is one of the oldest botanical gardens in the world. The Hortus is beautifully hidden

137

in the Plantage neighbourhood.
The rare and special plants that were brought back by the VOC from the tropics were taken into the collection here. Famous botanists, like Linnaeus did scientific research here. More than 8,000 different plants, among them many trees of more than a hundred years can be admired here on the grounds.
A speciality is the monumental Palm Hothouse (1912) with an extensive collection of rare cycad palms.
Also the three hundred year old Eastern Cape Breadtree (Encephalar tos altensteinii) can be admired in the Palm Hothouse. The Hortus has an area of 1,2 hectares.
The white plastered low building (1868) is the former lecture hall and is presently the Oranjerie of the Hortus. The building (1875) left of the entrance is built in chalet-style.
2A-K » Hugo de Vries Laboratory (J.M. van der Mey/ 1912) in the style of the Amsterdam's School.
On the other side lies the Wertheim Park (1812). This is the oldest park in Amsterdam. Later during this walk we will enter the park.

┌─── **The Plantage** ┐

The Plantage dates from 1682 when this area was divided into fifteen parks. The Plantage had a recreational function, especially for the well-to-do citizens. There was also a botanical garden set up (Hortus Botanicus). In the first half of the 19ᵗʰ century theatres and a zoo (Artis/1838) were also established here. At the end of the 19ᵗʰ century a start was made on building houses. We only find predominantly eclecticism-style of building in this neighbourhood. In comparison with other parts of the city, this part of the city still has a spacious atmosphere.

🚶 **We follow Plantage Middenlaan and pass Plantage Parklaan.**

138

Plantage Parklaan 9 » Here lived and worked from 1884-1916 Hugo de Vries (1848-1935), the discoverer of the mutation theory and Nobel prize winner.
🚶 **We continue on Plantage Middenlaan.**
4a » Desmet (A.L. van Gendt/ 1879, renovated in 1926).
Desmet was a theatre from 1867-1945 and remodelled into a cinema in 1946.
The art deco gable dates from 1926. Since 2001 radio and television studios are in this building. The former film hall is mainly kept in its original form. In the area of 150 m², there is a box-construction that makes the hall is now suitable for live pop-music registration for radio and television.
19 « Coach house (1880) with renaissance motifs. A garage is situated in the coach house.
27 « The former children's day care centre. Jewish and non-Jewish children were kept and cared for here until the beginning of World War II.
A German ordinance in 1941 decreed that only Jewish personnel was allowed to work at the day care centre. Since 1942 the building was an auxiliary to the Dutch Theatre. The parents waited in the theatre to be deported; and the children waited in the day care centre until they were thirteen years old. In January 1943 the matron Henriëtte Henriquez Pimentel, together with Walter Süskind and Joop Woortman, planned escape routes for the children to flee the day care centre. In September 1943, the day care centre was cleared out and its personnel was deported to Westerbork. Two child-care workers went undercover and survived the war.
22 »Café Eik en Linde.
Before World War II the café was part of the Dutch Theatre. The coffee room of the theatre was on the first floor.

☞ » **24 Hollandse Schouwburg - Dutch Theatre - (1891)**

Since 1961 the former theatre is a memorial to the remembrance of the Jewish Amsterdammers who were collected here to then be transported to one of the Nazi-concentration camps.

The neo-classical front gable is richly decorated and crowned with a pediment entablature. Around 1930 the theatre is thoroughly renovated. The gable remained original.

During World War II the German occupying force changed the name to Jewish Theatre and only Jewish actors could play for Jews only.

From 1942 the theatre was used as a place of deportation and more than 70,000 people were deported to one of the Nazi extermination camps.

As we enter the building, we come to a peaceful courtyard with two sober walkways.

On the remains of the walls of the former stage an obelisk is placed in the shape of a David's star. Behind it is the text: 'In remembrance of those who were carried off from this place 5700-5705 (1940-1945)'.

On the right hand at the exit of the theatre there is a showcase with an eternal flame burning with a name board behind it with all of the 6,700 family names of deported and murdered Jews engraved in it. These names are symbolic for all of the 107,000 Jewish victims from the Netherlands.

On the first and second floors there is an exposition about the persecution of the Jews during the II World War. The theatre is open daily, free of charge.

🕯 **When we leave the Theatre, we follow Plantage Middenlaan. We cross Plantage Kerklaan.**
36 » Asymmetric building (G. van Arkel/1892) in eclecticism-style with many neo-renaissance and a few art nouveau elements.
Note the neck-gable in the shape of stairs. Above the entrance a bay window is added. The date 1892 is next to the balcony.

41-41a « Main building of the zoo Artis 'Natures Artis Magistra' (J. van Maurik/1855).
45 « Rear-side of Artis library (G.B. Salm/1868).The eclectic building is built of yellow and red brick. The library has a large collection of scientific books on the natural sciences. Take note of the name plaques with names of scientists. You find them above the windows on the side of the street as well as on the side of the zoo. The works of the named scientists can be found in the library. The animal graffito's are by J. Groenestijn.
52 » Sint Jacobs-gesticht (W.J.J. Offenberg/1863), presently Retirement Centre St Jacob.
From 1688-1860 the Nieuwe Stadsherberg (the New City-inn) stood here. Three years later the Oudenliedenhuis Sint Jacob was built, which was replaced in 1986 by the present centre for the elderly.
The entrance gate is in eclecticism style with Saint Jacob in the top flanked by two elderly persons and reminds us of the former institution.
47 « Huize Weltevreden (± 1820) wooden house with a brick roof addition.
49 « Huize Welgelegen (± 1740), built of bricks. Unlike Huize Weltevreden, this house has a basement.
The wings of the dormer are decorated with Louis XIV ornaments.

🕯 **We walk further and look in Plantage Lepellaan:**
6 » Villa Coninck Westenberg (W. Springer/1874). A city villa built of brick and stone in eclecticism-style, with many ornaments, among others vases and statues.

🕯 **We continue on Plantage Middenlaan.**
60/62 » City villas (± 1875) in neoclassicism style.
At the height of Plantage Middenlaan nr. 62 we have a nice view through to the zoo.

☞ 53 « Artis Aquarium - G.B. Salm/1882

The eclecticism building, with lots of neo-classicism traits, is originally designed as combined housing for the aquarium, the museum and the lecture hall. The high stoop with a balustrade and steps on both sides is made of red sandstone. Six Doric pilasters carry the mainframe that is crowned with a pediment tablature. On both sides there is a corner pavilion with Corinthian pilasters and pediment tablature. The dome (on the Muidergracht) was a lecture hall until 1925, but since 1926 it is used as museum with diorama. The aquarium is exceptional and was the most beautiful in the world at the time of its opening. There is an ingenious filter system underneath the aquarium. In 1997 the building was fully restored. You can also see the water life of the Amsterdam canals.
80 » House (A.L. van Gendt/ 1885) with a mixture of different styles.
82-88 » House block (1886) in neo-Hollands renaissance style.

🚶 **We walk further. Immediately after crossing the bridge we turn left and cross at the pedestrian crossing.**
The Muiderpoort is on the right hand. Behind the gateway we can see the towers of the Tropics Museum.

☞ Muiderpoort - C. Rauws/1770

In 1811 Napoleon made his entry into the city of Amsterdam through this gate. The classicism gateway in Louis XVI style has a pediment entablature on both sides with Doric pillars. In the pediments are the city's coats of arms, the old with the cog ship and the new with the St. Andrew's crosses and the date 1770. Above the pediments runs a square balustrade with the eight-sided dome tower in the middle. The bell in the tower was cast in 1664. There were many gates that gave entrance to the city of Amsterdam in the 17th and 18th centuries. The Muiderpoort is the only remaining example.

🚶 **We turn left immediately and walk back on Plantage Middenlaan until Plantage Kerklaan.**
To the right we have a nice view of the Artis zoo. To the left we see many city villas in eclectic style.

🚶 **We turn right onto Plantage Kerklaan.**
36 » Former members centre (G.B. Salm/1871) of the zoo Artis. In this building the register of the population was kept from 1941 to 1968. During an attack of the resistance (in 1943) the building was severely damaged.

The corner pavilions show the original height of the buildings.

40 » Entrance Artis Zoo
On both sides of the entrance are neo-classicism gatekeeper's houses (1851). Note the two zinc eagles on the black gates.
Opposite side 61 » Plancius (1875). The building is constructed for the Jewish men's choral society Oefening Baart Kunst (practice makes perfect). Besides having a concert hall, there was also a conference room for the Jewish workers movement. Since 1999 the Nationaal Verzetsmuseum (National Resistance Museum) is located here.

⚲ **We turn left on Henri Polak-laan.**
Because of its many trees and large houses, the lane gives a spacious impression.
38-40 « Former church building of the Nieuw Apostolische Kerk (H.F. Sijmons/1913) in the style of H.P. Berlage. The church is symmetric and has two towers. The high staircase and the lead-glass windows give the building a stately alure.
6-12 « Former Jewish Portuguese Hospital (H. Elte/1916) in the style of H.P. Berlage. The building is asymmetric and has three top-gables and a bay window. Above the entrance we see a pelican feeding her young.

9 » De Burcht - H.P. Berlage/1900
This is the oldest trade union's building in the Netherlands and is built by the Algemene Nederlandse Diamantbewerkers Bond (ANDB) (Netherlands diamond cutters' union). The building is in the style of the Amsterdam's School and has five stories, crowned with a tower. The monumental stoop and entrance are striking. The union's monogram is above the door. The tower is integrated in the façade with a round window at the top with an emblem in the shapeis of a cut diamond.

De Burcht

The plain gable is crowned with flower motifs and initials of the trade union. On the first floor the windows are higher to improve the light fall.

⚲ **We turn left on Plantage Parklaan. We walk further and turn right at the end. We enter the Wertheim Park.**

☞ » Wertheimpark (1812)
This is the oldest park and was a gift from Napoleon to Amsterdam. Originally the park was the whole area between Plantage Middenlaan and the present Entrepotdok and was only open to members. In 1897 it was made an public park. Since 1982 the entrance is flanked by two white marble sphinxes.The original zinc examples from 1898 were removed in 1948 for safety reasons. In 1898 the park got the name Wertheim Park. Abraham Carl Wertheim (1832-1897) was a man of worthy endeavours for the state. As a banker and a Member of Parliament he made efforts for the poor of the city. Around the fountain (1898) his merits and virtues are

engraved in the hard stone basin. This basin is supported by eight marble pillars. His portrait medallion is on a granite obelisk, the other ornaments are in bronze. Again we see the pelican feeding her young, the symbol of the Portugees Israelite Congregation.

⚑ We pass the bridge (Sint Antoniesluis) and walk into Sint Antoniebreestraat.
6 » House De Pinto (see page 65).

⚑ We turn left and walk through the gateway of the Zuiderkerkhof.

Auschwitzmonument

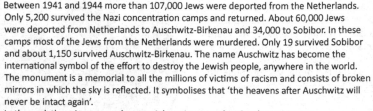

Between 1941 and 1944 more than 107,000 Jews were deported from the Netherlands. Only 5,200 survived the Nazi concentration camps and returned. About 60,000 Jews were deported from Netherlands to Auschwitz-Birkenau and 34,000 to Sobibor. In these camps most of the Jews from the Netherlands were murdered. Only 19 survived Sobibor and about 1,150 survived Auschwitz-Birkenau. The name Auschwitz has become the international symbol of the effort to destroy the Jewish people, anywhere in the world. The monument is a memorial to all the millions of victims of racism and consists of broken mirrors in which the sky is reflected. It symbolises that 'the heavens after Auschwitz will never be intact again'.
In the park there is an annual memorial service every last Sunday in January.

Auschwitzmonument (J. Wolkers/1993)

⚑ We leave the park and turn right on Plantage Middenlaan. We pass the bridge (Hortusbrug), cross left over the Muiderstraat via the tram rails and walk on the Nieuwe Herengracht.
« Hothouses of the Hortus Botanicus (1992).
63 » Dutch gable (± 1700) with basement, festoon around the attic window, a half-round pediment decorated with a flower motif.
61 » Dutch gable (± 1670) with half-round pediment and a festoon around the hoisting crane and attic window.

⚑ We turn right at the Jonas Daniël Meyerplein.
7 » Outbuildings and synagogue.

⚑ At the corner we turn right on Mr. Visserplein. We walk straight on and cross the street at the traffic lights. We turn left and walk along the Dutch Film and Television Academy. We cross Valkenburgerstraat and walk straight into the Jodenbreestraat.
4 « The Rembrandthuis + museum (see page 66).

Now we are in the churchyard of the monumental Zuiderkerk (see page 65).

⚑ We walk straight in to Zandstraat. We pass Zanddwarsstraat and leave Zandstraat. We turn right on Kloveniersburgwal.
On the opposite side of the Kloveniersburgwal we see the former Lutheran church, now the Compagnie Theatre. Next to it, on the right side, is the rear gable of the East-India House.

⚑ We turn left and cross the bridge (Bushuissluis).
On the bridge we see the Waag to the right.

⚑ We walk straight on Oude Hoogstraat.
24 « East- India Huis (see page 49).
22 « Gateway Walenkerk (see page 48).

⚑ We walk straight into Oude Doelenstraat, pass the bridge (Varkenssluis) and go in Damstraat. We walk straight on and arrive back at the Dam.

Groenburgwal

 # Museum Quarter

V ia Spuistraat and the Herengracht we walk to the Museum Quarter. This district was laid out in the 19th century and is centre of art and culture. We walk past the Rijksmuseum, the Van Gogh Museum, the Amsterdams Stedelijk Museum and the Concertgebouw. Then we walk to the largest park in the city, the Vondel Park.

We finish this walk with a visit to the Leidseplein and the Leidsestraat, one of the busiest areas of the city.

Max Euweplein

🚶 4.2 miles (6,8 km)

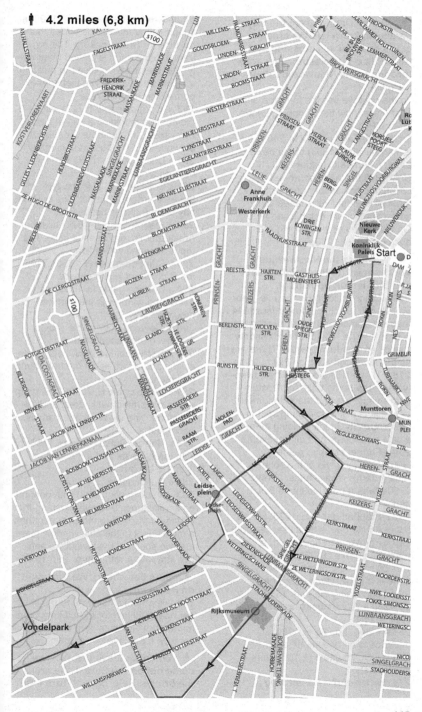

✝ On the Dam we face the Royal Palace and turn left. We cross at the pedestrian's crossing and turn right on Paleisstraat. We walk through to the Nieuwezijds Voorburgwal.

To the right we see the former main post office, now the Shopping centre Magna Plaza.

On the left hand at nr. 234-240 is the former building (1903) of the newspaper Algemeen Handelsblad. Until 1970 this neighbourhood was called the 'newspaper quarter'. The most prominent Netherlands' daily newspapers were established here. On both sides of the building are neck-gables (± 1750).

✝ We cross the Nieuwezijds Voorburgwal, follow Paleisstraat and turn left on Spuistraat.

210 » Office building Bungehuis (gebr. Van Gendt/1932). The lower façade is made of granite and the upper façade is of limestone. The door and window frames are made of bronze. There are no further decorations on this building.

218 » This building is more than twenty years the home base for Amsterdam's squatters and the autonomous. Vrankrijk is a self-governing spot in the centre city. In the building there is a café and rooms for cultural events.

230 » Former stepped gable (± 1625) in the style of the sober Amsterdam's renaissance. About 1750 it was renovated into a Dutch gable.

232 » Stepped-gable (± 1625) in sober Amsterdam's renaissance style.

249 « Former warehouse with a trapezium-gable (1639). Above the cornice moulding of the first story there is a gable stone with a blue round containing the date 1639.

251-253 « Warehouses (± 1680) with spout-gable.

255 a « Spout-gable (± 1630), entrance is on basement level.

255 b « Dutch gable (± 1630) has three crests.

274/corner of the Raamsteeg »

Shop/dwelling (G. van Arkel/ 1898) in Jugendstil. Van Arkel designed this building for Stähle bakery. The entrance to the shop is placed diagonally. The bay windows give the building a picturesque aura. The tiletableaux portray the baker's trade.

263 « Cornice-gable (1723) with in the cornice moulding a keg of beer, two vases, and the date. The top is crowned with the bust of a woman.

271 « Dutch gable (1687) with the date on a ribbon.

281 « Building (1910) in the style of the Amsterdam's School. The built out bay story (right) is noticeable.

294 » Stepped-gable (1627) in sober Amsterdam's renaissance style. The top is crowned with a lion.

296 » Stepped-gable (± 1650). The top is crowned with a sphere.

298 » Cornice-gable (± 1650) with half-round window in the cornice moulding.

300 » Elevated neck-gable (1642) with decorated scroll stones.

302 » Neck-gable (± 1650) with three swans and a fortress in the half-round pediment.

289 « Dutch gable (± 1680) ''t Schaep' with a decorated neck, crest and gable stone. The lower façade has lovely decorations.

295 « Narrow Dutch gable (± 1750) with three crests and a gable stone with 'De Loosman'.

299 « Dutch gable (± 1720).

303 « Neck-gable (1693) with decorated scroll stones and eye-catching fruit motifs. In the half-round pediment has a motif. Next to the attic window there are two sculpted oval windows and two streamers with 'anno' and '1693'.

✝ Spui lies ahead. We turn right on Heisteeg.

The alley thanks its name to the corner house ''t Hayblock' (heiblok= drop hammer) which was here in the 16th century. It has been torn down.

✝ When we leave the alley we come out on the Singel. We cross the bridge (Heibrug) and turn left on the Singel.

⸸ At the height of Singel 418/420 we turn right on Dubbele Worststeeg.
The alley is named after Laurens Dubbelworst, who lived here until 1672.
In this narrow and quiet alley we pass « the warehouse De Ravenhorst (± 1650). At the end of the alley, to the right side on nr. 364-370, are the Cromhouthuizen (1660), where the Bible's Museum is now established.

⸸ We turn left on the Herengracht and pass the Beulingsluis.
On the left side we have a nice view through to the Singel.
To the right is the lovely building Herengracht 380-382 (1890).

⸸ We continue walking and pass the Beulingstraat.
The street is named after the influential merchant Gerrit Jansz Beulink, who lived here around 1600. On the corner of the Beulingstraat are two lovely houses.
27 Neck-gable (1649) with a half-round pediment and a wooden under façade.

Beulingstraat 25 and 27

25 Neck-gable (1653) in the style of the Holland's classicism. Note the festoons, the dates, the sculpted oval windows and the decorated scroll stones.

⸸ We follow on the Herengracht and walk to the Koningsplein. We turn right and cross the bridge.
The bridge (P. Kramer/1921) is built in the Amsterdam's School style. On the corners of the bridge there are granite animal figures. The wrought iron balustrade is very lovely.

⸸ Immediately across the bridge we turn left and follow the Herengracht on the right side. We walk on to number 466 and then turn right on Nieuwe Spiegelstraat.
To the left we pass the Spiegelhof, where there are predominantly galleries and antique shops.

⸸ We cross the Keizersgracht and follow the Nieuwe Spiegelstraat.
45/corner Kerkstraat « Cornice-gable (± 1680) with a wooden store front and a lovely wooden built-out shop window. The high stoop leads to a higher story on the Nieuwe Spiegelstraat. The entrance to the shop is on the Kerkstraat.
64 » Neck-gable (± 1700) with decorated scroll stones with fruit motif, gable stone and half-round pediment. The lower façade is worked.
66 » Dutch gable (± 1700) with decorated neck and a half-round pediment. Facing brick with the civic crest of Amsterdam.
68 » High Dutch gable (± 1750) with decorated neck, half-round pediment and gable stone.
Ahead of us we have a beautiful view of the Rijksmuseum.

⸸ We leave the Nieuwe Spiegelstraat. We cross the Prinsengracht and walk straight into the Spiegelgracht.
The canal is excavated in the 17th century as a connecting canal between the Prinsengracht and the Lijnbaansgracht further on.

6 » Dutch gable (± 1675) 'Kaap de Goede Hoop' with a decorated neck and crest. Has a gable stone with the depiction of a three master ship.
9 « Dutch gable (1764) in Louis XV-style. With three crests and a gable stone.
13 « Warehouse (± 1750) with a cornice gable.

☞ 31/corner Lijnbaansgracht 287 « former one-house on a courtyard Nootebomme Uytkijk (1774)

The courtyard originally had six rooms for the 'destitute of the Low-German reformed faith'. The gable stone refers to the courtyard house.

⋔ We continue walking and reach the Weteringsschans. We cross it, go over the museum bridge and cross the Stadhouderskade.
Now we are right in front of the Rijksmuseum. This is the border between the 'old' and the 'new' city.
The underpass seems like an en-trance way to Amsterdam-Zuid. The architect Cuypers intended it like that.

☞ Rijksmuseum - P.J.H. Cuypers/1885

The building (P.J.H. Cuypers/1885) in a combination of neo-renaissance and no-gothic styles is built of red brick, granite, limestone and sandstone. The museum is in a garden which gives the impression that it is 'free' of its surroundings. The building is symmetric and the middle section is accentuated by two towers. On the corners two lower towers are placed. The underpass at the middle of the building connects the Stadhouders-kade with the Museumplein. The museum is richly decorated with sculptures, paintwork and stained-glass windows.
The Night Watch hall (1906) is famous, where the 'Night Watch' Rembrandt van Rijn can be admired. In the museum many exceptional pieces and masterworks can be seen by among others Rembrandt van Rijn, Johannes Vermeer, Frans Hals and Jan Steen.

⋔ We walk through the underpass under the Rijksmuseum.
As soon as we arrive at the Museumplein we find ourselves, or rather it feels like we are, in another part of Amsterdam. The museum square is under construction now for more than 125 years and is regularly a point of discussion. The square is almost totally redesigned from 1996-1999 by a Danish landscape architect Sven-Ingvar Andersson. He choose the theme 'space/emptiness' as a starting point.
The square makes a spacious impression with the strolling promenade between the Van Gogh Museum and the Stedelijk Museum and the extensive lawns and play area. Right in front of us you find the play fountain. In the summertime the fountain offers refreshment for man and dog, while it can be skated on in the wintertime.

⋔ We walk further and walk on

the footpath.
On the right side are a great number of houses designed by the architect of the Rijksmuseum, Cuypers.
On the right we pass the main building of the Van Gogh Museum (1973). As we continue walking to the left we pass the new wing (1999) of the Van Gogh Museum. name 'the oyster' is designed bythe Japanese architect Kisho Kurokawa.

♟ **We walk straight on.**

The Concertgebouw - A.L. van Gendt/1883
The building in the style of Viennese classicism is built of sand and brick.

Concertgebouw has brought forth a number of famous conductors, including Willem Mengelberg and Bernard Haitink.

♟ **We turn right on Van Baerlestraat, walk straight on and then turn right on Paulus Potterstraat.** In this street there are two important museums.

☞ 13 » Stedelijk Museum - A.W. Weissman/1895
This building in the style of the neo-renaissance is 100 metres long and

Above the main entrance is a pediment entablature in which the Muses are depicted. At the top is a harp in gold leaf. Furthermore, there is a classical gallery of pillars and on both sides are half-high towers with a balustrade. At the windows there are statues of Bach, Beethoven and the Dutch composer Sweelinck.
The Grote Zaal (Main Hall) has 2,000 seats, the Kleine Zaal (Recital Hall) has 450 seats. The building is famed for its perfect acoustics. The large concert organ is also special. The

36 metres wide and has many decorations. In the niches along the gable are images of architects and artists including: Hendrick de Keyser, Jacob van Campen and Joost Jansz. Bilhamer.

☞ 7 » Van Gogh Museum (1973)
♟ **At the pedestrian crossing between the Stedelijk Museum and the Van Gogh Museum we cross the Paulus Potterstraat and walk straight through into the Van de**

Veldenstraat. We cross Jan Luijkenstraat and turn left on P.C. Hooftstraat.

The street dates from 1873 and is named after the famous Dutch literary writer Pieter Cornelisz Hooft (1581-1647). It is one of the most exclusive shopping streets in Amsterdam. There are many luxury clothing and fashion shops. The Amsterdam jet set shows itself here often in the street and the percentage of expensive auto-mobiles is very high.

We walk on, cross the Van Baerlestraat and continue on the P.C. Hooftstraat. At the end of the street we walk straight into the Vondel Park. At the intersection we turn left (the pond is on the right hand) and walk straight on. We pass (right) a blue bridge. We walk straight on and at the signpost 'Osdorp/Geuzenveld' turn right. We pass the pond.

To the left is the restaurant Het Melkhuis (1874). The restaurant is built in Swiss style. In the 19th century there was a meadow here and the cows grazed between the tables of the restaurant. The guests could get sweet milk and sour cream in beer glasses. The old cart and antique milk cans remind us of that time.

We turn right and walk to the other side of the pond.

To the right is the entrance to the Openlucht Theater. In June, July, and August, there are open-air (weather permitting) concerts on the square.

We walk straight on and pass the bandstand (J.D. Zocher/1874) to the left. On the right is the:

☞ Blauwe Ronde Theehuis - H.J.A.B. Baanders/1937

This is a building with a very special shape in the style of the Nieuwe Bouwen. The tea house consists of three saucers supported by steel columns. Because of its unusual construction, it affords a prime view of the Vondel Park.

(If you want to visit the tea house and then re-continue the walk, you have to first walk back and then:)

Next to the tea house we turn left and cross the little bridge. We walk straight on and leave the park for now. We have reached the Vondelstraat and turn right.

The architecture in this street is basically a design by P.J.H. Cuypers.

☞ 140 « The Hollandsche Manege - A.L. van Gendt/ 1882

In 1882 this house was renovated to become the director's home and riding school. Van Gendt was inspired by the Spanish Reitschule in Vienna. If we walk through the monumental entrance we reach the actual ménage building. In 1882 the garden that used to lie here is partly covered with a

---

The Vondel Park

The planning of the park was an initiative of a group of well to do businessmen from this neighbourhood. The park is 48 hectares and is laid out in English landscape style: many winding paths, lawns, ponds, and unusual buildings.

The park got the name Vondel Park in 1867 when the statue of the famous Netherlands poet Joost van den Vondel (1587-1679) was placed in the park.

The Vondel Park - J.D. Zocher/1864

glass roof that is supported by half-round iron ribs. The space breathes out 19th century atmosphere and resembles an orangery. Only the elite of the city could become a member of the riding school in the 19th century. Note the high inside riding course and how lovely the different decorations and horses' heads are.

In the middle of the left side wall there is a grandstand where the orchestra played. The other three grandstands were removed to make more space for the riding track. When we leave the area of the riding track, we can go up the decorated stairs to the first floor. Here we find the foyer and the restaurant that provide a good view of the riding track.

Please note the doorframes which are decorated with pediments.

⋔ We leave the Hollandsche Manege and follow the Vondelstraat on the right side.

77-79 » Double city villa (P.J.H. Cuypers/1881), with an asymmetric gable. Above the right door a bay window is built that is crowned with a tower. Architect Cuypers lived in this villa from 1881-1893.

^ Vondelkerk - P.J.H. Cuypers/1872

The Vondel church is a neo-gothic cross-basilica with a nave and transept. The church gives a compact impression and so it fits into the street scene. The interior traces back to the French gothic period. The parsonage is on Vondelstraat 108. The tower was lost to a fire in 1904, but was rebuilt in a design by Joseph Cuypers.

In 1892 cracks were found in the vaulting and after inspection it was found that the church was not in such good condition. In 1978 it was such a ruin that it had to be closed. A project developer who owned it, wanted to demolish it. Private organisations and individuals were able to keep it from demolition. In 1986 the church

was reopened after restoration. The Vondel church no longer functions as a church. The office room is rented out and occasionally the transept is rented out to cultural and social organisations.

75-73 » House Nieuw Leyerhoven (P.J.H. Cuypers/1876) Has an asymmetric gable, towers, bay windows and balconies.

⋔ We turn right and return to the Vondel Park. We turn left.

☞ The Paviljoen - W. Hamer/1883

The eclecticism building with many Italian neo-renaissance traits was built as a place for holding board and committee meetings for the originators who founded the Vondel Park in 1864. The building is symmetric and is 35 metres wide and 10 metres deep. The two stone stairs lead to the terrace with a balustrade in the middle. There are towers on both corners. The coat of arms of the city of Amsterdam is placed on the roof. The lions have two different dates, namely 1864 and 1880.

The year 1864 stands for the date when the contract was signed with the architects for the Vondel Park. The year 1880 stands for the date when the contract was signed with architect W. Hamer.

⋔ We walk to the T-crossing and turn left under the viaduct. We continue walking.

The noticeable building to the left is the former Amsterdamsche Huishoud-school (domestic science) (C.B. Post-humus Meyjes/1895). The building in chalet style is built of brick and has five floors. The top floors have lovely wooden balconies and bay windows with wooden trimming.

⋔ We continue walking straight on and come close to the main entrance to the park.

1 » Former home of the gate-keeper (1890) in chalet style.

The imposing entrance gates of the Vondel Park were placed in 1883 for the occasion of the World Fair that was held that year in Amsterdam.

🚶 **We leave the Vondel Park and cross the Stadhouderskade and walk straight on to the Max Euweplein.**
This residential/shopping square (1991) is built around the former koepelgevangenis (domed prison) (A.L. van Gendt/1843). The square is named after Max Euwe; world chess champion (1935).

🚶 **We cross the Max Euweplein to the right.**
On the Kleine Gartmanplantsoen/ Weteringschans 29 is on the other side:

The Barlaeus Gymnasium - W & J.B. Springer/1885
The building in eclecticism style with the accent on neo-classicism has two wings and a corner pavilion that is crowned with a pediment entablature. On the building many subjects of the classic sciences are depicted. Above the entrance is the motto 'Disciplina vitae scipio' (science is life's staff). On the first floor are portraits of Sophocles, Cicero, Vondel, and Huygens and on the second floor reliefs depicting the sciences.

☞ **Weteringschans 20 »**
Paradiso - G.B. Salm/1880
The former church building is in eclecticism style. At first sight the building doesn't look like a church; because the front building hides the actual church behind. The former church auditorium has an intimate feeling. There are balconies on both sides of the auditorium. Since 1968 the building is named cultural centre Paradiso. Many artists and musicians from in and out of the country perform here.

🚶 **We turn left on Kleine Gartmanplantsoen.**
40 « Cultural centre De Balie (1845). De Balie is situated in the former court hall. The building was formerly

Paradiso

connected with the domed prison next door.
On the other side »

☞ **Cinema City-Theater - J. Wils/1935**
The cinema is built in the style of Russian constructivism. The City-Theater is completely restored from 2007-2009.

🚶 **We walk straight on and reach the**

┌──── **L e i d e s e p l e i n** ┐

Until 1862 the Leidsepoort stood here. At that time the square mainly served as a parking spot for carts and wagons.
In 1874 the square got its present function. The Leidseplein along with the Rembrandtplein is the entertainment scene of Amsterdam. The year-round street-artists perform outside. It is worthwhile to just look around.

23 « Former department store Het Hirsch-gebouw (A.Jacot/1913). The building is inspired by a department store in London (Selfridge's) and Chicago. Note the 40 metre high dome.

28-30 » The American Hotel (W. Kromhout/1902). Is in a style combination of art nouveau and early Amsterdam's School.

26 ^ Stadsschouwburg - (gebr. Springer & A.L. van Gendt/1892)

The theatre, built in the style of neo-renaissance, has a division that can be seen from the outside: a public section and a stage section. The stage tower is built in brown brick, the public section in smooth red brick with stone parts. The stories are accentuated with horizontal cornices. The staircases project outward and have little towers with Old-Holland's ornaments. Each rank had their own entrance. Nowadays the main entrance at the front is used for everybody.
The theatre is kept in the original state and is one of the most beautiful theatres in the Netherlands. The interior lay-out is not changed much since 1892.
In 1998 the entrance, passageway, and raised porch were renovated.

꜠ **We turn right, cross the pedestrian's crossway and walk halfway across the square.**
24 « Neck-gable (± 1665) in Holland's Classicism. With pilasters, decorated scroll stones and a half-round pediment.
20-22 « Cornice-gable (± 1775) with a high wooden under façade.
18-12 « Four stepped-gables (1666) with wooden under façade.

꜠ **We walk further and enter the Leidsestraat.**
Watch out for the tram, because this one rides back and forth on single tracks in the street.
The Leidsestraat is a busy shopping street. Next to a large array of shops, it also has some interesting gables.
81/corner Prinsengracht » Dwelling/ shop; bakery (1896) in Jugendstil with bay windows and a little tower.
44 « Dutch gable (± 1650) with a festoon under the attic trapdoor and

next to the attic window two triangular windows.
Leidsestraat/corner Keizersgracht
455 « former department store Metz & Co (see Keizersgracht 455).
27 » Wide Dutch gable (± 1700 with gable stone 'De Huys Duynder Visser'.
25 » Neck-gable (± 1700) with the coat of arms of Amsterdam in the decorated scroll stones. The top is crowned with a half-round pediment.
11-13 » Sober stepped-gables (± 1650).

꜠ **We walk further and reach the Koningsplein. We cross the bridge (Koningssluis) and walk straight into Heiligeweg.**
The road is named after the pilgrims who in the 14th and 15th centuries gathered at the Kapel Ter Heilige Stede (Chapel of the Holy City). The chapel was on Kalverstraat.
Nowadays the Heiligeweg is a busy shopping street that connects Kalverstraat with the Singel.
35 » Wooden store front (G. van Arkel/1890) in neo-renaissance style. Like in most of the buildings that Van Arkel designed, his name is engraved somewhere on the façade. On this building it is on the top-side of the left door.
21-25 » Former music instrument store Kettner Kettner (A.J. Kropholler & J.F. Staal/1906) in Berlage style. In the gable there are three tile tableaux with the names of three kinds of instruments.

☞ 19 » Het Rasphuispoortje - H. de Keyser/1603

The gate gives entry to the Kalvertoren, but it used to be the outer gate of the Rasphuis. In the Rasphuis (1595-1892) convicts had to rasp hardwood from Brazil. On both sides of the gate with a rounded arch are Doric half-pillars and the relief is on a console. On the relief a wagon loaded with Brazilian hardwood is depicted. The driver is taming the wild animals with a whip. Above the relief is the motto: 'Vertutis est domare quae cuncti pavent' (it is worthwhile to tame that what is feared).

In the top of the gate the city virgin is seen punishing two naked convicts. The inscription is 'Catigatio' and the date 1663.

The Rasphuispoortje now is an entrance to the:

☞ « Kalvertoren

This modern shopping centre has three stories and thirty specialised shops. The restaurant Kalvertoren

has a brilliant view of the historic city centre.

Entrances are in the Kalverstraat, Heiligeweg and the Singel.

1 » (corner Kalverstraat)
Store building (G. van Arkel/1891) in neo-renaissance style. Note the gables of red brick and the gable tops with stepped-gables and little towers.

🚶 We turn left and enter Kalverstraat. We walk through this street and return again to the Dam.

Vondelpark - Blauwe Ronde Theehuis

Leidsestraat

Canal Guide

Venice of the north

Amsterdam is world famous for its canals and monumental mansions on the canals. In 1582 the Italian writer Guicciardini called the city Amsterdam the Venice of the north. The writer meant the similarities between Amsterdam and Venice in the areas of (sea) trade, tolerance, cosmopolitism, and art in the broadest sense of the word.

The origin of the canals goes back to the medieval city centre that was formed by the Singel, the Kloveniersburgwal and the Geldersekade. During the city expansion plans of 1598 and 1609 the four concentric (main) canals took shape.

City architect Hendrick Jacobsz. Staets received orders from the city council to widen the Singel and to construct three canals around the Singel. Staets went to work in an almost classical manner. The four main canals became a ring of canals around the old city centre and consisted of Singel (1425, widened in 1586/1609), Herengracht (1586/1609), Keizersgracht (1612), and Prinsengracht (1612).

Between 1662 and 1665 the main canals were connected to the Amstel. The main canals were intersected by the smaller radial canals, like the Brouwersgracht, the Leidsegracht, and the Leliegracht.

In the working-class area the Jordaan eleven radial canals were built, six of which were filled in again in the 19th century for hygienic reasons. Other radial canals were filled-in to make the city more accessible. When the Rozengracht (1890) and the Warmoesgracht (1895) were filled in, a tram connection was laid out to the western part of the city.

Other examples of filled-in canals are the Elandsgracht, the Lindengracht, the Vijzelgracht and the Nieuwezijds Voorburgwal.

The main canals and the radial canals are connected to each other by streets, alleys, and historic bridges.

The four main canals have a combined length of 10 kilometres, more than 2,000 houses and larger buildings border them. 1,600 of these houses have received the designation of national monument.

Herengracht corner Beulingsluis

Singel

The Singel is the oldest canal and was excavated in 1425. Until the 15th century the Singel was the city borderline of Amsterdam. Because of the extensive city expansion plans, the Singel was widened in 1586 and in 1609. The Singel encircles the western part of the historic centre city and runs from the IJ to the Muntplein. There the Singel leads to the Binnen-Amstel.

Singel 104-106

☞ 2 De Kruiwagen - J. Loots/1606

Is one of the oldest and widest stepped-gables in Amsterdam with a wooden lower façade. When the dwelling/warehouse was built, it was outside of the city gates and on a piece of land outside the dike. The owner, Hendrick Jansz. Cruywagen, had a shop here in ship's materials. For this reason the hoisting hook is extra strong. The name of this large warehouse derives from the gable stone above the first floor. This stone is added by the owner in 1641. The large centre frame with the hoisting trapdoors is made into the gable later.
6 Neck-gable (1740) has decorated scroll stones and a half-round pediment. The side windows are smaller than the centre windows.
7 This gable is only 1 metre wide and is the narrowest rear gable in Amsterdam. The front gable is on the Jeroensteeg and is broader there. The narrowest front gable is on the Oude Hoogstraat 22.
8 Cornice-gable (± 1800) has the inscription in the cornice moulding 'God is mijn burg' (God is my refuge).

☞ 11 Ronde Lutherse Kerk - A. Dortsman/1668

This second Lutheran church (the first is Singel 411) is built in the style of sober classicism. The copper dome roof is conspicuous with a small tower on top in the shape of a lantern that has a swan as a weather vane. In 1822 and in 1993 the church was caught in terrible fires. In 1826 the church was rebuilt and completely restored in 1993. Presently the church is used as a congress centre and concert hall.

Lutherans

Lutherans have been in Amsterdam since 1520. After the reformation, in 1604, they were only allowed to hold services in a warehouse on the spot of where the Round Lutheran Church is now. The city council relaxed their ordinance in 1632 because of economical and political reasons. Amsterdam held intensive trade relations with the Baltic Sea area where the Lutherans were in the majority.

19-21 Dutch gable (± 1647). The centre Dutch gable dates from about 1760 and has Louis XV decorations. The inscription 'Vita hominum similis Naviganti' means 'Life of man is like that of a sailor'. Until 1647 brewery De Os was situated in this building and numbers 23-27. The peak of the roof runs parallel with the Singel. This is because the building was built so close to the city's wall that the entrance had to be made on a side street.

☞ 24 Vriesland (1770)

Cornice-gable in Louis XV style, has a straight cornice moulding. The balustrade has a raised centrepiece with a portrayal of a ship. It is crowned with a crest.

☞ 36 Zeevrugt (1763)

Cornice-gable has an open balustrade in Louis XV style. The raised centre has a crest and is richly decorated with an image of Mercury, with a purse in his hands and a rooster at his side. The straight cornice is decorated with small pilasters and the name Zeevrugt. In the door frame there is a sailing ship in the crest.

40 Cornice-gable (1735) has a decorated bell-shaped riser in Louis XIV style. Under the raised section there are carved tassels. On top there are two corner vases.

42 Cornice-gable (1810) has a straight cornice moulding. The hoisting hook protrudes from the roof.
45 Cornice-gable (1725) in Louis XIV style has a decorated elevation in the shape of a bell. There is an emperor's crown at the top.
56 Cornice-gable (1725-1750) has a decorated elevation. The cornice moulding has decorations in the Louis XIV style.
60 Cornice-gable (1745) in Louis XIV style, has a semi-circle shaped centrepiece with a richly decorated raised upper side. On the left side there are two children figures. The door frame has two Corinthian pilasters.
64 Stepped-gable (1637). The upper side is still original in Amsterdam's renaissance style with a gable with a man's head between two draped sheets. The window arches are decorated with shell motifs. At the top there is a vase. The bottom part of this stepped-gable dates from 1800. The house has inside shutters and a hoisting hook.
74 Neck-gable (1660) has decorated scroll stones and next to the attic window two decorated oval windows. In the gable stone a stage-coach is depicted pulled by two horses and the legend: 'De Haagsche postwagen'. From 1660 the stage-coach to The Hague started here.
75 Neck-gable (1723) has sculpted oval windows, a half-round pediment and a wooden under façade.
77 Neck-gable (1744) has decorated scroll stones and the date 'anno1744'. In the crest is the text "T Duyts Connon'. Above the hoisting hook there is a half-round pediment and a gable stone depicting a part of a canon. A vase is at the top.

☞ 83-85 corner Lijnbaansteeg, het Oude Veerhuis/ De Zwaan - J. van Campen/ 1652

This originally neck-gable in the style of Holland's classicism is re-built into a spout-gable in the 18th century.

style. In the decorated scroll stones there are representations of three heads with huge noses.

131/corner Nieuwe Spaarpotsteeg House (1615); through the centuries changed and renovated.

132 Cornice-gable (± 1730) of sandstone and four windows wide the cornice moulding is decorated as well as the door frame.

134 Cornice-gable (1740) with a raised cornice moulding and a high crest. In the cornice moulding there are four decorated joists. At the top there are two corner vases.

135 Neck-gable 'De Rouaense Boeijer' (± 1740), in Louis XIV style. With decorations around the hoisting hook, decorated scroll stones, and two vases on the corners.

137 Elevated cornice-gable (± 1740). There is a loft trapdoor and two windows in the cornice. The façade of the basement is decorated.

☞ 140-142 Huis De Dolphijn - H. de Keyser/1600

The house is built in the style of Amsterdam's renaissance. This was originally a double stepped-gable with dolphins in large scroll stones. The broad pilasters on the ground floor bear the coupled pilasters of the first floor. In the 17th century the house is split into a house with a side house. Since that time the one on the left is called the Gilded Dolphin and the one on the right The Little Dolphin. Frans Banningh Cocq (1605-1655) known from Rembrandt's painting the 'Night Watch' lived in this house.

145 Dutch gable (1680) has scroll stones and crown in the style of Louis XVI. In Amsterdam there are not many Dutch gables with Louis XVI decorations.

159 Side-gable (1745). The neck-gable is on the Torensteeg. The windows are decorated.

164 Cornice-gable (1780). The cornice moulding has two protruding girders, three carved stones, and four festoons. The outer two festoons are

The front façade, in the Lijbaansteeg, is a pilaster-gable with Ionic pilasters and festoons. The heavy oak under façade dates from the 17th century. In the Lijnbaansteeg there is a gable stone with the text 'De Swaen'. The stone refers to the first owner, Nicolaas Swaen. Singel 83 got a wooden store front in the 19th century. The windows were lowered. Originally the entrance to Singel 83 was a gateway. The gate disappeared in the renovation in the 19th century.
The colourful painting was added in 1998.

87 Neck-gable (1725) in Louis XIV style has a bust of Mercury in the top.

90 Neck-gable (1730) in Louis XIV-style. With decoration in the scroll stones and around the hoisting hook. The top is crowned with a half-round pediment.

104-106 Dutch gables (1743) in Louis XIV style. This is the highest twin Dutch gable in Amsterdam. The gables are decorated and have a vase on thetop.

116 Neck-gable (1752) in Louis XV

topped with a bull's head. The owner of this house was a butcher.

166 Until 1634 an alley ran here. The house is built in the alley. It is one of the smallest gables in Amsterdam. The front façade is 1.85 metres wide and the building is 16 metres deep. Towards the back the building keeps getting wider. The rear façade is 5 metres wide.

176 Cornice-gable (± 1775) in Louis XVI style. The straight cornice moulding has a pediment entablature.

186 Cornice-gable (1740) in Louis XIV style, is of sandstone with a decorated cornice moulding. The hoisting hook is wrought into the shape of a head and above it is a statue of Mercury. Above the centre window is a decorative vase.

187/corner Raadhuisstraat 2 Het Witte Huis (1899) is in Jugendstil. The lower façade is of hard stone decorated with animal and plant motifs. Above the windows are cemented arches of yellow and green bricks. The bricks of the floors above are white glazed. On the corner the top floor has a balustrade.

188 Neck-gable (1737) in Louis XIV style has a half-round pediment and decorated scroll stones. On the gable is a gable stone with a red oil windmill ('De Roo Oly Molen').

192 Neck-gable (1739) in Louis XIV style has a half-round pediment. The grape bunches under the pediment refer to the commissioner who was a wine merchant. In the left scroll stone it says 'Anno' and in the right '1739'.

200-208 Driekoningen building - Three Kings - (1921) in the style of the Amsterdam's School.

210 Warehouse (1790) has a straight cornice-gable and two entrance doors.

239 Het Bungehuis (A.L. Van Gendt & W. Klok 1932) This is an office building with seven floors (including the basement), made completely of stone. The lower façade is of yellow/gray granite. The upper floors are of limestone. The doors, frames, and windows are made of bronze. The commissioner of the building (NV Bunge's Handelsmaatschappij) didn't want any decorations of sculpture or paint work. For this building 20 houses were torn down.

250-256 Handelskantoor (J. van Rossem & W. Vuyk & A.L. van Gendt 1912) in the historicism style. Above the cornice there is a balustrade. Between the windows of the first and second floors there are pilasters and under the windows of the third floor there are festoons. The façade is of stone. The building now functions as the main post office.

258 Neck-gable (1660) has horns of plenty on the scroll stones. There are festoons under the windows. The attic window is round and has a sculpted frame. There is a pediment entablature on the top.

265 Former stepped-gable (1620) in Amsterdam's renaissance style. The stepped-gable is removed from this house and is given a sideways roof. The door frame has Louis XVI decorations and dates from 1790.

288 Cornice-gable (± 1750) in Louis XIV style with a large crest.

292 Cornice-gable (1740) in Louis XIV style. Above the right cornice moulding with four decorated girders we see a balustrade with a decorated central elevation and on each corner a vase. On the roof there are two decorative chimneys. Furthermore there are two hoisting hooks and a door-section with a half-round pediment held up by two pilasters and a richly decorated transom.

318 Cornice-gable (± 1750) with a bell-shaped top.

320 Elevated cornice-gable (± 1750) in Louis XIV style.

322 Elevated cornice-gable (± 1750) has a decorated cornice moulding and a vase on the top.

326 Neck-gable (± 1725) has decorated scroll stones and a half-round pediment.

328 Elevated cornice-gable (± 1750) in Louis XV style.

330 Cornice-gable (1650) with a bell-shaped top.
340 Building (1919) in the style of the Amsterdam's School.
354 Dutch gable (1679) has a year ribbon, festoons and a half-round pediment.
356 Dutch gable (± 1750) has a shell motif in the top.
370 Dutch gable (1650) with festoons around the hoisting hook.
389-391 Dutch gable twins (1680) with medieval window divisions.

☞ 390 Elevated cornice-gable - De Bouwkonst (1700)
In Louis XIV style with a lovely door frame.In the gracefully worked area there are figures of a woman with two children. Above the semi-circular elevation there are figures of Apollo and Minerva. In the corner of the cornice there are pieces of drawing paper. This refers to the builder, who was an 'architect'. The top is crowned with a heavenly sphere.
410 Neck-gable (1647) in Holland's Classicism with Doric pilasters and a circular window.

☞ 411 Oude Lutherse Kerk - P. de Keyser/1632
The church in sober classicism is built on an irregularrectangular terrain. That is why the two side aisles with top-gables lie on the Singel. The third aisle lies on the Spui. On the Spui we find sideways roofs (the ridge of the roof runs parallel tot the street or canal) above the third and sixth windows with top-gables.
412 Elevated neck-gable (1647 in Holland's Classicism. With Ionic pilasters, decorated oval windows and a medieval window division.

421 Het Doelengebouw (1733)
Since 1612 this is the building of the Handboog of Sebastiaansdoelen. Behind the building were the shooting ranges where the marksmen could

practice. The building became a lodging house in 1733. This is the date of the present gable with a sideways roof and two dormer windows. In the middle the cornice has a raised section containing the coat of arms of the city of Amsterdam. Under the middle window on the third floor is the coat of arms of Doelen and of a number of the leaders of militia. Since 1862 the building is used by the University of Amsterdam, who established the university library here in 1880.

☞ 423 Militiabuilding former tack or bus-barn - H. de Keyser/1606

In this building the weapons and the ammunition of the militia were stored. The trapezium top-gable in Holland's renaissance style was finished with brick-on edge coping on both sides and contains the date 1606 and four lion heads. The cornice moulding is decorated with a medallion and various round shapes.
In this building the weapons and ammunition were stored that were necessary for the defence of the city. The building is now used by the library of the University of Amsterdam.

432 Neck-gable (1725) with sculpted oval windows, decorated hoisting hook, and a half-round pediment.
434 Dutch gable (1680) has a gable stone and a half-round pediment.
436 Dutch gable (± 1680) with two oval windows and a half-round pediment.
440 Dutch gable (± 1750) with a richly decorated bell-shape.

☞ 446 De Krijtberg - A. Tepe/1881

In 1654 three houses were bought by Father Petrus Laurentius, a Jesuit missionary. The large house, De Cruytbergh, was used as a hidden church. Because of the growth of the parish, a new roomier gallery church was built in 1677. In 1835 the original house and the neighbouring coach house were demolished to enlarge the church. At the parsonage (left) the original height and breadth can be seen. After 1853 the confession of the Roman Catholic faith was allowed again in Netherlands. In 1881 A. Tepe designed the present neo-gothic city church on the spot where the houses 442, 444 and 446 Singel were. The stepped towers are 50 metres high. The front façade is symmetrical and has four high pointed arch portals.

Above the doors there is a pointed arch window. The two middle entrances give way to a broad nave. The side doors open onto the narrow aisles. These are just wide enough for the processions. The façade is made out of machine-made bricks and is beautified by balustrades. The nave stands out high against the neighbouring houses. The church has several galleries that can be reached by staircase towers.
447 Cornice-gable (± 1850). The façade dates from 1875 and is in the style of the Holland's mannerisms.
450 Stepped-gable (1642) in Amsterdam's renaissance style and has a wooden under façade from 1750.
451-459 Elevated cornice-gable (H. Leguit/1905) in the style of Holland's neo-renaissance, built for the population register and police station. The gable is of hard stone, the decorations are of sandstone. Above the windows relieving arches are placed.
452 Cornice-gable (1639/renovated 1839) is from the Mennonite congregation. In 1607 a barn was built on this spot which functioned as a meeting place. The first brick building was built here in 1639. In 1839 the church got its present form. This church is a good example of a hidden church.
454 Neck-gable (± 1740) with the stoop and entrance opening onto a separate spot. This is because the passageway is right next to it.
456 Stepped-gable (1607) in Holland's renaissance style. The stepped-gable has stone bands and blocks. The under façade is changed in the period 1750-1800.

☞ 460 Nuerenberg/Odeon - P. Vingboons/1662

The name of the building comes from the Greek 'odeion'. This high, wide and graceful Dutch gable in the style of Holland's classicism is built for the merchant Gilles Marcelis and was the house of a tradesman until 1838. Af-ter 1838 the building got a cultural use and served as concert hall, theatre and cinema. The gable is decorated with festoons, ornamented windows, and a decorated hoisting hook with a date stone underneath. The two sober pilasters support a half-round pilaster in the middle. The scroll stones have grape decorations the corners a little decorative tower. Under the scroll stones are two small decorated oval windows. The door with transom and windows are from 1800.

496 Dutch gable 'De Berg' (1739) in Louis XIV style. It is striking that the stoops are placed opposite each other to make entrance to the basement possible.

500 Neck-gable 'D' OudeSchelvis' (± 1750) has decorated scroll stones and a nameplate under the hoisting hook.

502 Spout-gable (1880) with decorative masonry and decorative wall anchors. The plinth and lintel are of hard stone.

☞ 512 Former Vaudeville Theater - I. Gosschalk/1861

The centre section of the electicism style is protruding and decorated. The ground floor is of hard stone and the other floors are plastered. The top floor (above the cornice moulding) is completely made of glass. The architect of this floor is G.B. Salm and is built by Photography Buttinghausen in 1879.

516-518 Warehouse Deen = dragt (1625) has a trapezium-gable with spiral-shaped ornaments and two spheres. The Dutch lion is at the top with the inscription 'D'Eendracht'. The façade and lintel from nr. 516 date from 1910.

Singel 140-142 Huis De Dolfijn (1600)

Herengracht

T he canal is named after the influential Heren XVII (17 Gentlemen) from the Dutch East India Company (VOC). The Herengracht was excavated already in 1586, but at the time of the city's expansion around 1609, it was extended to the Amstel River. To cover the high costs of laying out the canal, the city council offered large tracts of land for sale to the rich merchants. At that time the merchants mostly lived around the Old Church and on the Warmoesstraat. The parcels of ground were sold under conditions. In this manner only rich merchants were considered, they had to pay for the paving of the quay and their houses themselves, it was not allowed to subdivide the parcels, nor was it allowed to build a drawbridge across the canal. The Herengracht became the main trade centre of the city in the 17th century. The buildings are imposing and show much French influence. The Louis-styles are seen here often.

Between the radial canal, the Leidsegracht and the river Amsted lays the *Golden Bend*. Here on large parcels of land are the largest and most luxurious 'city palaces' that were built in the 17th century.

Herengracht 170 Huis Bartolotti (1617)

7 Dutch gable (± 1760). The height (3 m) and breadth (12 m) and the three-window-frame under the attic window still date from the 17th century. The Dutch gable is added in about 1760.

10 Cornice-gable 'De Burch' (± 1750). The name of the house comes from 'God is my fortress' by Martin Luther. The doorframe is in the Louis XV style.

14 Cornice-gable 'De Zon' (1767) in Louis XVI style of sandstone with slightly curved windows. The top is decorated with a pediment entablature containing bowed palm branches and a sunflower. This refers to the name of the house.

21 Neck-gable (± 1694) with decorated scroll stones and in the half-round pediment the depiction of a fish. This refers to the name of the first owner, the merchant Hendrik Visser (fisher).

26 Cornice-gable (± 1800) with in the cornice moulding oval windows and decorated joists. Between the door and the transom there is a half-round, decorated frame.

33 Neck-gable (1680) in Louis XVI style, is crowned with horns of plenty. Fruit motifs run along the neck. In Roomolenstraat it has a lean-to building.

35 Neck-gable (± 1725) has decorated scroll stones and at the top a half-round pediment with a shell motif. On the side façade there is a lean-to building with a door in the middle.

37-39 Balimore (1750 and 1753). Both warehouses have Dutch gables instead of the usual spout-gable. The attic trapdoors are coupled.

38 Stepped-gable (1614)

This stepped-gable, in a mixture of Amsterdam's renaissance style and the sober Haarlem's renaissance style was originally twins with number 36. This can be seen by the half of a year stone (16) in the right hand corner. The large steps have spiral shaped scroll stones and on the top a pediment entablature. The windows are in niches. The wooden under façade is

rebricked in the 18th century.

40 Cornice-gable (1790) is of sandstone in Louis XVI style with a straight, decorated cornice moulding. It is one of the few late 18th century dwellings in Amsterdam. This is a double house, built during the French period. The windows on the first floor are so-called French windows with half-round transoms.

43-45 Ware houses 't Fortuin and the Ark Noach (1590)

They are bricked over wooden warehouses. Brick walls are hanging on a wooden frame. The medieval window division is noteworthy. Number 43 has stone bands between the floors.

48 Cornice-gable 'De Drie Heuvelen' - The Three Hills - (± 1760), is built of sandstone. The cornice moulding has a balustrade and on the corners there are decorative vases. In the middle the balustrade is interrupted by a decorated and raised centrepiece in Louis XV style. In the crest there is a depiction of three hills.

The owner of the house that was here first was called Nicolaas van der Heuvel. He named the house 'De Drie Heuvelen'.

54 Cornice-gable (± 1750). This house was renovated in 1867 when decorations were added in various Louis styles. Above the door there is a balcony and in the middle a curved pediment. The stately 18th century gable is still original.

56-58 Cornice-gable (± 1650). In about 1795 the stepped-gable is replaced by a cornice-gable with a floor. By the relief arches above the windows on the first floor and the three centred arches above the second floor windows it is clear that these are 17th century houses.

59 Elevated neck-gable 'De Hond' - The Dog - (1659) has Ionic pilasters (pilaster-gable). The name is derived from a (removed) gable stone with a picture of a dog. The date stone (1659), the two sculpted windows, the festoons between the windows, and the half-round pediment on the top are original. There is a dolphin in the carved scroll stones.

60 Cornice-gable 'De Coningh van Vranckrijk' (1734). The cornice moulding of sandstone has an impressive entrance section with a bust of Louis XIII, (the king of France).

The entrance has Ionic pilasters on both sides. The porch is richly decorated.

61-63 Twin neck-gables (1666) are in the style of Holland's classicism. There are festoons around the hoisting hook, on the top a half-round

pediment and two sculpted oval attic windows. Nr 61 still has the original window placement: one wider middle window with a smaller window on both sides.

70-72 Pilaster-gable (1640) in the style of Holland's classicism. The basement forms a pedestal on which the façade stands. The pilasters are standing at an unequal distance from each other. The hoisting hooks on both sides of the houses are in a half-round pediment. The hoisting trapdoors are underneath. The middle part of the gable is a story higher and is crowned with a pediment entablature with a coat of arms shield. Under the entablature are four sculpted windows (so-called cows-eyes). During a renovation in 1760 the stairs leading to nr 70 disappeared and the entrance was brought back to street level.

☞ 77/corner Korsjespoortsteeg, stepped-gable (1632)

Top-pilaster-gable is in the style of sober Amsterdam's renaissance. The bottom step has S-shaped scroll stones. The upper floors of the side façade lean on beam heads. The house has two lean-to buildings: one on the Herengracht and one on the Korsjespoortsteeg. The under façade on the Herengracht dates from the

18th century. The back part of the house is on the Korsjespoortsteeg 22.

81 Stepped-gable (± 1625)

Is in sober Amsterdam's renaissance style. The bands and blocks are of sandstone. This is a merchant's house and that means that the building was a home as well as a warehouse. The ground floor was used for living and office and the rest of the floors were for the storage of goods. The warehouse trapdoors are vertically connected and are made of a wooden construction. The hoisting hook is right above them.
The date 1590 is painted on the house which suggests that possibly an older house was here before.

84-86 Former stepped-gable twins (1615)

Are in the style of the Holland's renaissance. These were the first houses built after the city expansion of 1613. Both houses have lion masks in the gable.
Nr 84 has almost the original gable.
Nr 86 received a new Dutch gable in the 18th century. The wooden under façades were covered with brick in the 18th century.
89 Neck-gable (1672), rebuilt according to a drawing from 1768 of a mansion from 1672.
91 Elevated neck-gable (1657). Has decorated scroll stones and a half-round pediment at the top. There are festoons above the outside windows on the second floor and above the middle window there is a date stone. The neck has Ionic pilasters. The first and second floors have Doric pilasters.
97 Eclecticism-gable (± 1865) Has ornament in various Louis styles. The coach house (former) is in the under façade. The gable stone depicting a salmon refers to the warehouse that was on this spot.

100 Stepped-gable 'De

Dubbele Adelaar' (± 1615)

Is in Amsterdam's renaissance style. Has large steps and scroll stones. The bell-shaped top with a pediment entablature dates from a later time.
105-107 This is the spot where the only German bomb fell in the Amsterdam city centre during World War II.

☞ 120 Stepped-gable 'De Coningh van Denemarken' - King of Denmark - (1615)

This is a good example of the transition from baroque Amsterdam's renaissance style to sober Amsterdam's renaissance style.
The house has a wide gable and large steps and scroll stones. The bottom of the façade is renovated in 1800 and then got a door in Louis XVI style.
The roof over the hoisting hook is seldom seen on dwellings, these were more often used on warehouses.
131/corner Bergstraat Low Dutch gable (± 1650) with stoop in front.
152 Former stepped gable (± 1620) with a medieval window division. Much was changed on this building.
155 Warehouse (1760) with Dutch gable.

157 Warehouse Het Keyserrijk (1725) has a decorated Dutch gable and a coach house.

160 Cornice-gable (±1760). The cornice moulding has four decorated joists and above that a crest with decorations in Louis XV style. On the corners there are two decorative vases.

164 House Messina (1743) in Louis XV style. The door is framed with pilasters that support the main frame, decorated with vases and a sculpted oval window. Above the cornice moulding there is an open balustrade with a crest and vases.

166 Cornice-gable 'Soli Deo Gloria' (to the sole glory of God) (± 1725) with a countered cornice moulding and a crest in Louis XIV style. In the relief there is a basket with thistle flowers, coming from the coat of arms of the owner, Pieter Elias.

☞ 168 Het Witte Huijs -The white house- P. Vingboons/ 1637

This house, in the style of Holland's classicism, is the first neck-gable that was built by in Amsterdam by P. Vingboons. The gable is totally made of sandstone. The scroll stones have a simple curved shape. On the top is a pediment entablature with two corner vases. On the neck the family's coat of arms is held on both sides by lions. The family coat of arms by the window is changed in the period 1728-1734. At that time also the windows were made higher so that the window pediments disappeared. The interior dates from 1728-1733.

☞ 170-172 Huis Bartolotti - H. de Keyser/1617

This stepped-gable in Amsterdam's renaissance style is designed for beer brewer Willem van den Heuvel. He took on the name Guillelmo Bartolotti, because he inherited the trade's house Bartolotti under the condition that he would take the name Bartolotti. In his time he was one of the richest Amsterdammers.

The outside windows of the house are placed crookedly in able to accommodate the 'small bend' on the Herengracht. The text under the balustrades means, 'by ingenious diligence' and 'through faith and honesty'. On the ground floor the façade has Tuscan pilasters and on the floor above Ionic. The house received a side-house in 1689 that is why there is a door put in on the right side. The roof has two large corner chimneys. Furthermore the gable has masks, vases, and a half-round broken pediment.

179 De Grooten Heer (C. Posthumus Meyjes/1901). In 1900 nine old houses were demolished to build this house.

182 De Sonnewyser (1772) This house has the oldest cornice-gable in Louis XVI style of Amsterdam. A double stoop leads to the door. The sculpted strip above the door consists of circles. Above the cornice moulding a decorated elevation is placed with a hewed out family coat of arms. The middle window above the door is framed and contains a sculpted sun and the line, 'Sole Justitia Dirigitur Mola Fortunae', which means: 'The wheel of fortune is moved forward by the sun of right-eousness.'

203 Het Koopmanshuis - The Sales-man House - (1618) in Amsterdam's renaissance style. The house is still mostly in original state. By the middle windows on the top floor it is evident that warehouse trapdoors were here that gave entrance to the warehouse attics. The stepped-gable is of brick with large steps and scroll stones and a broken top pediment. The gable has double pilasters.

206 Pierson & Co bank building (A.L. Van Gendt/1918) in historicism building style. By the use of pilasters, festoons, a balustrade and vases the building looks older than it is.

218-220 Stepped-gables 'Vader' and 'Zoon' - Father and Son - (1616) in Amsterdam's renaissance style. This double house, (nr 220) with side-house (nr 218), has stepped-gables of unequal size. The side-house is joined to the main house in 1920.

☛ 243 De Transvaalsche Boer (1900)

Late 16th century corner house, origi-nally a cigar shop, De Transvaalsche Boer. The small statue of the South-African farmer (wood carver J. Zeits) refers to the Farmers War 1899-1902. The house was renovated in 1900 by architect G.A. van Arkel. Especially the bright green and ochre yellow are eye-catching.

250 Cornice-gable (1740) with a door in Louis XV style the cornice-gable has a decorated elevation.

252 Cornice-gable (1730) with a deco-rated elevation.

257 Pilaster neck-gable (1660) of sandstone. The door section is in Louis XV style (1770).

269 Stepped-gable (1656) in almost original state.

272 Former stepped-gable (1625) in Amsterdam's renaissance with a bell-shaped gable.

274 Elevated cornice-gable 'D' Witte Leli' (1739) in Louis XIV style has

windows and a half-round elevation in the cornice moulding and the image of a lily with the text: 'D' Witte Leli'. Above that is an open sculpted balus-trade with a crest and corner vases.

281-283 Twin neck-gables (1660) in the style of Holland's classicism with decorated scroll stones. The tops have a half-round pediment, the hoist-ing hooks are decorated with flower streamers and underneath sculpted windows on both sides. The gable of nr 283 is still is in original state, in 1987 the gable of nr 281 was restored to its original state.

☛ 284 Huis van Brienen (1728)

Made from sandstone the cornice-gable is in Louis XIV style. The cor-nice moulding has twelve small

Herengracht 243 De Transvaalsche Boer

171

windows with a balustrade above, and a decorated centre section with two corner vases. The middle windows have beautiful window frames. The interior dates from 1728.

308 Dutch gable (1740) in Louis XVI style with a curved cornice pediment and crest. The top centre window is larger than the other windows; there must have been a second warehouse trapdoor here.

309-311 Low Dutch gables (rebuilt/1935) with wide store fronts.

314 Cornice-gable (± 1725) with small decorated scroll stones and a neck/bell-shaped elevation.

320-324 Cornice-gable (J. Duncker/1912) of sandstone in historicism (18th century) style.

329 Neck-gable (1690) 'de Vogelstruys' with a depiction of an ostrich. In the neck a round decorated window with leaf motifs; around that a garland.

331 Dutch gable (1750) has a decorated neck with a vase on top. High stairs with a service entrance and decorated door frame.

334 Stepped-gable (1627) in Amsterdam's renaissance style has on the highest step a top-pilaster, two lion heads and above the round arches two children's heads.

336 Elevated cornice-gable (1627), rebuilt (1745) in Louis XIV style. The elevated cornice mould-ing in the shape of a clock is made of wood with baroque ornaments.

338 Cornice-gable (1740) is made of sandstone with decorated joists and elevation. On the top is a coat of arms shield. The door has a beautiful frame.

342 Cornice-gable (1720) in Louis XIV style. The windows have a unique shape; especially the middle windows are richly decorated. Above the straight cornice moulding a balustrade is added with a vase on the corners and in the middle a closed elevation with a crest and coat of arms.

346 Wide stepped-gable 'De Oranjeappel' (± 1625) in the style of Amsterdam's renaissance.

352 Cornice-gable (1740) of sandstone with a bell-shaped top and a bust.

☞ 361 Stepped-gable De Sonnenberg (1655)

In the style of Amsterdam's renaissance. The under façade is wooden with a lintel. The hoisting trapdoor has two openings for light with a top-pilaster above it. The size of the stepped-gable was typical for 17th century houses.

☞ 364-370 Cromhouthuizen - P. Vingboons/1660

Neck-gables of sandstone in the style of Holland's classicism are commissioned by Jacob Cromhout. The difference in the height of the gables is noticeable. The gables of nr 368-370 are lower than nr 364-366. The gables each have a pediment entablature at the top. Above the windows are fruit motifs, festoons and various year stones. The Bijbels Museum is established in the buildings.

365 Low Dutch gable (± 1750); was a stepped-gable in the 16th century.
367 High Dutch gable (± 1750) has a wooden under façade.
369 Neck-gable (1740) has lean-to building on the Wijde Heisteeg.
374 Cornice-gable (1730) has an elevated cornice moulding and decorated joists.
376 Cornice-gable (± 1740) of sandstone with a bell-shaped elevation and on the top it has vases and statues.
378 Neck-gable (± 1750) has scroll stones and corner vases.

380 NIOD - A. Salm/1890

Is in a combination of neo-styles. The front façade is of sandstone taken from the French renaissance of the 16th century. The house is richly decorated inside and out. In the back in the garden is a coach house annex stable that was built in French-gothic style (very unusual for Amsterdam).

The garden can be reached via a gate and side entrance.

Since 1997 the Netherlands Institute for War Documentation (NIOD) is housed in this building.

☞ 386 Pilaster cornice-gable - P. Vingboons/1663

Is in the style of Holland's classicism with a large pediment entablature with representations of weapons. Under the pediment are composite pilasters. The pilasters underneath are Doric. Between the pilasters are festoons. The door frames and the window frames are 18th century.

388 Pilaster neck-gable (1655) in the style of Holland's classicism. Made from sandstone with decorations in the neck. It has corner vases, decorated scroll stones and a pediment entablature with shell motif.

☞ 390-392 Twin neck-gables - J. Vingboons/1665

Are of sandstone in the style of Holland's classicism. In the scroll stones are shields, figures of men and women. The cord, that is held by the figures in nr 390, is the symbol of the marriage bond. The hoisting trapdoors are decorated with festoons; on the top is a pediment entablature.

Herengracht 388-390-392

394 Dutch gable 'De Vier Heems-kinderen' (1671) is in the style of Holland's classicism. The gable is decorated with flower and fruit motifs and crowned with a half-round pediment. There are festoons around the opening for the hoisting hook and a decoration. The lower part of the gable is decorated with festoons and a gable stone. The portrayal on the gable stone is of the four Heems-kinderen on the horse Beyaert.
On the side of the Leidsegracht there is a lean-to building with a door. The stairs lead to the upstairs houses.
395 Tower has a stepped-gable (W. Vuyk & H. van Rossem/1882) in a combination of neo-styles.
396-398 Neck-gable twins 'de 2 ge-zusters' (1664) with beautiful windows and two lean-to buildings.
399 Cornice-gable (1725) in Louis XIV style with stoop and a lovely door frame.

☞ 402 Neck-gable - J. Vingboons/1665

In Holland's classicism. The stoop in Louis XV style is beautifully sculp-tured, but dates from a later period. Nr 400-408 were built identically by J. Vingboons, but only nr 408 and 402 have been saved. Both houses still have the sculpted scroll stones.
409-411 Twin neck-gables (1670) entrance stoop and basement, dec-orated scroll stones, and a pediment entablature in the top.

☞ 412 Cornice-gable - P. Vingboons/1664

In this cornice-gable in Holland's clas-sicism style there are eight pilasters in the middle section. The lower four are composite pilasters and the upper four are Corinthian pilasters. In the pedi-ment tablature there was an alliance coat of arms.
415 Stepped-gable (1898) in neo-gothic style.
416 Pilaster neck-gable (1667) with decorations and a half-round pediment.

426-428-430 Building (1901) in Jugendstil has a diagonal entrance and a half-round bay window.
427-429 Neck-gable (1715) in Louis XIV style. The scroll stones have a motif of acanthus leaves and flowers.
431 This is the rear-side of the Men-nonite church on Singel 452. The iron fence dates from 1840.
433 Cornice-gable (1725) in Louis XIV style with a coat of arms shield in the decorated elevation.

> ## The Golden Bend
>
> This part of the Herengracht that runs from the Leidsestraat to the Vijzel-straat is also called the Golden Bend. In the golden age the rich ship owners from the East India Company (VOC) had large city palaces built. The gables are almost all in the Louis (XIV, XV, and XVI-) styles.
> Not only in the Golden Bend, but also on the other canals, the stately elegance of the French architecture of the 17th century can easily be recog-nised.

446 Cornice-gable (± 1725) in Louis XIV style. Has a straight cornice moulding and a balustrade with a coat of arms shield decorated with a crown on top in the closed centre section. The lowest floor has a porch with four Doric pilasters in the middle with a balcony above.
450 Cornice-gable Huis van Deutz (P. Vingboons/1663) This straight cornice moulding is built of stone with grooved pointing. The only decoration on this house is the door section with a balcony above.
458 Cornice-gable (1875) in neo-styles is decorated with festoons. There is an elevated half-round pediment with two vases. The en-trance section is lovely with double pavements.
460 Cornice-gable (± 1750) has a straight cornice moulding and eleva-tion. The half-round window on the

first floor is built in the same design as the front door. The stoop fence is in empire style.

462 House Sweedenrijk - A. Dortsman/1671

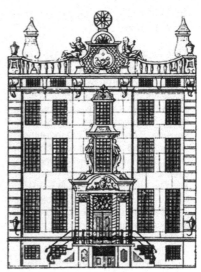

The cornice-gable is in the style of Holland's classicism and is of sand-stone with grooved pointing. The straight cornice moulding has oval windows and above that a balustrade with two statues with in the middle the family coat of arms, cornered by two vases. The door section with statues and pilasters is still original.

466 Cornice-gable De Arend (1858) in historicism style with decorative vases and a pediment entablature.

468 Cornice-gable (1670) has a cornice moulding and a balustrade with four vases.

475 House on the Golden Bend - Huis De Neufville (1731)

This is one of the most beautiful houses on one of the most beautiful spots in Amsterdam. The cornice-gable is

of sandstone in Louis XIV style. Note the decorated centre section. Above the double staircase the door frame is flanked by Corinthian pilasters. The window above has a woman's figure on both sides. The balustrade is richly decorated and has a closed crest with an alliance coat of arms and on both sides the figure of a woman. On the corner of the balustrade are two vases with two decorative chimneys behind them. In 1772 all of the residents of this building were killed in the big fire in the theatre (see Keizersgracht 384).

☛ 476 House de Vicq (1670)

The cornice moulding in the style of Holland's classicism in Louis XIV style has a curved balustrade with the coat of arms of the De Neufville family, which is encircled by statues of Mercury and Venus. Above is a large eagle with decorative vases on both sides.

479 Cornice-gable (1725) in Louis XIV style has a decorated door section and also decorated joists. It has a double stoop with a former service entrance.

480 Cornice-gable (1650) has a double stoop (harp motif) and a decorated door section with Ionic pilasters.

There is a decorated elevation in the top with a vase.

☞ 482 Building De Bazel - K.P.C. Bazel/1926

The building is 100 m wide and has ten floors, of which the top two floors are indented. The lower part of the building is made of the magma stone seyenite. The façades are indented vertically and are made out of various materials. Presently the building is used as city archives.

493 Double house (1766) in Louis XV style with a sandstone gable. The pediment entablature contains the alliance coat of arms. Behind the façade there is a straight cornice moulding with decorative vases. On the roof there are two corner chimneys. The middle windows are decorated and the door section has a beautiful frame. The transom above the door in the Louis XV style is added in 1940.

495 Double house (1725) of sandstone in Louis XIV style, has a decorated elevation with an open balustrade where the family coat of arms and two vases with fruit are placed. The middle window on the first floor is decorated. The wrought iron balcony has the text 'Omnia orta occidunt' that means 'Everything which comes up, must go down'.

497 Double house (1667) with pediment entablature. In this house the museum Kattenkabinet is established. After the cat John Piermont Morgan III died in 1984, a collection of felines was set up here. In the dining room a changing exhibition can be seen.

499 Double house (1667) in Louis XV style has decorated door and window section. There is a double stoop with the former service entrance. Formed twin houses with nr 497.

502 Cornice-gable (1672) in Louis XVI style. The balcony is supported by two pillars. The oval windows on the roof are put in after 1869. The coach house is on Keizersgracht 607. Since 1927 this house is used as the residence of the mayor of Amsterdam.

504 Neck-gable (1650) with animals in the scroll stones and a half-round pediment on the top.

506 Neck-gable (1680) has lion's claws in the scroll stones. The pediment is gone.

507 Double house (1650) has Corinthian pilasters crowned with a pediment entablature. The double stoop has harp shaped railings and a former service entrance.

508-510 Twin neck-gable (1688) is in the style of Holland's classicism. This neck-gable twin has a brick façade and at the top scroll stones depicting sea gods. Above there is a half-round pediment.

527 Cornice-gable (1770) in Louis XVI style. The gable has a crosswise roof with two corner chimneys. The second and third floors have Ionic pilasters and above that a pediment entablature representation of an eagle with spread wings.

This part of the Herengracht originated after the city expansion of 1664. From 1612 the pieces of land were parcelled out in standard sizes. The narrow alleys and compact buildings made way for wider canals and more spacious buildings.

539 Double house (± 1700) In Louis XIV style, is of sandstone with decorated elevation with statues. Double stoop and decorated door section.

543 Double house (± 1680) in Louis

XV style is of sandstone with decorated elevation with family coat of arms. Double stoop and worked door and window section.

548 Double house (± 1750) has decorated elevation and a vase on the corner. Double stoop. The door section is supported by Ionic pilasters with decorated windows above.

554 Double house (± 1650) in Holland's classicism. Is of sandstone with a decorated elevation with statues and two chimneys. It has a double stoop with decorated door and window section. Festoons decorate it.

556 Double house (1740) in Louis XIV style with two chimneys on the roof. Double stoop. Door and window section are decorated.

564 Cornice-gable (± 1725) is of sandstone with a bell-shaped top with two figures of women and on the top a vase. The hoisting hook is decorated with a festoon.

565 Neck-gable (± 1690) with vases in the scroll stones and a half-round pediment on the top.

567 Cornice-gable (± 1720) in Louis XIV style. Is of sandstone with a bell-shaped elevation with three vases.

568-570 Neck-gable twins (± 1725) have animal figures in the scroll stones. Two high stoops are placed sideways with the former service entrance.

571-581 These houses (1664-1667) are almost identical. The sale of the land parcels in 1664 was only

possible under specific architectural conditions: height, construction under one cornice, and identical windows. The pediment entablature was added to nr 571 in 1800.

Nr 573 is built for Mayor Cornelis de Graeff. Nr 579 has festoons at the entrance and a statue of the Archangel Michael, who caught a dragon. They rest on the head of an elephant. The elephant's head is the trademark of the cake bakers and refers to the first owner of the building, a rich cake baker.

580 Cornice-gable (± 1670) in Louis XVI style. With a closed elevation has decorated doors and window section. It has a double stoop with a former service entrance.

592 Mansion (1670) with a richly decorated bell-shaped elevation. The former service entrance is under the high stoop.

☞ 605 Museum Willet - Holthuysen (1687)

The house is renovated in 1739 in Louis XIV style. The cornice-gable has a sideways roof with two dormer windows and two corner chimneys as well as a sculpted door and window frames. The house is open to the public because Mrs. Willet declared in her will (1895) that to the city could inherit the house under the condition that it became a museum. The interior dates from 1739 and 1865.

607 Dutch gable (± 1670) in the style of Holland's classicism with a pediment entablature on top. On both sides there are triangular attic windows. The neck is decorated. The hoisting hook is decorated with festoons and a date ribbon.

609-611 Combined houses (± 1740) in Louis XV style with an elevation of sandstone. The doorframe is also of sandstone.

615-617 Combined houses (1767) crowned with a pediment entablature.

Keizersgracht

The canal is excavated in 1612 and named after the German Emperor Maximilian I, who borrowed more than 10,000 Flemish pounds from the city council of Amsterdam to pay for his struggle against the rebellious Flemish in1488. In the 17th century many of the rich ship owners established themselves along the Keizersgracht.

Keizersgracht 176 (1904)

5 Neck-gable (1725) with decorated scroll stones and hoisting hook.

12 Neck-gable (± 1725) with baroque decorations around the hoisting hook and in the scroll stones.

16 Neck-gable 'd Nootenboom' (1743) in Louis XIV style. Is in almost original condition. The scroll stones and crane are decorated. Under the high stoop is the former service entrance.

19 Dutch gable (± 1750) with decoration around the hoisting hook, half-round pediment with the family coat of arms, and a stoop.

22 De Zaaier of St. Ignatiuskerk (J. van Straaten/1837). The upper part of pediment, decorated cornice and tower are lost from this neo-classicism church. On this spot there was a hidden church of the order of Jesuits who were predominately visited by the poor parishioners from the Jordaan.

24 Warehouse De Jonge Moor (± 1750) with a cornice-gable and cornice moulding. The ground floor served as coach house.

29 Neck-gable (1692) with a date in the half-round pediment. The scroll stones have the family coat of arms of Jan Trip and his wife M.C. Nijs.

31 Former stepped-gable (1628), since the end of the 18th century converted to a cornice-gable. In 1911 story was built on top. Above the cornice moulding windows are made. The doorframe dates from beginning of the 19th century. The stoop dates from the beginning and has carved stone steps.

☞ **40-42-44 De Groenlandse Pakhuizen (1621)**

De Groenlandse Pakhuizen

The warehouse trapdoors are coupled vertically. Next to the attic trapdoors on all of the three warehouses are two little windows. The hoisting hooks are broad and have a little roof. The warehouses were commissioned to be built by the Norwegian or Greenlandic Whaling Company.

Until 1685 the whale fish liver oil (100,000 liter) was stored in sixty pits made of masonry on the ground floor. The attics were used to store the other parts of the whales. The whales were caught in the sea around Greenland. In 1819 the whaling stopped in Amsterdam.

50 Dutch gable 'Het Mededogen' (1622) with a gable stone.

60 Elevated cornice-gable (± 1750) with decorated joists.

62 Neck-gable (± 1667) in the style of Holland's classicism. The neck-gable has a half-round pediment. The scroll stones are decorated with fruit motifs. On both corners there are vases. The gable has two pilasters running through.

64 Former stepped-gable (1619) was renovated in (1738) into a neck-gable in Louis XIV style. At the time of the renovation in 1738 the house was enlarged with two floors. This made it the highest merchants' house in Amsterdam. The top is decorated with sculpture work, in the scroll stones there are figures of children.

68 Dutch gable (± 1775) with crest in the style of Louis XV.

71 Wide cornice-gable (± 1740) with decorations dating from around 1850.

77 Cornice-gable (± 1755) with straight cornice moulding in Louis XV style. The cornice moulding has four carved joists with a balustrade above. In the middle of the balustrade there is a raised closed centrepiece with coats of arms and a crest.

84 is rebuilt in 1934. The 18th century top of sandstone with decorations of the neck-gable come from a demolished building on the Zeedijk 9.

86 House (± 1880) in eclecticism style with many decorations, including the four lion heads on the ground floor.

88 Neck-gable (1718) portrays The Three Kings in the pediment.

95/corner Herenstraat 40 Dutch gable (1686). In the Herenstraat the gable is crowned with a half-round pediment and decorated with fruit motifs. Next to the attic window are two small sculpted oval windows. The wooden under façade has a diagonal entrance. On the Keizersgracht there is a lean-to building.

101 Cornice-gable (± 1715) has a wide closed cornice moulding. The middle section is semi-circled and has a statue. On the corners are the mythological figures of Neptune and Aphrodite. Under the crane are illustrations of a cat on a plate and the head of John the Baptist.

102 Former Remonstrant's church De Rode Hoed (1630). This is presently a

Keizersgracht 123 (1622)

cultural centre. At the time of the restoration in the 1980s the organ (1719) was preserved.

104 Dutch gable (± 1675). The gable top dates from the 19th century. The story has pilasters that carry the relief arches.
In the 17th century gable stone there is the illustration of a red hat. This hat refers to a milliner who was established here before 1630. The hat was originally placed in the gables of nr 102-104-106.

105 Cornice-gable D' Bruynvis (1763)

In the style of Louis XV. The door has a beautiful frame and the windows are decorated. Above the cornice moulding is a balustrade with decorative vases.In the middle there is a representation of a brown whale.
In 1940-1942, Keizersgracht 103 was added to nr 105. Originally the gable that was originally three windows wide, is enlarged to five windows.

107 Cornice-gable (± 1760), renovated in 1933 for the broadcasting association AVRO.

108 Elevated cornice-gable (± 1750) with two decorated joists and a decorated hoisting hook.

110 Dutch gable (1759) in Louis XV style with a crest on the top.

111 Elevated cornice-gable (± 1750) of sandstone with a decorated joists and a decorated window above the front door.

112 Cornice-gable (± 1745) with a crest in the cornice moulding in the shape of a clock. There is also an alliance coat of arms and a double eagle in the moulding.

115 Cornice-gable (± 1750), renovated in 1895.

117 Former stepped-gable (1618) in the Amsterdam's renaissance style, renovated in about 1750 into a cornice-gable with a bell-shape on the top.

119 Elevated cornice-gable (± 1740) has decorated joists and a vase on the top.

121 Cornice-gable 'De Sterre' (1618). The entrance dates from the 18th century. The window above the door has decorative wrought iron. The arch above the door is carried by two Ionic columns. In 1633 Agneta Deutz was born here. She later founded the courtyard facility on the 855-899 Prinsengracht.

☞ 123 Huis met de Hoofden -The House with the Heads- (P. de Keyser/1622)

The stepped-gable in the style of Amsterdam's baroque is richly ornamented with busts, lion masks, obelisks, scroll stones and date stones and a broken half-round pediment. On the first floor the wall pillars are disguised as wide Doric pilasters, above that there are double pilasters. On both sides of the stepped-gable are balustrades. This makes the house look larger. The door section has a low double stoop with 17th century railings. Behind the gate (right) is a passage that leads to the coach house. Above the gate is the room of the coachman. This is one of the three houses in Amsterdam with a side-house, a forerunner of the double house. The name of this house refers to the six busts: Apollo with laurel wreath (arts), Ceres with ripe sheaves (agriculture), Mars with helmet (war), Minerva (wisdom), Bacchus with grapes (wine), and Diana with half moon (hunting). According to the legend the maid chopped off the heads of six thieves.

124-128 Het Wapen van Benscop (± 1750) with decorated joists, doorframe, and window of the first floor.

127 Wide cornice-gable (± 1725) with decorated joists and Ionic pilasters beside the door.

133 Wide stepped-gable (1620) in the sober Amsterdam's renaissance style. The gable is four windows wide and has wide steps with sandstone scroll stones. There is a pediment entablature.

135 Cornice-gable (± 1750) with decorated joists and on the top an eye-catching crest.

137-139 Cornice-gable twins (1738). The cornice-gables have a circle-shaped elevation with a decorated clock.

141 Stepped-gable 'De Dubbele Arend' (1620) in the style of Amsterdam's renaissance. The façade is of painted brick with decorations of mountain stone. The stepped-gable has beautifully decorated steps. The reconstruction of the top in 1878 was not carried out in style. The house is so broad that an extra wall pillar had to be added in the middle. The first owner was a member of the family Hasselaer. They had a beer brewery in the Hasselaersteeg by the name of The Double Eagle. The house is named after the brewery.

149 Cornice-gable (± 1750) with a statue of 'D' Koning van Zweden' (the king of Sweden). This statue used to be on the gate of the 17th century building that stood here.

150 Neck-gable (± 1730) has decorated scroll stones and a half-round pediment.

158 Elevated cornice-gable 'In de stadt van Rissel' (1721) in Louis XIV style with a decorated top.

161 The blue sign with a double 'L' is a district's sign from the period 1852-1875. Then the city was divided into fifty districts and this kind of sign marked the areas.

170 Stepped-gable (1620) in Amsterdam's renaissance style. This house is often renovated.

172 The house (± 1750) has a lean-to building on the Keizersgracht. The wooden under façade continues over to the side façade.

175 Cornice-gable (± 1715) in Louis XIV style with raised cornice moulding and an open balustrade. In the middle of the balustrade the hoisting hook and coat of arms are installed. On both sides are decorative vases. Since 1933 this house is part of nr 177. The entrance was moved to street level and the stoops were removed.

☞ 176 Eerste Hollandsche Levensverzekering Bank - G.A. van Arkel/1904

(First Dutch Life-insurance Bank). The building in Jugendstil has a front façade of stone. There are decorations next to the entrance. In the mosaic on the Keizersgracht and under the bay window we see scenes of a dying woman while showing her child her life-insurance policy. The tower on the corner has two dome-like roofs with on top of that a high spire that is open on the rear side. The domes are connected by a nameplate with wrought iron art nouveau letters (EHLB) Eerste Hollandsche Levensverzekerings Bank.

☞ 177 House Coymans - J. van Campen/1625

The house is built in the style of Holland's classicism, and is the only dwelling in Amsterdam that is built by Jacob van Campen. The commissioners were the Coyman brothers. Behind the cornice-gable there are two identical houses. On the first floor Ionic pilasters are used and on the second floor Roman composite pilasters. The gable is twice as wide than it is high. The middle section juts forward slightly and is half the breadth of the gable. From construction date these houses have their entrance at

street level, there is no basement and also no warehouse attic. In the 19th century the attic is raised.
Since 1868 the house is used as a school.
178 Neck-gable (1620) in Louis XIV style with decorated scroll stones and door section.
190 Cornice-gable (± 1720) in Louis XIV style. Of sandstone with decorated joists in the top, a coat of arms, helmet, and two men's heads.
192 Cornice (± 1750) in Louis XIV style. With decorations around the attic trapdoor and a bell-shaped cornice moulding with a crest.
194 Cornice-gable (± 1750) in Louis

XV style. With decorations around the attic trapdoor and a bell-shaped top with crest.
196 Cornice-gable (± 1740) in Louis XIV style. Of sandstone with bell-shaped top and two corner vases.
199-197 These buildings (1898) are part of the shopping arcade on the Raadhuisstraat. On the corner the building has a small tower.
203 Double house (1734) has a shared gable, seven windows wide. Under both hoisting hooks there is an empty coat-of-arms shield. Above the cornice moulding there is a closed elevation. The frame of the door dates from the time of building.

Westerkerk (1620)

The design is by the city architect Hendrick de Keyser in a cruciform basilica with two transepts. The top gables of the transepts have pediment entablatures, round arch niches, and oval openings. It took from 1620 until 1630 to build the church. While the building was in progress Hendrick de Keyser died on May 15, 1621. His son Pieter de Keyser continued the build.
The church is 5858 metres long, 29 metres wide and 29 metres high, and has 36 windows. The 85 metre-high tower (1638) is not according to the original plans of Hendrick de Keyser. The Westertoren is the highest tower in Amsterdam and consists of square segments stacked above each other in classicism style with balustrades. On the corners are vases and spheres. The tower is crowned with the emperor's crown. There are 49 bells in the belfry including the 7,500 kilogram heavy bell that strikes on the whole hour, dating from 1636.

Interior: the main organ (1686) is built by Roelof Barentz. Duyschot and has magnificent organ shut-ters painted by Gerard de Lairesse. The pulpit and the richly carved inner portals date from about 1630. The original brass chandeliers were sold in 1830. The present, lovely examples are replicas that replace the 19th century gas chandeliers. In 1906 a memorial stone for Rembrandt van Rijn was installed. Supposedly Rembrandt was buried on October 8, 1669 in the Westerkerk, but nobody knows in which spot.

It is possible to climb the tower with a guide from April - October.
Open: Mon-Sat 10AM-5:30PM

Between 203 en 205 Small coach house (± 1750). This belonged to a building on the Herengracht.
The building was demolished for the widening of the Raadhuistraat.
208 Dutch gable (± 1750) in the style of Amsterdam's renaissance. In 1750 the stepped-gable from 1652 was changed into the present Dutch gable.
209 Cornice-gable 'De Hoop' (1743) in Louis XIV style. Above the cornice moulding there is a broken pediment with an open balustrade on both sides and a decorative vase on the corners. In the pediment the symbol of the hope is depicted: the figure of a woman with an anchor in her hand. The gable is decorated with blocked corner pilasters.
214 Raised pilaster neck-gable (1656) with a decorated date stone and a half-round pediment.
218 The Redemptorist Monastery (1850).
220 De Redemptoristenkerk - (Th. Molkenboer/1852).
The Redemptorist church (also called Our Lady of the Immaculate Heart). The neo-gothic church has no towers. Beside a high nave, lower side aisles were built. The façade is of brick with parts of stone. The pointed arch portal is of stone. The gable tops of the nave and aisles are decorated with tracery. Five earlier buildings in this spot were all destroyed by fire.
Presently the Syrian-Orthodox church and the Roman Catholic Surinam fellowship hold their services in this church.
221 Cornice-gable (1747) in Louis XIV style. Of sandstone with decorated elevation and family coat of arms in the cornice moulding. Note the two chimneys
225 Cornice-gable 'De Kooper Moole' (1746) in Louis XIV style. The door frame has composite pilasters and a curved pediment with crest. In the pediment stands 'De Kooper Molen 1746'.
In the top part of the pilasters are the coat of arms and initials of the first

owner and his wife.
239 Cornice-gable 'De Zon' (± 1740). In the elevation above the cornice moulding we see a sunburst.
240 Graceful Dutch gable (± 1750) in Louis XV style with asymmetric decorations.

☞ 244-246 Twin cornice-gable(± 1730)

In Louis XIV style. This is one of the most beautiful twin cornice mouldings in Amsterdam.
The cornice moulding has windows, decorated joists and an attic trapdoor. Above that is a richly decorated elevation with an open balustrade, hoisting hook and a decorative vase at the top. The door framing dates from the time of building.
247 Dutch gable (± 1760) with a bust on top. It probably represents Prince Maurits and the bust comes from the building that was there earlier. It was returned in the 18th century. The scroll stones are decorated.

248 Cornice-gable (± 1710) in Louis XIV style with a closed balustrade above the cornice. In the cornice there are two coat-of-arms shields with the date underneath in Roman numerals.

260 Cornice-gable (± 1750) with bell-shaped wooden cornice moulding with crest.

263 Cornice-gable (± 1735) with an elevated half-round cornice moulding. The family coat of arms is under the decorated hoisting hook. The top and corners are completed with a decorative vase.

265 Cornice-gable (± 1740) in Louis XIV style with decorated joists and a closed cornice moulding.

284 Elevated cornice-gable (± 1765) in Louis XV style. The cornice moulding has decorated joists. There are windows in the cornice moulding and an attic trapdoor. Above that is an elevation with a curved balustrade with a crest on top. Figures of children seal the corners.

292-294 Neck-gable twins (± 1730) with decorated scroll stones and hoisting hooks, half-round pediments and four corner vases.

316 Building William Koch (1935) in historicism style. On the Keizersgracht we see the side façade and the stairs with the entrance to the basement underneath. The windows get smaller towards the top. The front side is on Berenstraat with a stepped-gable. The building looks older than it really is.

317 Cornice-gable (± 1713). The façade is brick and has a decorated joist that supports the cornice moulding. The cornice moulding has a sandstone decorated elevation that is semi-circular in the middle. The ornaments are attributes from trade, water nymphs, and four vases in the middle.

The commissioner for this renovation in approximately 1713 was C. Brandts. He spent a great deal of his life in Russia and was friends with Tsar Peter the Great. In 1716 Peter the Great came to visit him in this house.

☞ 319 Elevated neck-gable - Ph. Vingboons/1639

This house of sandstone, is built in the style of Holland's classicism and is the first small house where Ph. Vingboons used a pilaster gable. On the bottom floor he used Tuscan pilasters and on the two floors above Doric pilasters were used. On the outside sections the pilasters are connected by cornice mouldings. Above the windows on the second floor there are pediment entablatures. The middle section is left free to make hoisting easier. On both sides of the attic trapdoor there are oval windows with sculpted frames. The hoisting hook is decorated with a festoon. The neck has four scroll stones, corner vases, and a pediment entablature.

322 Dutch gable (± 1750) in Louis XV-style. The doors date from the construction date and have exquisite woodcarvings. The Dutch gable is decorated with a curved cornice cap.

☞ 324 Felix Meritis - J. Otten Husly/1787

The building is built for meetings of the cultural society Felix Meritis (Success through Merit). It is built in classicism Louis XIV style. Note the Corinthian half-columns, the richly decorated pediment entablature and the cornice-gable with the partial open balustrade. The entrance is accentuated by large festoons. The halls were designed for concerts and cultural gatherings. These cultural meetings ended in 1888. The building was sold to a printing business and the interior was almost completely removed. A great fire destroyed a great deal of the front façade in 1932. The building was bought by the Communist Party in the Netherlands (CPN) in 1946. Both the interior as well as the exterior was restored.
In the 1970s Felix Meritis became a cultural centre again. In 1998 the building was restored.
328 Spout-gable (1914) in historicism style.
365-367 Cornice-gable (± 1725) with a special entrance. It is a gate from a hotel on the Oudezijds Voorburgwal. The gate has the name of that hotel, "s Heeren Logement', with above it a pediment entablature with two lions and the emperor's crown.
384 Gateway to the former theatre (J. van Campen/1637)

On this spot in 1617 in a wooden building the first theatre in Amsterdam was opened. This was replaced in 1638 by a stone building. The building was destroyed by fire on May 11, 1772. The new theatre was built on the Leidseplein. The stone gateway (1637) survived the fire and has three arches with fencing. The pilasters with Ionic capitals carry the pediment entablature. In the courtyard behind the gate are statues of three Dutch poets: Pieter Cornelisz. Hooft, Joost van den Vondel and Samuel Coster. The theatre was founded after an idea from Coster.A charity organisation, the Roman Catholic Oude-Armenkantoor, (1772) was built where the theatre was.

☞ 387 'De Vergulde Ster' - J. Vingboons/1668

Elevated neck-gable in the style of Holland's classicism. Festoons are placed around the hoisting hook and above the windows of the first and third floors. Under the scroll stones are two oval windows with sculpted frames. The windows on the second floor are decorated with half-round pediments. The hoisting trapdoor has a date stone underneath and a pediment entablature above. The neck-gable is crowned with a half-round pediment. On the left side of the house is a gate that is decorated with a gable stone depicting a star.

396 House (1897) with a wooden peaked roof.

401 Huis 'Marseille' - Ph. Vingboons/1665

Elevated neck-gable in the style of Holland's classicism.
Figures of children are sculpted in the scroll stones. Under the scroll stones are two oval windows with sculpted frames. The first floor has Doric pilasters and the second and third floors have Ionic pilasters. In the neck Corinthian pilasters are used. The cornices between the floors are interrupted at the centre section. This is probably to prevent goods from being damaged during hoisting. There are festoons above the windows on the second floor. The top is crowned with a half-

round pediment in shell motif. Above the under façade there is a gable stone with the name of the house and a relief of the city of Marseille. The first owner was a merchant with trading interests in Marseille. The warehouse Maarseveen next door (nr 403) originally belonged to this house.
Huis Marseille has a beautiful interior and is open to the public.

441 Neck-gable (1684) decorated with festoons and on the top a half-round pediment.

442 Cornice-gable (± 1740) of sandstone with a closed cornice moulding and two vases on the top. The windows and door are decorated.

444-446 Combined cornice-gables (± 1730) in Louis XV style with closed straight cornice moulding and crest (nr 446).

452 Wide cornice-gable 'Het huis van bankier Fuld' - The house of banker Fuld - (1650), is renovated in eclecticism style in 1860. It has many decorations and two chimneys.

453 Elevated neck-gable (1669) there is a festoon around the hoisting hook. The scroll stones are decorated and the top is crowned with a half-round pediment.

455 The building is commissioned by the New York Life Insurance Company. The American eagles and the letters N and Y refer to the American client. The gable is richly decorated with entablatures and half-round pediments. On the corner there is a tower with a clock. Metz & Co bought the building in 1908. In 1918 the whole building is remodelled into a department store. The glass pavilion on the roof dates from 1933 and is designed by Gerrit Rietveld, the famous Dutch designer. Especially lovely is the 19th century stairwell that is still completely intact. Since 2012, the fashion store Abercombe & Fitch is located in this historical building.

465 Neck-gable (± 1675), decorated with festoons and in the top a half-round pediment.

486-488 Neck-gable twins (1686)

with a gateway between the two houses. The gateway is decorated with a gable stone. Both gables have decorated oval windows next to the attic window and corner vases. The scroll stones are decorated and there is a half-round pediment with shell motif at the top. On nr 488 the festoon around the hoisting hook is still there and a date ribbon adorns the gable.

493 Double warehouse Indië (A.N. Godefroy/1860). There are not many double warehouses in Amsterdam. The name is in the cornice.
There are decorative wall anchors.

503-505 Neck-gable twins (± 1675) with on the top half-round pediments with shell motif. Until 1825, number 501 formed triplets with nr 503 and 505.

504-506 Neck-gable twins (1671). The hoisting hooks are decorated with festoons. There is a pediment entablature at the top. Nr 506 has a store front from 1896 and nr 504 still has the original stoop in front of the entrance.

524 Cornice-gable 'Het Geloof' (1758), with straight cornice moulding and decorated joists and windows. The figure that depicted 'Faith', is lost. Together with nr 526 'Hope' and 528 'Love', these houses formed triplets.

529 Cornice-gable (± 1760). John Adams lived here between 1781-1782. He was the first American ambassador of the USA in the Netherlands and later the second president of the United States of America.

535-537 Low neck-gable twins (± 1700) with two stoops placed crosswise.

546 Dutch gable (± 1760) in Louis XV style with a half-round pediment with a large crest. The decorations on the pediment run around to the hoisting hook. The scroll stones are also decorated in Louis XV style. Under the hoisting hook are still two original hoisting trapdoors; both the attic as well as the third floor served as a warehouse attic. This house used to be one of triplets (± 1675) with nr

544 and 548. But this house was completely remodelled around 1760 and given a Dutch gable.

555 Office building (J.B. Posthumus Meyes/1917). Is in historicism style. The house looks older than it is. Note the pediment entablature with depiction and the two large chimneys.

558-560 Combined cornice-gables (± 1700). The memorial stone is a reminder of the fact that the writer/lawyer Jacob van Lennep lived here from 1830 until his death in 1868. Jacob van Lennep is responsible for the first tap water here that was filtered through the sand dunes. The poor no longer had to drink the contaminated salt water from the canals. Van Lennep got the nick-name 'Mozes van de Woestduin' (Moses from the wild dune).

565-567 Cornice-gable (± 1680) with a coach house next to the steps.

566 Protestants Keizersgracht Church (gebr. Salm/1888) in neo-gothic style. The church is restored in 1958.

573-575 Building Nederlandsch Indische Escompto Maatschappij (J.A. Van Straaten/1909). Cornice-gable (± 1750) with many decorations, Corinthian pilasters and a pediment entablature.

587-589 'De Bazel' (K.P.C. Bazel/1919) (see page 176).

596 Cornice-gable (± 1740) in Louis XIV style. With a straight cornice moulding with above that a closed decorated elevation. The emphasis lies on the protruding centre section.

Keizersgracht 548-546-544

The door has lanterns on both sides. The double stoop has decorated fence work (± 1800). There are four large windows on the Nieuwe Spiegelstraat.

604 Cornice-gable 'Int Derde Vredejaer' (1670). This double mansionin the style of Hollands classicism is only three windows wide. The straight cornice moulding has a decorated elevation of brick with an inscription of the house name. The name refers to the year of the building, which was the third year after the Second English War. (1665-1667). The trapdoor to the warehouse attic is disguised in the gable.

606-608 Neck-gable twins (± 1730) in Louis XIV style. These are the largest neck-gable twins in Amsterdam. There are decorations around the hoisting hooks and crests at the top.

607 Coach house (1672). This is the coach house of 502 Herengracht. The building is almost 15 metres wide. It has three dormer windows and three hoisting hooks. On the top floor goods were stored.

609 Sandstone cornice-gable (C. Outhoorn/1862) with a straight cornice moulding in eclecticism style. Before 1861 this building used to be a warehouse/stable with the name 'De Spook' (The Ghost).

611-613 Neck-gable twins (1716) in sober Louis XIV style. The scroll stones were freely obtainable in the trade, the so-called trades scroll stones. In these houses the first city museum of Amsterdam was established since 1863. The owner C.J. Fodor was an art collector and he gave his collection to the city of Amsterdam after his death. He stipulated that the buildings on the Keizersgracht had to be turned into a museum. Now the Fodor Foto Museum is established in these buildings.

615 Neck-gable (± 1715) in Louis XIV style with a curved cornice top pediment. The hoisting hook has a decorative framing. On the scroll stones Arion is sitting on dolphins with

a lyre and Triton with a horn.

617-629 Office building (P.J.S. Pieters/1912) in historicism style. The entrance door has a front stoop with on either side an elephant's head. The side wings each have two pilasters.

634-646 Neck-gable (± 1700). Together with nr 644, 646, and 648 these houses had eight almost identical neck-gables.

649 Neck-gable (± 1690) with decorated scroll stones, corner vases and next to the attic window two oval windows framed with sculpture work.

660 Building (1927) in the style of the Amsterdam's School. It has round bay windows on the corner.

661/corner Reguliersgracht Cornice-gable (± 1690). There are festoons on the front gable. The houses have a straight cornice and a sideways roof.

Corner Reguliersgracht 39

This shop/dwelling (± 1690) has a Dutch gable. There is a lean-to building on the side of the Keizersgracht. Because of its beautiful setting, this is one of the most photographed gables in Amsterdam.

664 Cornice-gable (± 1755) in Louis XV style. The elevated cornice has decorated joists with a semi-circular elevation containing a half-round window. The door dates from the time of the building.

666-668 Cornice-gable 'Zeerust' (C.B.P. Posthumus Meyes/1937) in historicism style. The date of building is on the gate work of the balcony.

☞ 672-674 Van Raey Huizen - A. Dortsman/1671

Twin cornice-gable is in the style of Holland's classicism. The façades are built of horizontally grooved sandstone. The doors are framed with pilasters. On the right cornice moulding there is a balustrade where the closed centre section curves in and contains the date. The whole is completed with statues of Ceres and Minerva (nr 672) and Mars and Vulcanus (nr 674). The two double stoops date from the 18th century and replaced the head-on stoops. The painter Ferdinand Bol lived at nr 672 until 1680. He rented the house from the owner Van Raey, who lived at nr 674. Presently the Museum Van Loon is situated at nr 672. The interior is worth seeing. The show-gable of the coach house is still in the garden (Kerkstraat 261).

676 Waalse kerk - Walloon church - (A.N. Godefroy/1855), built of sandstone in eclecticism style. In 1861 the church is rebuilt in a different style after being damaged by fire.

695 Neck-gable (± 1690). This neck-gable has decorations around the hoisting hook and the sandstone scroll stones contain figures.

707-709 Corner building (1905) in art nouveau style with round bays and a small tower.

708 Dutch gable (± 1670) in Holland's classicism with decorative bunches on the sides and a pediment entablature on the top. The bird on top of the pediment is of later date. Next to the attic window are two smaller windows.

713-715 Office building (C.B.P. Posthumus Meyes/1905) in historicism style. By using stepped-gables the building looks much older.

716 Dutch gable (1671). This plain Dutch gable is possibly one of the first Dutch gables in Amsterdam. The high wooden store front dates from the 18th century. The living quarters can be reached via stairs above the lean-to building on the Reguliersgracht. There is also a sculpted oval window.

Keizersgracht 672-674 (167

727 Neck-gable (1697). Together with nr 725 and 723 forms neck-gable triplets.

730-732-734 Cornice-gable - A. Dortsman/1671

This house is in the style of Holland's classicism of sandstone. The emphasis is put on the middle house by the double stoop, the decorated doorframe, and the decoration of the window on the first floor. There is a balustrade above the cornice moulding.

743 Wide cornice-gable (± 1670) with a double stoop and a basement.

750-752-754 Cornice-gable/neck-gables (± 1680). Originally these were neck-gable triplets. Around 1800 nr 754 was changed into a cornice-gable

755 Former coach house (± 1700). In 1906 a lot was changed during a renovation.

756 Cornice-gable (1738) in Louis XIV style. The straight cornice moulding contains two windows. The top has a balustrade that is open on either side and closed in the middle. Note the decorated cornice moulding and the crest. The fencing on the stoop is decorated. The doorframe is sculpted.

757 Double house (± 1670) with a pediment entablature above the cornice with a window and a statue on both sides.

759-761-763 Neck-gable triplets (1704).

766 Bakery/dwelling (G. van Arkel/ 1894) in Jugendstil. Above the door the first and second floors have decorated balconies. The third floor has a tower that is supported by a stone socle that is decorated with a sun. The top of the tower is exuberantly decorated. The left side has a bay window extension on the first and second floors and on the third floor there is a balcony. The building is a national monument and was restored in 1960.

778-786 Neck-gable quintuplets (1688) with half-round pediment tops with shell motifs. The scroll stones are richly decorated. Nr 782, 780, and 778 retained their decorative vases. Only nr 780 still has the original entrance with stoop.

818 Dutch gable (1672) with a top pediment entablature. The hoisting hook and trapdoor have festoons around them. On both sides of the attic window are two small oval windows.

822 Dutch gable (1672) with a half-round pediment. The hoisting hook and trapdoor are decorated with festoons. Next to the attic window are two decorated oval windows. Under the windows of the third floor are festoons.

Keizersgracht - Leidsegracht arched bridge

Prinsengracht

The canal is designed in 1609 and finished in 1612 and named after Prince William of Orange (William the Silent 1533-1584), the national hero who resisted the Spanish rule in the Netherlands. The Prinsengracht is the longest of the four main canals. Along the quay are many houses and warehouses. There are many houseboats moored on the canal.

Prinsengracht 2 (1641)

2 Stepped-gable (1641)

In sober Amsterdam's renaissance style. There is a head of a girl on the top pilaster above the attic trapdoor. The gable has a stone with the date 1642.

On the Prinsengracht the upper floors are supported by protruding beams. The under façade is of wood and is hardly changed. The stoop is incorporated in the lean-to building.

In the basement remains can still be seen of the escape tunnel from the Roman Catholic hidden church on the other side (7 Prinsengracht).

4 Narrow Dutch gable (± 1775) in Louis XV style. On the middle of the gable we can see that this was originally a stepped gable from 1655 in sober Amsterdam's renaissance style. It is one of the narrowest houses in Amsterdam.

7 Dutch gable (± 1750) with a postal horn in the doorframe. This refers to the rich history of the building. Until 1687 this was where the horses were stabled for the ferry barge service to Haarlem. In 1687 the stables were rebuilt into a hidden church and the postal house became the parsonage.

In 1863 the Augustine parish moved to the newly built Post Horn church on the Haarlemmerstraat.

8 Neck-gable (± 1660) with richly decorated scroll stones and a half-round pediment with shell motif. Under the attic trapdoor there are two horns of plenty. Next to the attic window are two sculpted oval windows. Under the attic window is a representation of a cloth with three rings.

10 Two elevated neck-gables (± 1660). In Holland's classicism.

14 Cornice-gable (± 1760). The cornice moulding is made of wood and has two attic windows and two hoisting hooks. The house is four windows wide (normally a cornice moulding is only two or three windows wide).

Noorderkerk 1620)

This Reformed Church was the first church to be built for the protestant worship service in Amsterdam and is in the style of Holland's renaissance.

The church is octagonal (Greek cross) with four equal aisles. The small wooden tower has an open cupola.

Note the typical renaissance expressions like the pediment, the scroll stones, the decorative vases and the tops of the gables with balustrades.

The church is restored between 1993 and 1998.

1 Stepped-gable (1620) in sober Amsterdam's renaissance style has a wooden under façade.

9 Dutch gable (1747) in Louis XIV style.

15 Neck-gable (1701) in Louis XIV style with scissors and a plane in the pediment.

16 Neck-gable 'Fortuin' (1726) in Louis XIV style. The gable stone depicts Fortuna and attributes from the woollen cloth industry.

17 Dutch gable (1765) in Louis XV style with an Easter ox in the crest.

18 Neck-gable (1718) with the date 1718 and a hen in the top.

19 Neck-gable 'Het Witte Lam' (1736) has a lam in the half-round pediment.

20 Neck-gable (± 1720).

21 Neck-gable De Rotterdamse Schuyf (± 1720).

22 Neck-gable (± 1650) with pilasters and a pediment entablature.

25 Neck-gable (± 1740) in Louis XIV style, has Corinthian pilasters and scroll stones with a diamond motif. The top is finished with ornaments.

27 Neck-gable (±1740) in Louis XIV style. With decorations around the hoisting hook, on the scroll stones and at the top.

36 Elevated neck-gable 'De Veersack' (1650) in Holland's classicism has a pediment entablature on the top. The gable has four Ionic pilasters, a date ribbon and a gable stone. On the gable stone there is a bag full of feathers. Under the attic trapdoor there is a festoon. The scroll stones have fruit motifs. Under the scroll stones are decorated oval windows. It is possible to see that there was once a store downstairs because the under façade is made of wood.

84 Dutch gable (1658) in Louis XIV style with festoons and a gable stone with the date. There is a high wooden under façade with basement.

86 Dutch gable (± 1650) with a high wooden under façade. In the 19th century the Dutch gable is made more sober.

☞ 89-133 Van Brienens Gesticht 'De Star' - A. van der Hart/1804

This courtyard almshouse was built at the place where the beer brewery De Star once was. The date is under the clock.

In the middle building the Roman Catholic chapel and the regents' room were situated. On three sides of the courtyard are the houses for Roman Catholics. The regime of the alms-house was strict. There is a pump and a lantern in the middle of the courtyard.

Open: Mon-Fri 6 AM-6PM, Sat 6 AM-2PM, Closed Sunday. Free entry.

92 Elevated neck-gable (1661). The neck has two Ionic pilasters and two oval-shaped sculpted windows. Under that are two Tuscan pilasters running down two floors. The top is crowned wit a half-round pediment.

94 Neck-gable (± 1680). In the neck there are two sculpted oval windows and on the top a pediment entabla-ture. The under-façade is wooden.

106 Dutch gable (± 1680) with a high wooden under-façade and a rotated stoop.

126 Cornice-gable (1775) in Louis XV style has windows in the cornice moulding, decorated joists and decorations around the attic trapdoor. Above the cornice moulding is a bell-shaped elevation. The wooden deco-ration is carved in the shape of a man's head. There are vases on the corners.

135 Dutch gable (1772) has a Jacob's staff in the top.

155 Warehouse (1700) has a spout-gable and a half-round pediment.

159-171 Zonshofje (1764)

The courtyard is built at the place where the small church building De Zon (1671) of the Mennonite congregation stood. Later this church was used by the Frisian Mennonites and was called Noah's ark. In the courtyard a gable stone is placed showing that the Sun shines on Noah's ark. At the time of its opening in 1764 the Sun's Almshouse was very progressive. The little houses were 'built respectably and hygienically', had modern sanitary fittings and were occupied by Mennonite ladies of fifty years or older.

The courtyard is open to the public and worth visiting.

Open: daily 10 AM - 6 PM

162 Dutch gable (1725) with wooden under façade and two variously placed stoops.

168 Warehouse (1650) with wooden under façade and a pediment tablature on the spout-gable.

175 Stepped-gable (1661) in sober Amsterdam's renaissance style. There are three gable stones with the inscriptions: 'Out Schaep', 'Jong Lam', and 'De Bonte Os anno 1661'. Shop sells coffee and tea since 1870.

180 Dutch gable (± 1765) with mahogany wooden under façade.

189-193 Warehouse triplets 'Geloof', 'Hoop', and 'Liefde' (1725), have decorations of sandstone and spout-gables.

211-217 Four identical warehouses (1690) with spout-gables. The spiral-shaped decorations are of sandstone.

224 Neck-gable 'De Hoop' (1727) in Louis XIV style has a gable stone depicting a woman with an anchor; this symbolizes hope. Above the hoisting hook are the date and a bird.

226 Neck-gable (1733) in Louis XIV style with gable stone depicting a vat of tobacco and tobacco rolls.

235 (1649) & *237* (1873). Until 1871 the Nieuwezijds Huiszittenhuis was housed. This institution was in charge of doling out bread, butter, cheese, herring, peat and other comestibles to the poor. Nr 235 has a portrayal of two men and a dog in a boat in the pediment. They represent the founders of the city. According to the story they floated around rudderless in a cog ship for days. They were blown on to the delta lands of the IJ and the Amstel.Nr 237 is remodelled in 1837 into a fire department barracks by W. Springer. Now they are made into living quarters. The windows and doors have a semi-circular shape. The middle section is three windows wide and there is a balustrade at the top.

252 Neck-gable (1730) has a lean-to building and the entrance to the upper floors are on the Lauriergracht.

☞ 263 Het Anne Frankhuis (1635)

This house, as is nr 265, built by Dirk van Delft. At the time of the renovation in 1740 the annex was built and the front façade was renewed. During a second renovation in 1840 the top-gable was replaced by a straight cornice moulding. In 1940 Otto Frank established his spice trade in this building. In 1942 Otto Frank went into hiding with his family in the upper section of the annex. After World War II the building was in very bad shape. The Anne Frank Foundation that was established on May 3, 1957, restored the building. Furthermore, the buildings Prinsengracht 265-275 and Westermarkt 16-20 were bought, after which in 1960 the museum could be opened. From 1997-1999 the building next to the Anne Frank House is demolished and a modern wing to the museum was built. During this time the interior on 263 Prinsengracht was restored to the state when Anne Frank was hiding there.

276 Dutch gable (1680). Above the wide under façade the gable has pilasters and a gable stone. In the 19th century the spout-gable is replaced by Dutch gable.

277 Former second city meat hall (1814).

278 Double warehouse (1680) with a trapezium-gable. Because of the two garage doors we assume it was in use as a coach house. The large windows were placed in the 19th century.

279 Westerkerk (H. de Keyser/1620) (see page 183).

281 Sexton's house (1656).

289 Neck-gable (± 1725) with decorated scroll stones and a half-round pediment.

299 't Casteel van Beveren (1720) in Louis XIV style. The elevated cornice moulding has a window and the inscription 'Casteel Beveren'. There is a vase on both corners and in the centre.

300 Dutch gable (1755) with a wood-

en under façade. Above the door a fox is depicted with a bird in its mouth. Under the hoisting hook there is a gable stone with a fox. The basement has wrought iron work in Louis XV style.

305 Cornice-gable (± 1730) with a bell-shaped top.

307 Elevated neck-gable (1725) with a half-round pediment.

327 Warehouse D' Nieuw Goudsbloem (1710) has a spout-gable and a pediment entablature.

328 Asymmetric house (1905) in Jugendstil. Note the balcony above the round bay windows.

331 Warehouse (1970!) in historicism style.

349 Warehouse (1650) with Dutch gable and a half-round pediment on the top.

355 Dutch gable twins (±1740).

360 Warehouse (1700) with spout-gable.

378 Shop/dwelling with Dutch gable (1710). In the 19th century the original neck-gable was remodelled into the present sober Dutch gable.The building has two lean-to buildings. On the Prinsengracht there are two small round windows next to the attic window. On the Passeerdersgracht there are two small oval windows and a diagonal entrance.

385-393 Nieuwe Suykerhofje (1755) Small courtyard almshouse (six houses) founded for Roman Catholic elderly women.

400 J. van Noortschool (1925) in the style of the Amsterdam's School.

414-416 Building (1925). In the style of the Amsterdam's School.

☞ 434-436 Former Paleis van Justitie - Hall of Justice - (1825)

In the period 1825-1829 this former orphanage is changed radically. The exterior has Corinthian pilasters. The cornice moulding is of stone and the elevation above is closed in the middle section. Both outer sections are finished off with a balustrade. The gate of the corner pavilion (nr 434) has gable stones showing how orphans receive doled out food and clothing.

438 Narrow warehouse (1737) has spout-gable and gable stone.

440 Cornice-gable (± 1740) in Louis XIV style with a bell-shaped elevation.

450 Shop building (1896) with wooden decorations. On the corner it has three bay windows and a little tower.

452 Cinema) De Uitkijk (1902) has an attic window on both sides of a date stone.

454-456 Neck-gable twins (1685) in Holland's classicism have sculpted oval windows and half-round pediments on the top.

472 't Lam (1740) with an elevated cornice moulding, two corner vases and a crest.

504-506 Huis van Locatelli (1860). Has a straight cornice and decorated dormer windows. The famous Italian composer Locatelli (1695-1764) lived in this house. The gable stone on nr 506 is a gift from Bergamo, the city where the composer was born. From 1863-1871 the painter Jozef Israëls (1827-1911) lived here, also.

530 Single house (1674) has a straight cornice and date stone.

531/corner Runstraat Neck-gable (± 1730) has two corner vases and a representation of an elephant.

534-536 Warehouses Het Lam and De Star (1670), has a spout-gable and is almost in original state.

540-542 Building (1918) is in the style of Amsterdam's School with a store front and doors of mahogany wood.

548 Warehouse (1630) with spout-gable.

550 Neck-gable (1703) with stoop and basement. It has the original window divisions, year ribbon, and a pediment entablature on the top.

552 Neck-gable (1698) has original window divisions and a pediment entablature on the top.

556 House (1699) with a Dutch gable-like top, crowned with a pediment entablature. House is radically reno-

Prinsengracht 556 (1699)

vated in the 18th and 19th centuries.

579 Dwelling/shop building (1905) in Jugendstil with a stepped-gable. There is a picture of a lion with arms in the gable.

582-584 (1665) Originally both of these houses had a neck-gable. Around 1770 nr 582 is renovated into a Dutch gable in the Louis XV style.

612 Building (1920) in the style of Amsterdam's School. Note the middle section with bay window and the two little towers on the top.

644 a and b/Vijzelstraat 2 Former Walloon Orphanage (A. Oortsman/ 1669). The low section has a sideways roof and a straight cornice moulding. The section on the corner has a large hipped roof, straight cornice moulding and on the corners protruding brick decorations. This building has been the Walloon Orphanage since its founding until about 1965.

646-648 Houses (1680) have decorated dormer windows and front-on placed stoops. The storefront dates from 1850. The building is an imposing corner house with various shops and a café on the ground floor and living quarters on the upper floors.

650 Neck-gable (± 1725) in Louis XIV style with richly decorated scroll stones and decorations at the top with the date.

659-661 Warehouse De Keizerskroon (± 1650) with a trapezium spout-gable.

672 Low Dutch gable (± 1680) with little round windows next to the attic window. It has a front-on stoop and basement.

681-693 Seven neck-gables (1715). Each has the name incorporated of one of the seven provinces. This refers to the Republic of the Netherlands when these provinces united. The middle house, Gelderland, (nr 687) is different from the other six houses in that it has two vases on the top and a double stoop.

692 Dutch gable (± 1680) with bunched grape decorations around the gable and entablature. Stoop with service entrance.

698-700 Dutch gable twins (± 1680) with fruit motif decorations. The half-round pediment has the shape of a shell. The window division of the first, second and third floors is still authentic (one wider window between two narrower ones). Above the attic window is a hoisting trapdoor that is replaced by a window. The wooden store front is of a later time. On the Noorderdwarsstraat there is a service entrance.

715 Warehouse Curaçao (1790) in Louis XIV style has a richly sculpted Dutch gable. This house was originally on the Dam until it was taken down and moved to this spot.

721 Cornice-gable (± 1750). The cornice moulding has an attic trapdoor in the semi-circular middle elevation. In the middle of this elevation is a hoisting hook. Between the attic trapdoor

and hoisting hook are decorations. Both corners are supported by decorated girders.

733 Warehouse (1649) has a spout-gable.

739-741 Building De Amsterdamsche Melkinrichting (Ed. Cuypers/1880) in neo-renaissance. The roof has a small tower and the façade is richly decorated.

747-755 Neck-gable quintuplets (± 1700) in Louis XIV style with decorated scroll stones and two stoops.

☞ 756 Church De Duif - The Dove- (1857)

The church is built in neo-classicism style. The front façade and the ground plan are inspired by baroque churches in Italy, France and Belgium. The front façade is covered with sandstone and brick. Note the Doric pilasters, the statues of saints, the mosaic with the text 'In loco isto dabo pacem' (here I will give you peace) and the cross on the gable top. In the pediment tablature there is a dove covered with gold-leaf. Between 1998 and 2002 the church was totally restored and various frescos were discovered. The church now has the function of a cultural centre. On Sunday worship services are still held.

767-769 De Ziekenverpleging - Nursing of the sick (J.H. Leliman/ 1856). The most striking aspects of this eclecticism building are the horizontal lines, the rounded windows on the first and second floors and the sandstone entrance.

768 Wide Dutch gable (± 1750) has hoisting hooks and a half-round pediment in shell motif.

771-773 Warehouses (1655) with spout-gables. They are still original.

780 Do not be misled! This is a reconstructed building (1975) in accordance with plans of an 18th century Dutch gable.

795 Cornice-gable (± 1785) in Louis XVI style.

800 Building (1940) in historicism style.

802 Building (1905) in Jugendstil with a narrow tower and balconies.

805-807 Dwelling/shop (1851) has a richly worked wooden store front. In the cornice above the under façade there are busts depicting the colonies. The cornice of the wooden under façade also has decorated joists. The human heads refer to the lands where the colonial products were bought. There are leaded glass windows under the cornice. Above in the cornice you find the name of the company and the colonial products that were for sale.

808/Utrechtsestraat 119 Dwelling/ shop (1906) with bay windows, balconies, and a round tower at the corner. It is decorated with a tile-tableau.

809 Low house (1665) with a sideways placed roof. Typical 17th century building style, because then they did not build high. Among other things, the wooden store front was renovated in 1750.

812-814 Church building (1910) with bay window with a balcony above.

833-835-837-839 Neck-gable quadruplets (± 1660) have decorated scroll stones and coat of arms in the half-round pediments. There are stoops and entrances to the basements.

834 Pilaster-gable (1890) the ground floor has two arched windows with a balcony above. On the top floor there is a pediment entablature, on the roof there are two small oval windows.

836-838-840 Former neck-gable triplets (± 1740) in Louis XV style. Nr 838 is renovated in 1800 when most of the decorations were removed.

851 Neck-gable (± 1725) with decorated scroll stones and a pediment entablature.

☞ ## 855-857-897-899
Het Deutzenhofje (1695)
This courtyard housing was founded for aged house-maids in 1692 with the legacy from Agneta Deutz. The entrance gate has a frame of stone, a plate with the date (1695) and the figure of a child in marble with the text 'Agneta Deutz laat hier haar liede en godsdienst blijken/den armen tot een troost, tot voorbeeld aan den rijken/ Anno 1695' (Agneta Deutz shows her love and faith here /Is a comfort to the poor, an example to the rich). Above are the coats of arms of both husbands of Agneta Deutz. The ornaments on the entrance port were restored in 1999.

860 Building (1920) in the style of the Amsterdam's School.

901-903-905 Neck-gable triplets (± 1710) with stoops and a basement. The window division on the second floor is in original state.

927 High and wide building (1870) in neo-renaissance style with decorations on the pediment entablature.

959-961 Neck-gable twins (1691) with decorated scroll stones and a half-round pediment. The port dates from 1875.

999 Warehouse (1675) with four half-round hoisting trapdoors and spout-gable.

1001-1005-1007-1009 Former neck-gable quintuplets (1675). Nr 1003 is renovated in 1800 and received a straight cornice. The scroll stones on the other four are decorated. The stoops to the entrance date from the building time.

Amstelveld and Amstelkerk (1670) (see page 130).

1075 Warehouse (1690) with spout-gable.

1089-1091-1093-1095 Neck-gable quadruplets (± 1770). Three houses still have the half-round pediments. On nr 1095 this was removed in 1904. All of the four houses have two small decorated oval windows on the top floor. On nr 1089 and 1091 the roof is elevated after a renovation and can be seen behind the neck-gables.

1099 Dutch gable (1745) in Louis XV style with a crest on the top.

1115-1117 Neck-gable twins (± 1730). Nr 1115 has a half-round pediment with a shell structure. On nr 1117 the pediment is empty.

1123/corner Amstel 284 House (1769). Above the door to the upper stories there are two small decorated oval windows. Under the stoop is the second entrance. The house has a lean-to building and on the roof a dormer window with decorations.

Prinsengracht 10 - 8 - 6 - 4 - 2

Prinsengracht

Radial Canals

The radial canals are excavated in the 17th century to connect the four main canals with each other. The artisans from the higher middleclass lived and worked on the radial canals. In the 19th century a few of the radial canals were filled in for reasons of health (the canals also functioned as sewer) and for traffic-technical reasons.

Reguliersgracht 92 (1675)

Egelantiersgracht

This canal is named after the bush-rose eglantine and is excavated between 1614 and 1620. Mostly artisans and working-class lived along this canal.

2-6 Gunters & Meuser (1917). The building is in the style of the Amsterdam's School and is symmetric. The façade is expressive and has wrought iron decorations on both sides.
8 Stepped-gable (1649) in sober Amsterdam's renaissance. The wall anchors have the shape of cloverleaves and on the two gable stones 'S Willebrordus' and 'D' Brovwer' can be read.
15 Neck-gable (± 1730) in Louis XIV style with decorated scroll stones and a half-round pediment at the top. Two sideways placed stoops and a gable stone depicting a carpenter in his shop with the inscription: 'De ionghe timmerman'.
17 House (H.P.Berlage/1891) in a combination of Holland's and Italian renaissance style. Because he added a few of his own styles, this house could be eclecticism style.
21 Low Dutch gable (± 1680).
23 Low neck-gable (± 1730) with a half-round pediment in shell motif.
42-44 Warehouse twins Jonge Bernhard and Koophandel (1680). Nr 44 still has the original stepped-gable, but has been removed from nr 42.
47-49 Neck-gables (± 1730) with decorated scroll stones. Nr 47 has

a decorated half-round pediment; nr 49 a half-round top with a wooden store front.
50 Dutch gable (± 1780) with stoop, basement, and a crest on the top.
63 Low Dutch gable (± 1750) has a gable stone with a falcon. It was once twins with nr 65, which can be seen by the gable stone that has 'anno' and half of a lion mask.
66-68-70 Neck-gable triplets (1735).

☞ 105-141 St-Andrieshofje (1617)

This is the oldest courtyard almhouse still in existence in Amsterdam. It was built to house Roman Catholic widows. The blue tiled entrance leads to the courtyard. Like in most courtyards, there is a (18th century) water pump here in the middle. Note the three connected doors, of which the middle one is the entrance to the upstairs houses. On the gable stone (1620) Christ is depicted with the text 'Vrede sy met U' (peace be with you).
199 Cornice-gable (± 1750).
201-215 Cornice-gable quadruplets (± 1750) with high stoops.
221 Low Dutch gable (± 1720) with original window division.
223 Low Dutch gable (± 1740).

Bloemgracht

This canal was excavated in 1612 and is the oldest canal in the Jordaan.
Here mainly businesses were established that were specialised in colours and dyes for the woollen cloth industry.
Many tradesmen lived along the Bloemgracht which can be seen by the lovely mansions. That is why the canal is often mockingly called 'the Herengracht of the Jordaan'.

9 Neck-gable (± 1730) in Louis XIV style.
13 Dutch gable (± 1680).
15-19 Bibliotheca Philosophica Hermetica (± 1650) in the style of

Holland's renaissance. The library is specialised in old handwritten documents, of which many are from before 1550.
22 Dutch gable (1735) in Louis XIV

style.

30 Dutch gable (± 1775).

36 Raised cornice-gable (± 1775) in Louis XV style with a bell-shaped top.

45 Neck-gable (± 1725) in Louis XIV style.

55 Neck-gable (± 1725).

64 Dutch gable (± 1750).

75 Building (1977) in traditional building style.

77 Warehouse De Saaijer (1752) with Dutch gable and gable stone.

83-85 Neck-gable twin (± 1725).

86 Neck-gable (± 1725).

☞ **87-89-91 Stepped-gables De**

Blauwburgwal

Excavated in 1614 as a cross canal between the Singel and the Herengracht. The name comes from the dye works that were established here in the 17th century. The textile was usually coloured with blue dye.

☞ **22 Elevated Dutch gable (1669)**

This is the only elevated Dutch gable in Amsterdam. The side façade on the

Drie Hendricken (1642)

In sober Holland's renaissance style, with gable stones 'Steeman', 'Landman', and 'Seeman'. The wooden store front, the window cross with leaded windows and the shutters are all restored to the original state in 1947.

98-100 Church building (1928) of the Christian Reformed Church.

108 Wide neck-gable (1644) in Holland's classicism with Doric pilasters.

116 Gable with gable stone 'Godt alleen d'eere' (the glory to God alone).

124 Neck gable (± 1730).

Herengracht is stepped upward and outward. The building has two lean-to buildings; one on the Herengracht and one on the Blauwburgwal.

Brouwersgracht

Mainly beer breweries, leather tanneries, tar boilers, and fish liver oil processing factories were established on this canal, which was excavated between 1614 and 1620. (See for the buildings: Haarlemmerbuurt).

Lauriergracht

This is a connecting canal between the Lijnbaansgracht and the Prinsengracht.

2 Dutch gable (± 1700) in Louis XIV style with gable stone 'in 't Casteel van Malaga'.

8 Dutch gable (± 1700) with three crests. The Dutch painter and photographer G.H. Breitner (1857-1923) lived here.

9-11 Spout-gables (± 1650).

30 Warehouse (± 1750) with spout-gable.

19 Low Dutch gable (± 1700).

23 Neck-gable (1658) in Holland's classicism. Has lion heads in the scroll stones, an elevated under

façade, and a stoop.

37 This is the house where Batavus Droogstoppel lived, the protagonist in the novel 'Max Havelaar' by Eduard Douwes Dekker (Multituli). The book is one of the most important books in the Dutch literature.

62 Dutch gable (± 1750) with three crests and a diagonal entrance.

116 Classicism cornice-gable with a pediment entablature. The date of construction is unknown, but probably around 1700. In 1725 a Lutheran orphanage was established here.

Between 1858 and 1904 it was a lodging house for officers from the East Indies. The situation around the lodging house is not changed.

99-105 Former boy's orphanage De Platanen (± 1650) this large court yard home got its name due to the ten large oriental plane trees in the courtyard. Presently it is in use as a theatre.

107 Dutch gable (1775) has ten floors and is three windows wide. There are three crests on the top.

Leliegracht

This is a connecting canal between the Keizersgracht and the Prinsengracht, excavated between 1614 and 1620. For a long time the canal functioned as passage between the Jordaan and the city centre. The Leliegracht was the only radial canal that was connected with the Prinsengracht. Because of the connection with the Prinsengracht, which was in turn connected with the Amstel River, the canal functioned as a water input system of the city canals up and into the 20th century. There are mainly houses on this short canal with plain Dutch gables, cornice-gables, eclecticism-gables and a few neck-gables.

Looiersgracht

The canal was excavated in 1612 and is situated in the working-class district the Jordaan. Predominantly tradesmen in hides and skins (tanners) lived on this canal.

21 Neck-gable (1640) with a high wooden store front, date stones and on the top a pediment entablature.

Reguliersgracht

This canal, excavated in 1664, was named after the monastery of the Canons Regular that was here between 1395 and 1532. At the Kerkstraat six arched bridges can be seen. The Reguliersgracht is not connected with the Amstel. On the north end the canal was filled-in in 1874. This is where the Thorbecke-plein is now.

11-13 Warehouses De Zon en De Maan (± 1680) with spout-gables; crowned with an entablature.
34 Sandstone Dutch gable (1725). The top is crowned with an eagle. The house can be reached via two sideways placed stoops.
39 Dutch gable (± 1680). The gable is decorated and crowned with a half-round pediment. The building has a high wooden store front and two lean-to buildings; one on the Reguliers-gracht and one on the Keizersgracht.
57-59 Former workshop with living quarters (I. Gosschalk/1879) in German medieval style, Queen Anne style, and Holland's renaissance style. The joists under the window on the second floor are carved as heads.
92 Dutch gable (1675). Noteworthy here on this shop/dwelling, is the stork in the niche above the wooden store front. The stork refers to the known Amsterdam's liqueur distillery. There used to be a café in the vestibule. The lean-to building is on the side of the Prinsengracht.
98-100-102 Dutch gable triplets (± 1680) with decorated gables.

Leidsegracht

The Leidsegracht is one of the oldest radial canals and was excavated in 1612. The canal cuts through the Herengracht, Keizersgracht and Prinsengracht, and ends in the Singelgracht.

4 Neck-gable with decorated scroll stones, a festoon around the hoisting hook, and a pediment entablature. There are pilasters running on both sides of the three attic windows that are placed above each other. The stoop is placed sideways.

5 Elevated neck-gable (± 1675) has decorated scroll stones. The top is richly decorated with a crest.

7 Neck-gable (± 1675) with a sideways placed stoop, sculpted scroll stones, and a shell motif in the half-round pediment.

8 Narrow pilaster neck-gable (± 1675) with a pediment entablature, and a festoon around the hoisting hook.

10 Dutch gable (1665) with decorated scroll stones, festoons around the hoisting hook, dates in the top, and a pediment entablature. The oval windows are decorated with palm leaves. The high stoop is placed sideways

11 Neck-gable (± 1675) in which the scroll stones have two windows that are decorated with lizards. There is a pediment entablature.

13-15 Cornice-gable (1890) with pilasters in the door section.

16 Eclecticism building (1885) with bay windows in art nouveau style.

18 Eclecticism building (1884) in neo-renaissance-style.

20 Neck-gable (± 1780) with two small sculpted windows next to the attic window, decorated scroll stones with two corner vases, and a pediment entablature.

22 Neck-gable (± 1780) with a round top, two small sculpted oval windows next to the attic window, decorated scroll stones with two corner vases, and a high sideways placed stoop.

23 Neck-gable (± 1780) with sideways placed stoop, a half-round pediment and decorated scroll stones.

24 Wide neck-gable (± 1780) with

decorated scroll stones and a pediment entablature with shell motif. Next to the attic window are two small sculpted oval windows. Around the hoisting hook there is a festoon and two corner vases.

25 Neck-gable (1684) with stoop, decorated scroll stones, and a half-round pediment with shell motif and two corner vases.

27 Cornice-gable (1684) has a stoop and a date ribbon.

37 Dutch gable (1666) with gable stone 'De Haes'. The gable is decorated and has a festoon, a date ribbon with Roman numerals, and next to the attic window are two small triangular windows.

40 Cornice-gable (± 1660) with the name 'Campen' and two family coats of arms.

42 Dutch gable (± 1680) the gable is decorated, has two corner vases, and two decorated oval windows.

44 Dutch gable (1685) with a decorated neck and two corner vases. Next to the attic window are two triangular windows.

46 Dutch gable (± 1660). The gable is finished with a cornice and has two decorated oval windows.

48 Dutch gable (± 1660) with a decorated gable, two corner vases and two decorated oval windows.

53-55 Dutch gable (± 1660) with a decorated gable and next to the attic window two triangles with sculpted leaves.

54 Dutch gable (± 1660) with a decorated gable and two decorated oval windows.

58 Neck-gable (± 1660) with in the half-round pediment a family coat of arms. Two decorated oval windows.

68 Dutch gable (1660) with a high wooden store front. The half-round door is placed sideways. There is a lean-to building on the Prinsengracht side with a high stoop.

72 Wide neck-gable (1666) with a high wooden store front. The four scroll stones are decorated with leaves. There are two decorated (blind) oval windows.

76 and 86-88 Warehouses (1660) with spout-gables.

95 Cornice-gable (1680) with a high decorated cornice. The two hoisting hooks are decorated with heads.

Brouwersgracht

Beyond the City Centre

De Pijp

De Pijp lies south of the centre and developed because of the city expansion in 1875. The district has two areas: the Oude Pijp (from Stadhouderskade to the Ceintuurbaan) and the Nieuwe Pijp (from the Ceintuurbaan to the Rivierenbuurt). The story goes that the name 'de Pijp' has to do with the large chimney pipes that used to be here in the district. Other explanations are that the long streets are pipe-shaped or that this was the first neighbourhood to be connected to gas from the Pijpgascompagnie (Pipe Gas Company).

The names of most of the streets refer to the famous Dutch painters and architects of the 17th century: Jan Steen (1626-1679), Albert Cuyp (1620-1691), Ferdinand Bol (1616-1680), and Jacob van Campen (1596-1657). The paintings of these artists can be seen in the Rijksmuseum.

The Pijp has always had a mixture of ethnic groups. In the seventies and eighties of the last century many original residents moved to larger homes outside of the city. Students and people originally from Surinam, Turkey, and Morocco are presently the most important residents. Around 1980 an intensive city renewal plan is put into action. Many old dwellings are renovated and where necessary replaced by new buildings. More than a hundred different ethnic groups live here and there is a large number of internationally oriented shops here.
The Pijp is more than worthwhile to visit.

Albert Cuyp Market

Points of interest:

Albert Cuyp Market
Daily market, situated between the Ferdinand Bolstraat and the Van Woustraat. It is the largest and busiest market of the Netherlands and has a broad range of wares.

Heineken Brouwerij (1868)
Stadhouderskade 78.
The brewery is open to the public and gives insight into the brewing process of beer and the history of Heineken as a world famous beer brewer.

Amsterdam-Zuid

At the beginning of the 20th century the Amsterdam city council asked the architect H.P. Berlage to design a plan for city expansion. The basic principle of Berlage's Plan-Zuid was the classless society expressed by uniformity and a monumental style of building. It was the wish of Berlage that especially the working class could have roomy living quarters. Because the cost of the construction was higher than was estimated, the housing was unaffordable for the working-class.
Then Amsterdam-Zuid soon developed into a neighbourhood of the more well-to-do. Especially the Apollo neighbourhood and the streets around the Stadionweg are still popular and expensive areas to live. Berlage only designed Plan-Zuid.
More than thirty architects, among whom Michel de Klerk and Piet Kramer, executed parts of the plan in assignment of a few large housing cooperatives. The neighbourhoods with broad streets and large houses were built between 1917 and 1925. The blocks of houses are alternated with squares and parks. That is why the area has a spacious feeling.
The houses all have the known characteristics of the Amsterdam's School: protruding brick balconies, bay windows, stately porch-entrances, wrought iron work, decorations in stone, and leaded glass windows.

Rivierenbuurt

The Rivierenbuurt is built between 1917 and 1925 as a part of Plan-Zuid by H.P. Berlage. The streets in this neighbourhood are named after Dutch rivers (for example: Rijnstraat, Scheldestraat, and Maasstraat).

Points of interest:

Victoriaplein
The house with 12 floors (J.F. Staal/1932)
The building is standing on 896 piles. The house is called the Wolkenkrabber (Skyscraper) by the people and is built in a style combination of the Amsterdam's School and functionalism. Note the sober symmetric tower with apartments on both sides. Architect Staal used modern building materials like concrete, steel and glass sections.

Merwedeplein 37/2
The Frank family lived in this house from 1933 until July, 1942.
In 2004 this house is restored to the original 1930s style. The house has the function as a refuge for foreign writers who are not free to work in their own countries. The house is not open to the public. On the Merwedeplein is also a statue of Anne Frank (J. Schep/ 2004). Anne Frank looks back at her home one more time before she leaves for the place of hiding on the Prinsengracht 263.

*Vrijheidslaan 2-46/50-78 - Woon-
blokken -housing blocks-
(M. de Klerk/1923)*
These housing blocks were built
generally in the style of the Amsterdam's School. The large spacious
houses are lavishly decorated.
The façade on the Vrijheidslaan has
a cascade of balconies that are connected by half-round bay windows.

Java- and KNSM-eiland

The island is made in 1876 as a stretched out narrow artificial peninsula that originally served as a breakwater for the Eastern Trade Wharf. It is in the middle of the
IJ on the north side of the Oostelijke Eilanden.

The western part of the island is called Java-island, the eastern part KNSM-island.
The KNSM-island continues via Azartplein almost unnoticeably into Java-island.
Until the 1950s there was a lot of industry that was aimed at the former Dutch
colony Indonesia. The eastern part of the island the Koninklijke Nederlandse Stoom-
boot Maatschappij (KNSM) (Royal Dutch Steamboat Company) was established
that provided the regular boat service between Amsterdam and Indonesia.
When Indonesia became indepen-dent in 1948, the trade and travel with the former
colony died down. The industrial buildings and warehouses became empty in the
1950s and squatters, artists, and city nomads lived in them in the 1980s. The area
has been redeveloped in the1990s.
The difference between Java-island and KNSM-island is mainly the architecture. On
Java-island there is a different type of architecture every 27 metres. Many of the old
buildings are demolished and replaced by modern mansions.
Ultimately five residential areas arose which are connected by bridges and separated by four narrow canals. Within these areas there are five green areas: one city
park and four gardens, each representing a different season. The old buildings that
were spared are renovated and give the neighbourhood a nostalgic and modern
feeling. On the KNSM-island a great many of the old buildings were kept and integrated into the new housing estate.
The Java-island is 1300 metres long and 130 metres wide.The KNSM-island is 700
metres long and 150 metres wide. Java-island has two quays that run parallel with
the island. The orientation of the Sumatrakade is to the IJ, while the Javakade has
the view of the IJ harbour and the Oostelijke Handelskade. On the KNSM-island the
quays respectively change into the Surinamekade and the Levantkade. The Java-
island, is connected to the Oostelijk Handelskade via the Jan Schaeferbrug and is
within ten minutes walking distance from the Central Station. It can also be reached
by the (free) ferry.

Java-island

Java-island points of interest:

Jan Schaeferbrug (T. Verhoeven/ 2001)

This eye-catching bridge, shaped like a reptile, connects the centre of Amsterdam (Oosterlijke Handelskade) with Java-island. The bridge is 280 metres long and 20 metres wide and runs straight through the warehouse De Zwijger. Two sections in the middle can be removed to allow ships to pass through.

Connecting dam - Hoogtij (Diener & Diener/1996)

Hoogtij is a huge block Langhaus and a smaller block Hofhaus and connects Java-island with KNSM-island.

Javakade

Javakade distinguishes itself by varied architecture.

Javakade 700-728 - Building with the 'bar-code' façade. The shallow balconies are enclosed by steel fences. The entrance gate to the building is of an Indonesian Batik pattern.

Azartplein - SHB (J.W. Hanrath en D.F. Slothouwer/1918)

This is the only historic building on Java-island. It was the office of the Samenwerkende Havengebouwen (Cooperating Harbor Buildings). It is changed into an apartment building.

Vier grachtjes -Four Canals-

The four different canals divide the island and post-modernistic houses are built along them. There are connecting foot and bicycle bridges. The buildings on the Brantasgracht have a zigzagging design and crooked bay windows.

KNSM-sland points of interest:

Levantkade 1-5 Former captain's houses of the KNSM.
Levantkade 7- 43 Former harbour building of the KNSM, remodelled into houses.

KNSM-Laan, Levantkade - Piraeus (H. Kollhoff en C. Rapp/ 1994)

This building of 170x57 metres is built around an old harbour building of the KNSM. It is built of dark brick and consists of 304 apartments, two courtyards, and a few offices and businesses.

KNSM-Laan - Mien Ruys Plantsoen

This small former business park of the KNSM is designed in 1934 by the landscape architect Mien Ruys.

Levantkade - Barcelona (B. Albert/ 1993)
This circular building has 325 apartments, divided over two residential blocks. The residential blocks are connected by fencing with 48 focal planes.

Levantkade 265-271
These former harbour buildings are remodelled into houses.

KNSM-Laan - Emerald Empire (J. Coenen/1994)
The round building at the head of

KNSM-island has 224 apartments. The Emerald Empire is also called the Tower of Babel.

KNSM-Laan - Skydome (W. Arets/ 1996)
The tower is more than 60 metres high (twenty floors). Because of the three deep vertical grooves, it looks like four separate towers.

The gables are made of concrete elements that are covered with anthracite coloured rubber.

Seranggracht

The IJ

The IJ means 'the water' and is a former sea bay of the Zuyder Zee. In the 17th century the IJ was the mooring place of the VOC ships. During the industrial revolution in the middle of the 19th century the area around the IJ got a complete makeover. The IJ to the west ofAmsterdam was turned into polders. To insure the passage to the North Sea for the shipping, the North Sea Canal was excavated in 1876 between the IJ and IJmuiden. The canal is 17 kilometres (10.56 miles) long and is excavated by hand under poor social conditions. With the sand won by the excavation of North Sea Canal, three islands were filled-in in the IJ on which Central Station is built.
On the eastside of the IJ the Oostelijke Handelskade was laid out. The Java and KNSM islands were constructed in the IJ.

City Park Frankendael

During the first half of the 17th century Amsterdam expanded to the east. The polders to the east of the city centre were drained and the resulting ground became the property of rich Amsterdammers. This is where they built country homes with farms. The present Park Frankendael (7 hectares) lies in the Watergraafsmeer (east) that was drained in 1629. Franken-dael is the last remaining country paradise in Amsterdam of the forty country homes that were built in the 17th and 18th century. The park is named after Huize Frankendael built by Nicolaas van Liebergen in 1680. The house that was a recreation house was lived in by Van Liebergen especially during the summer months. The big remodelling took place in 1730 when Isaac Balden (rich silk broker) became the owner.

The lovely house with its richly decorated windows and two coach houses are recently restored to their original 18th century state. The left coach and the main house serve as official wedding locations. A restaurant is established in the right coach house. The park is also restored in authentic style. The two historic gardens, the style garden with the statue of Bacchus (autumn) and Ceres (summer) and the landscapes garden with the artificial ruin from 1820, are open to the public, free of charge. Furthermore there are many trees and bridges to be admired.

House Frankendael

Definitions

Accolade arches
See relief arches
Alliance coat of arms
Combination of (two) coats of arms, from families that are united by marriage.
Capital
Crown of a column.
Coach house
Combination of living quarters and a place for parking a carriage and/or horse.There are three kinds of coach houses:
- the coach house is behind the house on a canal and opens onto the parallel street
- the living quarters of the coachman are above the stable
- the coach house is under the same roof; in/or next to the façade are large doors.
Console
A decorated bracket supporting a cornice or a protruding joist.
Corbelled

Corbelling is used on the side façade of a 17th century corner house with a wooden frame. The protruding gable rests on theextending girders from the lower façade. On the front façade corbelling can only be used if the front is made of wood.

Crest
18th century decoration at the top of mainly Dutch gables or neck-gables.
Festoon

Decoration on the front façade in the shape of a streamer with a flower or fruit motif.
Hidden Church
In the 17th century the Netherlands had a state church, the Reformed Church. Catholics, Lutherans and Mennonites were tolerated. The church buildings of these denominations were not allowed to be recognised as such. Often these hidden churches were found in attics of warehouses. Examples of still existing hidden churches in Amsterdam are: Singel 452, chapel in the Begijnhof, Ons' Lieve Heer op Solder, De Rode Hoed.
Lean-to building (Pothuis)
A building that juts out of the basement and leans onto the corner house or house. It could be a space to keep pots and pans, or a workshop for an artisan. The lean-to buildings are built outside of the building line on the public street.

Median risolit
Middle window section juts out from the façade and runs all the way up to the top.

Medieval window placement
The windows are coupled horizontally and vertically.

Pediment
Crowning of a window, door, or top-gable in the shape of a triangle or a curve.

Pilasters
Decorations of wall pillars. Pilasters can be square, flat, or half-round columns. Their only function is for decoration. Pilasters come from the classic Greek and Roman building order and were often used in the 17th century.
-Tuscan pilasters have a round capital, smooth column and a high foot.
- Doric pilasters have a grooved column and a plain capital.

 - Ionic pilasters have a decorated capital with two large volutes. The columns have vertical grooves and are placed on a pedestal.

 - Corinthian pilasters have decorations of acanthus leaves on the capitals. The columns have vertical grooves and rest on a decorated pedestal.

 - Composite order combines the acanthus leaves and the volutes in the capital. The columns are grooved vertically.

Pilaster-gable
A gable that is decorated with pilasters.

Relief arches or accolade arches
Are used to transfer the weight of a door or window to the wall pillar. They have small white sandstone blocks in the middle and ends.

Risolit
A section high up that juts out across the entire gable. It is at least one window wide.

Roll ornament
Decorations along the gable top in sandstone block masonry in the shape of an S or C.

Scroll stones
Sandstone decorations that are attached at an angle of 90 degrees to a neck-gable. In the stepped-gables in the period of Amsterdam's renaisance sance small scroll stones were also used.

Shield with coat of arms
The sign on which the family coat of arms is painted.

Soapstone layer
A layer of soapstones in masonry of brick.

Stoop
A stone step/stairs/paving in front of a house.

Twins, triplets, and multiples
These are buildings next to each other with identical gables. Often one or more of these buildings have changes made during renovations. In Amsterdam there are more than 250 of these combinations.

Tympanun
The recessed face of a pediment (usually triangular) within the frame made by the upper and lower cornices.

Volute
Gable crowning of the spout, neck, and Dutch gables. It is a sandstone decoration in the shape of a spiral or a curl.

Wall pillar
On both sides of the window are brick wall sections. On pilaster-gables the wall pillars look like pilasters.

Window framework
A decoration around a window and/ or a door.

Index

Colophon

Amsterdam The Guide

Publisher
MokumBooks, Amsterdam
www.mokumbooks.com

ISBN
9789087780098

Text, compilation, research, design
Marcel Bergen & Irma Clement

Design cover and icons
Coen Pohl

Photography and illustrations
Marcel Bergen en Irma Clement;
Except for and with thanks to:
Rijksmuseum, John Lewis Marshall 5
Bureau Monumenten & Archeologie
van de gemeente Amsterdam 9
Artis 22
Caspar Philips 27, 28, 175, 182, 184, 190

Cartography
Blokplan

Sources and literature
J.G. Wattjes en F.A. Warners:
Amsterdams Bouwkunst en Stads-
schoon. Amsterdam, 1944.
D'Ailly: Historische gids van Amster-
dam. Amsterdam 1949
Bureau Monumenten & Archeologie
van de gemeente Amsterdam.

With thanks to
This guide is made possible by Dylan
Bergen, Darifa Bergen, Ilona Leenen,
Lex Vermeulen, Sien Kalkoven, Coen
Pohl.

Remarks and suggestions
Writing of this guide is done with the
greatest care for the correctness of
the given information. However,
details are subject to change and the
compilers can not be held responsible
for any incorrect information received
through this guide, or the conse-
quences arising from the use of this
book. Any corrections or suggestions
for following publications are very
welcome.

CPSIA information can be obtained
at www.ICGtesting.com
Printed in the USA
LVOW06s2354111017
552097LV00005B/16/P